BE

EQUIPPED

BE

EQUIPPED

ACQUIRING THE TOOLS FOR SPIRITUAL SUCCESS

OT COMMENTARY

DEUTERONOMY

Warren W. Wiersbe

David C Cook®
transforming lives together

BE EQUIPPED
Published by David C Cook
4050 Lee Vance View
Colorado Springs, CO 80918 U.S.A.

David C Cook Distribution Canada
55 Woodslee Avenue, Paris, Ontario, Canada N3L 3E5

David C Cook U.K., Kingsway Communications
Eastbourne, East Sussex BN23 6NT, England

The graphic circle C logo is a registered trademark of David C Cook.

LCCN 2010934944
ISBN 978-1-4347-0052-0
eISBN 978-0-7814-0561-4

© 1999 Warren W. Wiersbe

First edition of *Be Equipped* published by Victor Books®
in 1999 © Warren W. Wiersbe, ISBN 1-56476-704-3

The Team: Karen Lee-Thorp, Amy Kiechlin, Sarah Schultz, Jack Campbell, and Karen Athen
Series Cover Design: John Hamilton Design
Cover Photo: iStockphoto

Printed in the United States of America
Second Edition 2010

4 5 6 7 8 9 10

091213

CONTENTS

THE BIG IDEA

An Introduction to *Be Equipped*
by Ken Baugh

Simplicity is in. Believe it or not, it's actually becoming cool not to accumulate more stuff. It used to be that having more material possessions proved that a person was successful and important. There are certainly many people who still believe that, but I've noticed a trend where people who can afford more stuff are choosing not to buy it in order to live a simpler and stress-free life.

For example, I have a friend who not long ago was contemplating the purchase of a private airplane because it made sense for his transportation needs. However, as he thought more about it, he chose not to buy the airplane, not because he couldn't afford it, but because he didn't want to manage one more thing in his life. My friend wanted to simplify his life, not to make it more complicated. I suspect that many people are finally beginning to realize that more stuff does not lead to happiness and greater esteem. It just makes life more complicated.

Not long ago I was thinking of buying a computer software program (I know, it's not an airplane, but you gotta work with what you have). I chose not to buy it because I just didn't want the pressure of having to learn one more computer program. I'm beginning to realize, like my friend, that there's something to keeping life simple. I'm certain that Jesus would agree.

Jesus kept His life simple. Think about it. Jesus didn't own a home. He didn't have to worry about mortgage payments and upkeep. Jesus didn't own any land or animals that required His time and attention, and Jesus wasn't married, nor did He have a family to take care of. Instead, Jesus lived a simple life and proclaimed a simple message: "Repent, for the kingdom of heaven is near" (Matt. 4:17 NIV).

Perhaps the greatest example of Jesus' commitment to simplicity is seen in His encounter with an expert in Jewish law, who one day asked Him a complicated question: "Teacher, which is the greatest commandment in the Law?" Now, this was probably a loaded question, because these guys were always trying to trap Jesus into saying something that would discredit Him in the eyes of the people. But I love Jesus' reply, because it is not only profound but is also incredibly simple. "Jesus replied: 'Love the Lord your God with all your heart and with all your soul and with all your mind.' This is the first and greatest commandment. And the second is like it: 'Love your neighbor as yourself.' All the Law and the Prophets hang on these two commandments" (Matt. 22:36–40 NIV).

Pretty simple, huh? Jesus quoted Deuteronomy 6:5 as the "first and greatest commandment." This points to the Big Idea of Deuteronomy: obedience. If loving God is the greatest commandment, then obedience to God's commands is the greatest expression of love for God. Jesus said it well: "If you love me, you will obey what I command" (John 14:15 NIV).

And the greatest practical expression of my obedience motivated by love is to love my neighbor. John reminds us of this when he writes, "If anyone says, 'I love God,' yet hates his brother, he is a liar. For anyone who does not love his brother, whom he has seen, cannot love God, whom he has not seen. And he has given us this command: Whoever loves God must also love his brother" (1 John 4:20–21 NIV). Therefore, Jesus' response to this expert in the law sums up the entire teaching in the Old Testament in these simple instructions: Love God and love people. This was the essence of Moses' instructions to the Israelites as he equipped them to cross the Jordan River into the Promised Land.

So what does this mean for us today? Simply this: Obedience to God's Word is to be motivated by love. This was Moses' message to the Israelites, and it is the same message to you and me today. When people love God, they want to obey Him. Not because they have to, and not because they fear His reprisal if they don't. Instead, loving God flows from a relationship with God that He initiated with us. John explains, "We love because he first loved us" (1 John 4:19 NIV).

God's love equips God's people to obey God's commands. Therefore, the more I internalize God's love, the more I will want to please Him. How does a person internalize God's Word? Again, it's a simple process: Read it, study it, meditate on it, memorize it, and share it with others. God's Word is supernatural (2 Tim. 3:16–17; Heb. 4:11–12), and the more I get His supernatural truth into my heart, the more God will use His Word through the power of the Holy Spirit to transform my mind (Rom. 12:2). And the more my mind is transformed, the better equipped I am to obey God's commands and live for His glory.

It's simple but not easy. That's why we need the power of the Holy Spirit working within us. Let God's love fill your heart through the intake of His Word, and *Be Equipped* to obey everything He commands.

***

Dr. Wiersbe's commentaries have been a source of guidance and strength to me over the many years that I have been a pastor. His unique style is not overly academic, but theologically sound. He explains the deep truths of Scripture in a way that everyone can understand and apply. Whether you're a Bible scholar or a brand-new believer in Christ, you will benefit, as I have, from Warren's insights. With your Bible in one hand and Dr. Wiersbe's commentary in the other, you will be able to accurately unpack the deep truths of God's Word and learn how to apply them to your life.

Drink deeply, my friend, of the truths of God's Word, for in them you will find Jesus Christ, and there is freedom, peace, assurance, and joy.

—Ken Baugh
Pastor of Coast Hills Community Church
Aliso Viejo, California

A WORD FROM THE AUTHOR

Deuteronomy means "second law" or "repetition of the law." In this book, Moses reviews the law originally given at Sinai and applies it to Israel's life in the land of Canaan. It also contains instructions and exhortations concerning the conquest of the land and Israel's relationship to the inhabitants of the land.

The book of Deuteronomy may well be the longest farewell speech in recorded history. It's certainly the longest farewell speech found in Scripture. But it's much more than a farewell speech, because in this series of addresses, Moses sought to equip this generation for their new life in the Promised Land. One of the most important responsibilities of the older generation is teaching the younger generation the Word of God and the principles of godly living, and Moses fulfilled that task superbly. We have the same responsibility today (2 Tim. 2:2; Titus 2:1–8), and God calls us to be faithful (1 Cor. 4:2).

First, Moses reviewed the past and reminded Israel of God's faithfulness and their ancestors' unfaithfulness. Then he declared the law of God and the covenant the Lord had made with them at Sinai, because their obedience to this covenant would determine their success in the Promised

Land. The nation had been nomadic for forty years, but now they would enter their land and become an agricultural people as each tribe claimed its inheritance. Moses applied to their new situation the law He had given them forty years before.

If Israel obeyed God's covenant, God would bless them abundantly, and the nation would be a witness to the pagan nations around them. These peoples would then want to know the God of Israel, and the Jews could explain their faith to them. Moses urged his people to love the Lord, because love is the greatest motive for obedience. So important was the book of Deuteronomy to the Jewish nation that God commanded it to be read publicly during the Feast of Tabernacles at the close of each Sabbatical Year (Deut. 31:10–13).

But does Deuteronomy have a message for us today? Three facts would indicate that it does: (1) All Scripture is inspired and profitable, and that includes Deuteronomy; (2) Deuteronomy is quoted in the New Testament nearly one hundred times; and (3) Jesus quoted more from Deuteronomy than from any other Old Testament book. It was the book He used when Satan tempted Him (Matt. 4:1–11) and when His enemies questioned Him (22:34–40).

The church today needs to return to the principles of godly living explained in Deuteronomy. Only then can we move forward in victory, by faith in Christ, and claim the inheritance He has appointed for us. To love God supremely and our neighbors as ourselves, and to seek to glorify God in all that we do, is the essence of the message of Deuteronomy; and it's a message we need to return to as we face the challenges of the future.

—Warren W. Wiersbe

A Suggested Outline of the Book of Deuteronomy

Theme: Preparation for claiming the inheritance
Key verses: Deuteronomy 6:1–3, 23

I. Remembering God's Blessings (Deuteronomy 1:1—5:33)

    A. God led them (Deuteronomy 1:1—3:29)

    B. God came to them (Deuteronomy 4:1–43)

    C. God taught them (Deuteronomy 4:44—5:33)

II. Responding to God's Goodness (Deuteronomy 6—11)

    A. Loving God (Deuteronomy 6)

    B. Obeying God (Deuteronomy 7)

    C. Showing gratitude to God (Deuteronomy 8:1—10:11)

    D. Fearing God (Deuteronomy 10:12—11:32)

III. Reviewing God's Word (Deuteronomy 12:1—26:19)

    A. Worship and obedience (Deuteronomy 12:1—16:17; 18:9–22)

    B. Civil officials (Deuteronomy 16:18—17:20)

    C. Offerings (Deuteronomy 18:1–8; 26:1–19)

    D. Cities of refuge (Deuteronomy 19; 21:1–9)

    E. Waging war (Deuteronomy 20)

    F. Miscellaneous laws (Deuteronomy 21:10—25:19)

IV. Renewing God's Covenant (Deuteronomy 27:1—30:20)

    A. Obedience and disobedience (Deuteronomy 27—28)

    B. The terms of the covenant (Deuteronomy 29—30)

V. Replacing God's Servant (Deuteronomy 31—34)

    A. Moses encourages his successor (Deuteronomy 31:1–13)

    B. Moses warns the nation (Deuteronomy 31:14—32:52)

    C. Moses blesses the tribes (Deuteronomy 33)

    D. Moses leaves the people (Deuteronomy 34)

Chapter One

CATCHING UP ON THE PAST

(Deuteronomy 1—3)

Our journalism instructor taught us that the first paragraph of every news article had to inform the reader of the "who, what, where, when, and why" of the event being reported. Deuteronomy 1:1–5 isn't a news article, but it does just that. The people of Israel are at Kadesh-barnea in the fortieth year after their deliverance from Egypt, and their leader Moses is about to expound God's law and prepare the new generation to enter Canaan. Although Moses himself wouldn't enter the land, he would explain to the people what they had to do to conquer the enemy, claim their promised inheritance, and live successfully in their new home to the glory of God.

God was giving His people a second chance, and Moses didn't want the new generation to fail as their fathers had failed before them. Israel should have entered Canaan thirty-eight years before (2:14), but in their unbelief they rebelled against God. The Lord condemned them to wander in the wilderness until the older generation had died, with the exception of Joshua and Caleb (Num. 13—14). Philosopher George Santayana wrote, "Those who cannot remember the past are condemned to repeat it,"[1] so the first thing Moses did in his farewell discourse was to review Israel's past and remind the new generation who they were and how they got where they were (Deut. 1—5). Knowing their past, the new generation in Israel could avoid repeating the sins of their fathers.

ISRAEL MARCHING (1:6–18)

A grasp of history is important to every generation because it gives a sense of identity. If you know who you are and where you came from, you will have an easier time discovering what you should be doing. A generation without identity is like a person without a birth certificate, a name, an address, or a family. If we don't know our historic roots, we may become like tumbleweeds that are blown here and there and never arriving at our destination.

A father took his young son to the local museum to help him better understand what life was like before he was born. After looking rather glumly at some of the exhibits, the boy finally said, "Dad, let's go some-place where the people are real."

Like that bored little boy, many people have the idea that the past is unreal and unimportant and has no bearing on life today; and like that little boy, they are wrong. The cynic claims that all we learn from history is that we don't learn from history, but the mature Christian believer knows that A. T. Pierson was right when he said, "History is His story." The Bible isn't a boring museum where everything's dead. It's a living drama that teaches us about God and encourages us to obey Him and enjoy His blessings (Rom. 15:4; 1 Cor. 10:1–12). No book is more contemporary than the Bible, and each new generation has to learn this important lesson.

Israel at Sinai (vv. 6–8; see Num. 1:1—10:10).[2] After the nation left Egypt, they marched to Mount Sinai, arriving on the fifteenth day of the third month (Ex. 19:1), and there the Lord revealed Himself in power and great glory. He delivered the law to Moses, who declared it to the people, and they accepted the terms of the covenant. The Jews left Sinai on the twentieth day of the second month of the second year after the exodus (Num. 10:11), which means they were at Sinai not quite a year. While the nation was camped at Sinai, the tabernacle was constructed and the priests and Levites were set apart to serve the Lord.

Why did the Lord have the Jews tarry so long at Sinai? He wanted to give them His law and teach them how to worship. The Lord didn't give Israel His law to save them from their sins, because "by the works of the law shall no flesh be justified" (Gal. 2:16). Under the old covenant, people were saved by faith just as sinners are today (Rom. 4:1–12; Gal. 3:22; Heb. 11). The law reveals the sinfulness of man and the holy character of God. It explained what God required of His people if they were to please Him and enjoy His blessing. The civil law allowed Israel to have an orderly and just society, and the religious laws enabled them to live as the people of God, set apart from the other nations to glorify His name. The law also prepared the way for the coming of Israel's Messiah (Gal. 4:1–7), and the various tabernacle furnishings and ceremonies pointed to Jesus.

Knowing that wars and dangers lay before them, many of the people might have been satisfied to stay at Mount Sinai, but the Lord ordered them to move. Not only did the Lord command them but He also encouraged them: "See, I have given you this land" (Deut. 1:8 NIV). He promised to keep the covenant He had made with the patriarchs to whom He had graciously promised the land of Canaan (Gen. 13:14–18; 15:7–21; 17:8; 28:12–15; Ex. 3:8). All the army of Israel had to do was follow God's orders, and the Lord would give them victory over their enemies in Canaan.

Israel on the way to Kadesh-barnea (vv. 9–18; Num. 10:11—12:16). It wasn't easy for Moses to lead this great nation because he frequently had to solve new problems and listen to new complaints. Accustomed to the comfort of their camp at Sinai, the people resented the hardships of their journey to the Promised Land. They forgot the distress of their years of slavery in Egypt and even wanted to turn around and go back! They got accustomed to the manna that God sent them from heaven each morning and soon took it for granted, and they longed for the savory meat and vegetables they had enjoyed eating in Egypt. No wonder Moses got discouraged and cried out to the Lord![3] He wanted to quit and he even asked God to take his life (Num. 11:15)!

God's answer to Moses' prayer was to give him seventy elders to assist him in managing the affairs of the camp. Moses was a great leader and a spiritual giant, but even he could do only so much. He and the elders organized the nation by thousands, hundreds, fifties, and tens, with competent leaders in charge of each division. This created a chain of command between Moses and the people so that he didn't have to get involved in every minor dispute. He could devote himself to talking with the Lord and helping to settle the most important problems in the camp.

The charge Moses gave to the newly appointed leaders is one that ought to be heeded by everybody who serves in a place of authority, whether religious or civil (Deut. 1:16–18). The emphasis is on character and justice and the realization that God is the judge and the final authority. If all officials made their decisions on the basis of nationality, race, social position, or wealth, they would sin against God and pervert justice. Throughout the law of Moses, there's an emphasis on justice and showing kindness and fairness to the poor, especially widows, orphans, and aliens in the land (Ex. 22:21–24; Lev. 19:9–10; Deut. 14:28–29; 16:9–12; 24:17–21). Frequently, the prophets thundered against the wealthy landowners because they were abusing the poor and the helpless in the land (Isa. 1:23–25; 10:1–3; Jer. 7:1–6; 22:3; Amos 2:6–7; 5:11). "He who oppresses the poor reproaches his Maker" (Prov. 14:31 NKJV).

ISRAEL REBELLING (1:19–46; NUM. 13—14)

Kadesh-barnea was the gateway into the Promised Land, but Israel failed to enter the land because of fear and unbelief. They walked by sight and not by faith in God's promises. "See, the LORD your God has given you the land," Moses told them. "Go up and take possession of it. ... Do not be afraid; do not be discouraged" (Deut. 1:21 NIV). It has well been said that faith is not believing in spite of evidence—that's superstition—but obeying in spite of circumstances and consequences. How much more evidence did the people need that their God was able to defeat the enemy and give them their land? Hadn't He defeated and disgraced all the false gods of Egypt, protected Israel, and provided for them on their pilgrim journey? God's commandment is always God's enablement, and to win the victory, His people need only trust and obey.

Searching out the land (vv. 22–25; Num. 13). The first indication that the nation was wavering in faith was their request that Moses appoint a committee to search out the land. Israel would then know the state of the land and be better able to prepare their plan of attack. This is the approach any army would use—it's called "reconnaissance"—but Israel wasn't just "any army." They were God's army and the Lord had already done the "reconnaissance" for them. From the very beginning, God had told Moses that Canaan was a good land flowing with milk and honey, and He even gave the names of the nations living in the land (Ex. 3:7–8; see Gen. 15:18–21). Surely the people knew that the will of God would not lead them where the grace and power of God could not keep them.

When Moses spoke to God about the people's suggestion, the Lord graciously gave him permission to grant their request (Num. 13:1–2). God knows how weak we are, so He sometimes accommodates Himself to our condition (Ps. 103:13–14; Judg. 6:36–40). However, doing God's permissive will isn't quite the same as obeying His "good, acceptable, and perfect will" (Rom. 12:2). When God lets us have our own way, it's a concession on His part that should make us walk in fear and humility. Why? Because there's always the danger that we'll become proud and self-confident and start telling God what to do! Doing God's express will is the safest course because God never makes a mistake. Sometimes our desires and God's concessions combine to produce painful disciplines.[4]

The twelve men explored the land for forty days and returned to the camp with the enthusiastic, unanimous report that everything God had said about the land was true. The report shouldn't have surprised anybody because God's Word can always be trusted.

Rejecting the land (vv. 26–40). But then ten of the spies gave their opinion that Israel wasn't able to conquer the land because the cities were protected by high walls and there were giants in the land. The minority (Joshua and Caleb) boldly affirmed that the Lord was able to give His people victory because He was greater than any enemy. Unfortunately, the nation sided with the majority and became discouraged and even more afraid. Twice Moses told them not to be afraid (Deut. 1:21, 29), but his words fell on deaf ears. Instead of the leaders singing their victory song and marching forward by faith (Num. 10:35), they and the people sat in their tents complaining, weeping, and plotting to return to Egypt. With the exception of four men—Moses, Aaron, Joshua, and Caleb (14:5–6)—the entire nation rebelled against the Lord and failed to claim the land He had promised them. The Lord could bring them out of Egypt, but He couldn't take them into Canaan!

What was the cause of Israel's failure at Kadesh-barnea? "They forgot what he had done, the wonders he had shown them…. They did not remember his power" (Ps. 78:11, 42 NIV). God had demonstrated His great power by sending the plagues on Egypt and by opening the Red Sea so Israel could escape, and yet none of these wonders had really registered in the minds and hearts of His people. Even the miraculous provision of bread, meat, and water didn't increase their faith. They gladly received the gifts but failed to take to heart the goodness and grace of the Giver. Instead, they hardened their hearts against the Lord and developed "an evil heart of unbelief" (Heb. 3:7–19). If God's blessings don't humble our hearts and make us trust Him more, then they will harden our hearts and weaken our faith. Unless we receive His Word in our hearts and give thanks to God for His blessings, we become proud and selfish and begin to take the Lord's blessings for granted.

There's a difference between unbelief and doubt. Unbelief is a matter of the will; it causes people to rebel against God and say, "No matter what the Lord says or does, I will not believe and obey!" Doubt, however, is a matter of the heart and the emotions; it's what people experience when they waver between fear and faith (Matt. 14:31; James 1:5–8). The doubter says, "Lord, I believe; help my unbelief!" God seeks to encourage doubters and help them believe, but all He can do with rebels is bring judgment. At Kadesh, He decreed that the nation would wander for the next thirty-eight years (they had already been in the wilderness two years) until all the people twenty years and older had died. Then He would take the new generation—the children and teenagers whom the leaders said would be devoured by the enemy—and lead them into the land where they would conquer the enemy and claim their inheritance.

Attacking the enemy (vv. 40–46; Num. 14:40–45). When the Jews heard God's judgment declared, they tried to undo their sin in their own way, but they only made matters worse. "We have sinned!" they said, but it was a shallow confession that really meant, "We're sorry for the consequences of our sin." It wasn't true repentance; it was only regret. Then they tried to attack some of the people in the land, but their efforts failed and God brought about a humiliating defeat (Deut. 1:41–46). After all, the Lord wasn't with them and hadn't ordered them to fight. The whole enterprise was a feeble attempt on the part of the men of Israel to accomplish in their own strength what God would have accomplished for them had they only trusted Him. The only thing the sinful nation could do was submit to the discipline of God. They came home and wept, but their tears didn't change the mind of God. The nation wouldn't listen to God's voice, so He didn't listen to their voices.

Caleb and Joshua believed God, so God decreed that they would live through the wilderness wanderings and enter the Promised Land. But later, even Aaron and Moses rebelled against God and were kept out of the land (v. 37; Num. 20:1–13, 24). When God instructed Moses to provide water by speaking to the rock, he struck the rock and said, "Hear now, you rebels! Must we bring water for you out of this rock?" (v. 10 NKJV). Because he didn't believe God and glorify Him, Moses forfeited the privilege of leading Israel into the land.[5] His sin wasn't that of the doubter but of the rebel: He deliberately disobeyed God and exalted himself.

When Moses said that God was angry with him "for your sakes" (Deut. 1:37; "because of you," NIV), he wasn't excusing himself by blaming the Israelites. What this means is that the rebellious attitude of the people had provoked him into doing what he did and saying what he said. Moses had been grieved so often by the people's complaining and disobeying that it all finally came to a head, and he lost the meekness for which he was so well-known. Even the greatest spiritual leaders are but frail human beings apart from the grace of God, and many of them failed in their strongest points. Moses' greatest strength was his meekness, but he lost his temper. Abraham is known for his great faith, yet in a time of testing he fled to Egypt and lied about his wife. David's great strength was his integrity (Ps. 78:72), but he failed miserably and became a liar and a hypocrite, and Peter's great strength was his courage, yet three times he became afraid and denied his Lord. "Therefore let him who thinks he stands take heed lest he fall" (1 Cor. 10:12 NKJV).

ISRAEL CONQUERING (2:1—3:20)

This is a summary of the record given in Numbers 20:14—31:54, describing the people of Israel defeating nations and kings in their march to the

Promised Land. In this speech, Moses gave no details of what Israel experienced while wandering thirty-eight years in the wilderness.[6] During those years, Israel was out of God's covenant favor, and there's no record that they observed the Passover or even circumcised their sons. After Joshua led the nation across the Jordan River, he took care of those responsibilities and Israel was back in God's covenant blessing (Josh. 5). The people in Moses' congregation who were nineteen years old when the wanderings began were now fifty-seven (19 + 38) and certainly would remember those difficult years and tell their children and grandchildren about them.

Avoiding the Edomites (2:1–8; Num. 20:14–21). Moses was commanded by God not to declare war on the people of Edom and try to take their land. The Edomites were descended from Jacob's brother, Esau, and therefore were related to the Jews (Gen. 36). Moses at first tried a friendly approach, but the Edomites wouldn't accept their brothers on any terms, so Moses led the people by another route that bypassed Mount Seir. The Edomites should have shown Israel brotherly love, but instead they preferred to perpetuate the ancient feud between Jacob and Esau (Gen. 27; 32—33). Centuries later, Edom was still angry with Israel and rejoiced when the Babylonians destroyed Jerusalem (Ps. 137:7; Ezek. 25:12–14; Amos 1:11; Obad. 10–13).

Of all the problems we face in life, family disagreements are probably the most painful and the hardest to solve, and yet the Bible records so many of them. Cain killed his brother Abel (Gen. 4); Jacob and Esau were rivals; Jacob's wives competed with one another (Gen. 29—30); Jacob favored Joseph and therefore Joseph's brothers hated their youngest brother (Gen. 37); and David's father-in-law, King Saul, hounded him and tried to kill him (1 Sam. 19—20). Even in the Christian family, brothers and sisters in the local church don't always love one another. The Corinthian church was divided four ways (1 Cor. 1:12); the Galatian believers were biting and devouring one another (Gal. 5:15); the saints in Ephesus needed to be kind and forgive one another (Eph. 4:31–32); and in the Philippian church, two women were at odds with each other (Phil. 4:2–3). Family feuds and church disagreements are at least somewhat confined, but when entire nations cultivate and sustain hatred for one another and wage war, many innocent people are hurt.

Moses did the right thing by obeying God's command and deliberately avoiding a costly and unprofitable confrontation. "Blessed are the peacemakers: for they shall be called the children of God" (Matt. 5:9). "Let us therefore follow after the things which make for peace" (Rom. 14:19). There are times when avoiding conflict is cowardly, but there are other times when it's a mark of courage and wisdom (James 3:13–18; Matt. 5:21–26). Like James and John, we might feel like calling down fire from heaven on people who reject us, but it's better to follow the examples of Moses and Jesus and take another route (Luke 9:51–56).

One more factor in this "peacemaking" should be noticed: God had graciously cared for Israel and blessed His people even during their years of wandering, so there was no need for them to attack their brothers and exploit them (Deut. 2:7). God would give Israel all the land they needed without their having to go to war. If more individuals, families, and nations were content with the blessings God has given them, there would be less fighting among them.

Avoiding the Moabites and Ammonites (2:9–23). Just as the Edomites were not attacked and conquered because they were related to Jacob, so the Moabites and Ammonites were spared because they were the descendants of Lot, the nephew of Abraham (Gen. 19:30–38). God is supreme over all nations and assigns their territories according to His sovereign will (Acts 17:26–28; 2 Chron. 20:6). In fact, the Lord even helped these other nations defeat their enemies and take their land (Deut. 2:20–23). God is on His throne and deals with the nations according to His perfect will (Dan. 4:35). Neither the Moabites nor the Ammonites deserved this kindness, but the Lord sometimes blesses people because of their relationship to other people. Israel was certainly blessed because of God's covenants with Abraham and David, and the church is blessed today because of the Father's eternal covenant with Jesus Christ (Heb. 13:20).

It was a turning point in their history when the Jews crossed into the Zered Valley, for now the older generation was gone except for Moses, Caleb, and Joshua (Deut. 2:13–16). With their time of divine discipline ended, Israel could now look forward to defeating their enemies and moving into the land that the Lord had promised to them.

Defeating the Amorites (2:24—3:11). Sihon and Og were powerful kings in the region of the Amorites on the east side of the Jordan, and the Lord had determined to destroy them and their people. God's orders in 2:24–25 and 31 summarize the pattern Israel would follow in their conquest of the Promised Land. God would tell Joshua which city or people to attack; He would assure them of victory; and He would go with them to help them win the battle. Israel's defeat of Sihon and Og was especially important because it would send a message ahead to the nations in Canaan and bring fear to their hearts (11:25). By the time Joshua was ready to enter the land, the news of Israel's invincible march had already gone before them (Josh. 2:8–11; see Ex. 15:14–16).

As he did with the Edomites, Moabites, and Ammonites, Moses first made Sihon an offer of goodwill, promising to pass through the land peacefully and pay for whatever food and water the people consumed. However, the Lord wanted Israel to defeat Sihon and seize all his land, so he hardened the king's heart as He had hardened the heart of Pharaoh in Egypt.[7] When Sihon led his army out to attack Israel, God gave Moses a great victory and all the people of the land were slaughtered. This victory over Sihon gave the Israelites encouragement to confront Og, and they won that battle as well and took over all the land. The fact that the cities had high walls (Deut. 3:5) and that Og was a giant (v. 11) didn't seem to create any of the problems that the older generation had feared (Num. 13:28). God is bigger than the walls and greater than the giants!

Liberal critics of the Bible express concern at the way Israel destroyed entire nations, killed "innocent people," and confiscated their cities and their lands. But how "innocent" were these people? The critics of Scripture (and God) may not realize that the nations Israel encountered east of the Jordan and in Canaan itself were indescribably wicked. They were brutal people who sacrificed their own children to the false gods that they worshipped. Male and female prostitutes served in their temples and sexual intercourse was an important part of the Canaanite religion.

These people were not left without a witness from God in creation (Rom. 1:18ff.) as well as through the lives of Abraham, Isaac, and Jacob, who had lived in Canaan. Furthermore, the news of the destruction of Sodom and Gomorrah, the plagues of Egypt, and Israel's deliverance through the Red Sea (Josh. 2:8–11) came to the ears of these people and bore witness that Jehovah alone is the true God. God had been long-suffering with these wicked nations even in Abraham's day, but now their time had run out and their judgment had come (Gen. 15:16). If these evil civilizations had not been exterminated, Israel would have been in constant danger of being tempted by pagan idolatry. In fact, that's what did happen during the period of the judges, and God had to chasten His people to bring them back to the true God. Israel had important work to do on earth in producing the written Scriptures and bringing the Savior into the world, and imitating the pagan nations would have polluted Israel and threatened God's great plan of salvation for mankind.

ISRAEL PREPARING (3:12–29)

The victories over Sihon and Og, the two mighty kings of the lands east of the Jordan, were themselves preparation for the battles Israel would fight when they arrived in Canaan. The new generation was getting its first real taste of warfare and was quickly discovering that Jehovah could be trusted to overcome every enemy. All that the army had to do was obey God's orders, trust His promises, and courageously confront the enemy.

A second step of preparation for conquest was the settling of the two-and-a-half tribes in the territory that had been captured on the east side of the Jordan. This land was given to the tribes of Reuben and Gad and the half tribe of Manasseh. They especially wanted this land because they were herdsmen and the territory was suitable for their livestock (Num. 32). The two-and-a-half tribes were allowed to fortify the cities for their families to live in and also to build pens for their flocks and herds. But it was understood that the men of war in the tribes would cross the Jordan with the other tribes and help their brothers conquer the land. Once that was done and all the tribes had been assigned to their inheritance, the men of Reuben, Gad, and Manasseh could return home to their families (Josh. 22). The fact that Moses gave them the land and that the men were willing to leave their loved ones behind was evidence of their faith that God would give Israel the victory in Canaan.

Moses described this victory as "the Lord giving rest" (Deut. 3:20), a phrase that is used again in 12:10 and 25:19 and frequently in Joshua (1:13–15; 11:23; 14:15; 21:44; 22:4; 23:1). The book of Hebrews picks up the phrase and applies it to the spiritual rest we have in Christ because we have trusted His finished work on the cross (Heb. 3:11, 18; 4:1–11). Israel at Kadesh-barnea wanted to go back to Egypt, and the Jewish believers to whom Hebrews was written wanted to go back to the old life and the old religion. But there could be no rest in the Jewish religion that was about to pass off the scene, so the writer urged the people to go ahead by faith into the rest that only Christ can give (Matt. 11:28–30). Canaan isn't a picture of heaven; it's a picture of our spiritual riches in Christ, the inheritance that we have in Him.

A third step of preparation for conquest was the appointment of Joshua to succeed Moses and lead the nation into Canaan (Num. 27:18–23). At the command of the Lord, Moses publicly laid hands on Joshua and with the help of Eleazar the high priest consecrated him to his new office. Moses also began to hand over some of his authority to Joshua (v. 20 NIV) so that by the time Moses left the scene, Joshua was ready to take charge. However, Joshua was a man of great faith and experience and was fully qualified to lead God's people. He had served as Moses' servant (Ex. 33:11) and as leader of the army (17:8–16), and he had been on Sinai with Moses (24:13). At Kadesh-barnea he proved his faith and obedience by standing with Moses and Caleb against the ten spies and the whole unbelieving nation.

The only cloud over all this celebration of victory was that Moses wasn't permitted to enter the Promised Land because of his impetuous sin of striking the rock (Num. 20:1–13; 27:12–14). But even this sad note brought with it a trumpet call of encouragement in what Moses said: "O Sovereign LORD, you have begun to show to your servant your greatness and your strong hand" (Deut. 3:24 NIV). As wonderful as Israel's victories had been so far, they were just a small expression of the greatness and power of God, and Moses didn't want to miss any of the magnificent things God was going to do in Canaan. The Lord wouldn't permit Moses to enter the land, but before Moses died, he was allowed to see the land from the top of Mount Pisgah (Nebo; see 32:48–52; 34:1–6). Centuries later, Moses stood in the Holy Land in glory on the Mount of Transfiguration with Jesus and Elijah (Matt. 17:1–3).

All that Moses said in the first part of his farewell address prepared the way for his exposition and application of God's law, for history and responsibility go together. God had done mighty things for the people, both in blessing them and in chastening them, and the people of Israel had a responsibility to love God and obey His Word. Throughout this address,

Moses will frequently remind the Jews that they were a privileged people, the people of God, separated unto the Lord from all the nations of the earth. It's when we forget our high calling that we descend into low living.

The church today needs to catch up on the past and be reminded of all that the Lord has done for His people—and all that His people have done and not done in return for His blessings. If a new generation of believers is to march into the future in victory, they need to get back to their roots and learn again the basics of what it means to be the people of God.

QUESTIONS FOR PERSONAL REFLECTION
OR GROUP DISCUSSION

1. What was Moses seeking to do through this series of addresses recorded in Deuteronomy?

2. In "A Word from the Author," what three facts does Wiersbe give to prove the importance of the book of Deuteronomy? Which of these surprises or motivates you, and why?

3. What does this quote mean for your life: "Those who cannot remember the past are condemned to repeat it"? What prevents people from learning through history?

4. What was the purpose of the law-giving if it didn't save the Israelites from their sins? What role might studying the law have in our lives?

5. What difference do you notice in your life when you walk by sight and not by faith?

6. How can we encourage one another away from fear, unbelief, and dependence on sight, and toward trust and faith?

7. What is the difference between God's permissive will and God's "good, acceptable, and perfect will"?

8. Why did Israel fail so miserably to accept God's promises in faith and thus fail to move forward?

9. How is unbelief different from doubt? When have you experienced one or the other?

10. How would you answer the charge that Israel killed innocent people as they conquered the Promised Land? What benefit to the world came from destroying these other nations?

11. How does reviewing what the Lord did for His people (Deut. 1—3) affect you?

Chapter Two

THE GOD WE WORSHIP

(Deuteronomy 4—5)

T he people of Israel were blessed above all nations on earth, for they belonged to the true and living God and were in covenant relationship with Him. They were now preparing to enter the land God promised them when He called Abraham, the father of their nation (Gen. 12:1–3; 13:14–18), and part of that preparation was listening carefully to a farewell speech by Moses, God's prophet and their leader. After rehearsing the history of the nation (Deut. 1—3), Moses reminded the people of the character of the God of Israel and how they should respond to Him. If we don't know the character of the God we worship, how can we worship Him "in spirit and in truth" (John 4:24)?

GOD SPEAKS—HEAR HIM (4:1–2)

The eminent Jewish scholar Abraham Joshua Heschel wrote, "To believe, we need God, a soul, and the Word."[1] Another Jewish scholar, the apostle Paul, reached the same conclusion and wrote, "So then faith comes by hearing, and hearing by the word of God" (Rom. 10:17 NKJV).

The God who brought creation into existence by speaking the Word

(Ps. 33:6–9) has ordained that His people should live by hearing and obeying His Word.

The verb "to hear" is used nearly one hundred times in the book of Deuteronomy. The traditional Jewish confession of faith (Deut. 6:4–5) is called "the Shema," from the Hebrew word that means "to hear, to pay attention, to understand, to obey." To the Old Testament Jew and the New Testament Christian, hearing the Word of God involves much more than sound waves impacting the human ear. Hearing God's Word is a matter of focusing our whole being—mind, heart, and will—on the Lord, receiving what He says to us and obeying it. The Word of God must penetrate our hearts and become a part of our inner beings if it is to change our lives. That's what Jesus meant when He said, "Who has ears to hear, let him hear!" That statement is found at least eight times in the Gospels, so it must be important. (See also Deut. 29:4; Ezek. 12:2.)

Hearing and obeying the Word of God was Israel's very life (Deut. 4:1a). When God speaks, He sets before us life and death (30:15–20), and our response determines which it will be. "Keep my decrees and laws, for the man who obeys them will live by them. I am the LORD" (Lev. 18:5 NIV). The emphasis in Deuteronomy 4:1–2 and 5 is on commanding and teaching, for the Lord not only tells us what to do but He also explains the truth behind His commands. Jesus may have had this in mind when He told His disciples that He treated them like friends ("insiders") and not like slaves, because He explained to them what He was doing (John 15:14–15).

Not only was Israel's life dependent on obedience to God's Word, but so was their victory over the enemy (Deut. 4:1b). Apart from faith and obedience, Israel couldn't enter the land and defeat the nations that were strongly entrenched there. How could the Lord go before His people and give them victory if they weren't following Him obediently (1:30)? The ten spies who failed to grasp the power of God's promises led Israel into discouragement, defeat, and death because of their unbelief (Num. 13—14).

"And this is the victory that has overcome the world—our faith" (1 John 5:4 NKJV), and that faith is generated by the Word (Rom. 10:17).

Believers today must find their life and victory in God's Word. Unless we know what God commands, we can't obey Him, but if we know His commandments, believe them, and obey them, then His power goes to work in our lives. "And His commandments are not burdensome" (1 John 5:3 NKJV). Obeying the Lord becomes a joyful privilege when you realize that His commandments are expressions of His love, assurances of His strength, invitations to His blessing, opportunities to grow and bring Him glory, and occasions to enjoy His love and fellowship as we seek to please Him. God's Word is the open door into the treasury of His grace.

Moses added a warning against changing the Word of God, either by adding to it or by taking from it (Deut. 4:2; see 12:32; Prov. 30:6; Gal. 3:15; Rev. 22:18–19). The early manuscripts of the Scriptures were copied by hand, and it would be easy for the copyist to make changes, but God watches over His Word (Jer. 1:12) and judges those who tamper with it. The Pharisees in Jesus' day jealously guarded the Scriptures, yet they were guilty of taking away from the Word of God by replacing it with their own traditions (Mark 7:1–13). If God's Word is our life, then we're jeopardizing our own futures if we don't honor the Word and obey it from the heart (Eph. 6:6).

GOD IS HOLY—FEAR HIM (4:3–4)

Israel's persistent sin was idolatry and the immoral practices associated with it. While living in Egypt, the Jews got a taste of idolatry and even practiced it during their wilderness wanderings (Acts 7:42–43). When Moses was with God on Mount Sinai, the people in the camp were worshipping a golden calf (Ex. 32). Idolatry was a grievous sin because Israel had been "married" to Jehovah when the nation accepted the covenant at Mount Sinai, so their worship of idols was really adultery (Jer. 3; Hos. 1—2). It was a sin against God's love as well as a violation of God's law. The Lord finally had to send His people to Babylon to cure them of idolatry.

This may be why Moses brought up the tragedy of Israel's sins at Baalpeor (Deut. 4:3–4; Num. 25). This event was recent enough for the people to remember it. The false prophet Baalam had been hired by King Balak to curse the people of Israel, but each time Baalam tried to curse the Jews, he ended up blessing them (Num. 22—24). His curses didn't work, but he had a plan that did work. He and Balak invited the Jewish men to attend one of the Moabite religious feasts and encouraged them to participate to the full (Num. 25). This meant having intercourse with the temple prostitutes, and one man even brought his "date" back into the Jewish camp! The fact that God judged His people by killing 24,000 men indicates that many of the Jews eagerly participated in the wicked feast. What the enemy couldn't accomplish with curses and fighting he accomplished with compromise and "friendship."

The Jews who refused the invitation and remained true to the Lord were still alive, because the Word is our life, and obeying God's Word keeps us in fellowship with the Lord (2 Cor. 6:14—7:1). God's people must be careful not to become friendly with the world (James 4:4) or spotted by the world (1:27), because this leads to loving the world (1 John 2:15–17) and being conformed to the world (Rom. 12:2). This kind of lifestyle invites the chastening of God, for "the Lord shall judge His people" and "it is a fearful thing to fall into the hands of the living God" (Heb. 10:30–31).

To fear the Lord means to respect who He is, what He is, and what He says, and by our submission and obedience show Him that we love Him and want to please Him. He's the Creator and we're the creatures; He's the Father and we're the children; He's the Master and we're the servants. When we knowingly and willfully defy His authority, we tempt Him to discipline us, and our arrogance only leads to pain and tragic loss. It just isn't worth it. If you want to identify the blessings believers miss when they fail to fear the Lord, read and ponder these verses: Deuteronomy 6:24; Psalms 25:12; 31:19; 34:9; 112; 145:19; Proverbs 1:7; Isaiah 33:6; Ephesians 5:21; Hebrews 12:28–29.

GOD IS WISE—LEARN FROM HIM (4:5–9)

God's Word is the revelation of God's wisdom, and we need to know and follow His wisdom if our lives are to please and glorify Him. The world's wisdom is foolishness with God (1 Cor. 3:19), and those who follow it will be disappointed. In the Old Testament, the word "wisdom" has to do with character rather than human intelligence and describes the right use of knowledge. "Wisdom means being skillful and successful in one's relationships and responsibilities, observing and following the Creator's principles of order in the moral universe," says Dr. Roy Zuck.[2] Practicing God's wisdom means you don't just make a living, you make a life.

Why was it so important for Israel to know and obey God's wisdom? For one thing, this was the guarantee of their success in taking possession of the Promised Land (Deut. 4:5). When you read the book of Joshua, you discover that God had the campaign all worked out and Joshua simply had to discern God's will and obey it. The two times Joshua didn't seek God's wisdom, the nation experienced humiliating failure (Josh. 7; 9).

In knowing God's wisdom, the people of Israel would not only succeed in their mission but they would also be witnesses to the other nations (Deut. 4:6–8). The pagan nations in Canaan tried to obtain guidance from their false gods by means of sorcery and various forms of spiritism, all of which were forbidden to the Jews (18:9–14; Isa. 47:12–14). God's laws clearly revealed to Israel what was right and wrong and covered just about every decision they would have to make. Believers today have the complete Word of God and the assurance that if we obey what God has already taught us, He will give us the guidance we need in the special areas of life (John 7:17). People who live according to God's wisdom can't help but demonstrate to those around them that God is real and that following His wisdom brings blessing.[3] Everything about Israel's religion was so far superior to that of the surrounding nations that the unbelieving pagans couldn't help but be impressed: the presence of God in Israel's sanctuary, the divine laws governing their life, the guidance of God, and the absence of cruelty and impurity. The tragedy is that Israel got so accustomed to these blessings that they began to imitate their neighbors and lost their witness.

There's a third benefit that we enjoy when we follow God's wisdom: It helps to build godly homes (Deut. 4:9–10). Surrounded as they were by heathen people, Israel was always one generation short of losing God's blessing, and so it is with the church today (2 Tim. 2:2). If we don't teach our children about God and His Word, the day will come when a generation will arise that doesn't know the Lord, which is what eventually happened to Israel (Judg. 2:7–15). "Nevertheless, when the Son of Man comes, will He really find faith on the earth?" (Luke 18:8 NKJV).

How can believing parents best influence their children to trust the Lord and live by His wisdom? Moses gives the adults three suggestions: Be examples to your children; don't let God's Word slip from your minds and hearts; remember what the Lord has done for you in the past and share these experiences with your children. Every Jewish child in Moses' day was supposed to know the story of the exodus (Deut. 6:20–25; Ex. 10:1–2; 12:24–28; 13:1–16), and in the future, every child was supposed to know the significance of Israel's crossing the Jordan River (Josh. 4:1–7, 21–24). It's the responsibility of the older generation to instruct the younger generation and be an example and an encouragement to them (Deut. 6:1–3; 32:44–47; Ps. 34:11; 44:1; 71:17–19; 78:1–8; Titus 2:1–8). Parents must not turn this responsibility over to Sunday school teachers or Bible club leaders, as important as those ministries are, for dedicated Christian parents are God's first choice as teachers of their children. The sins of parents—especially spiritual neglect and bad example—may be imitated by the children and produce sad consequences later in life (Deut. 5:8–10; Ex. 20:5–6; Num. 14:17–18).[4]

GOD ALONE IS GOD—WORSHIP HIM (4:10–43)

The nations around Israel worshipped many gods and goddesses, but Israel was to worship only the one true God. "Hear, O Israel: the LORD our God is one LORD" is the first and basic tenet in the Jewish confession of faith, "the Shema" (Deut. 6:4–5), and the first of the Ten Commandments is, "Thou shalt have none other gods before me" (5:7). Why? Because all other "gods" are only the creations of sinful imaginations and aren't gods at all (Rom. 1:18ff.). To worship other gods is to worship nothing and become nothing (Ps. 115:8). One of the Hebrew words for "idols" means "vanity, nothingness." In his message, Moses gives several arguments to defend this warning against idolatry.

Israel's experience at Sinai (vv. 10–19). Moses reminded the people of the nation's awesome experience at Sinai when God made His covenant with them. The mountain blazed with fire and was covered with clouds and great darkness; thunder and lightning frightened the people; and after a trumpet blast that grew louder and louder, God called Moses to the top of the mountain (Ex. 19:16–19; Heb. 12:18–21). The people heard God speak the word but they didn't see any form of God. The Lord was making it very clear that Israel would be a people of the word, hearing their God speak but not beholding any form that could be copied and then worshipped (Deut. 4:12, 15). "He who can hear can see," said a Jewish sage, and he was right.

"You saw no form of any kind the day the LORD spoke to you at Horeb out of the fire" (v. 15 NIV). The conclusion is obvious: God forbids His people to worship visible representations of God or of anything God has made, whether humans, animals, birds, fish, or the sun, moon, and stars.

To worship the creation instead of the Creator is the essence of idolatry (Rom. 1:22–25). God made man in His image, but idolaters make gods in their own images and thereby cheapen themselves and insult God.[5]

Israel's deliverance from Egypt (v. 20). Moses had just mentioned all nations (Deut. 4:19), so he reminded the people that Israel was different from these other nations because Israel was God's chosen people and His special inheritance (Ex. 19:1–6). The Lord chose Abraham and his descendants to bring His blessings to the whole world (Gen. 12:1–3; John 4:22), and in order to accomplish that important task, Israel had to be a separated people. Each year when they celebrated Passover, the Jews would be reminded that they had been slaves in Egypt and the Lord had delivered them by His great power, and they were His people. It was when Israel began to imitate the other nations and worship their detestable gods that Israel ceased to be a nation devoted wholly to the Lord. Because they forgot their distinctive privileges, they lost their distinctive blessings.

The church today can learn a lesson from this. We're called to be a separated people who are not conformed to this world (2 Cor. 6:14—7:1; Rom. 12:1–2), and yet the trend today is for churches to pattern ministry after what the world is doing. The philosophy is that the church will attract more people if the lost feel more comfortable with the services. The tragedy is that the sanctuary becomes a theater and "ministry" becomes entertainment. But Scripture and church history make it clear that what G. Campbell Morgan said is true: "The church did the most for the world when the church was the least like the world." Jesus didn't compromise with the world and yet He attracted sinners and ministered effectively to them (Luke 15:1–2). Unless we are a separated people, devoted wholly to the Lord, we can never follow His example.

Moses' experience at Kadesh (vv. 21–24; Num. 20:1–13). When Moses smote the rock instead of speaking to it, God graciously supplied an abundance of water for His thirsty people, but He disciplined His servant who glorified himself instead of glorifying the Lord. God alone is God, and He alone must be glorified. "I am the LORD: that is my name: and my glory will I not give to another" (Isa. 42:8). Moses warned the people, "For the LORD thy God is a consuming fire, even a jealous God" (Deut. 4:24; see Heb. 12:29). God is jealous over His people the way a husband is jealous over his wife or a mother over her children. (See Deut. 5:9; 6:15; 13:2–10; 29:20.) He wants the very best for us, but when we deliberately go our own way, we grieve His heart and miss all He wants to do for us.

God's loving covenant (vv. 25–31). God made a covenant with His people and He expected them to keep it. The word "covenant" is used at least twenty-seven times in Deuteronomy and comes from the Hebrew word *berith,* which some scholars say means "to eat bread." In the East, when people broke bread together, they formed a covenant or treaty that they would help and protect each other (see Gen. 26:26–35). When God established His covenant with Israel at Mount Sinai, Moses and the Jewish elders ate before God on the mountain (Ex. 24:11). The terms of the covenant were simple: If Israel obeyed God's laws, He would bless them; if they disobeyed, He would chasten them. He would show His love to them in both the blessing and the chastening, "for whom the LORD loves, He chastens" (Heb. 12:6 NKJV).

Moses would elaborate on the details of the covenant later in his address (Deut. 28—30), but here he warned the people that they would be punished, scattered, and destroyed as a nation if they didn't take their covenant responsibilities seriously. This, unfortunately, is what happened. During the closing years of Solomon's reign, to please his many wives he introduced idolatry into the land (1 Kings 11), and this led to God's judgment and the division and deterioration of the nation (1 Kings 12). In 722 BC, Assyria captured the ten tribes that formed the northern kingdom of Samaria, and Babylon took the southern kingdom of Judah in 586 BC From AD 70 until May 14, 1948, when the modern nation of Israel was recognized, the Jewish people were dispersed throughout the world and had no national homeland.

The love of God (vv. 32–43). When you're raising small children, you use rewards and punishments to teach them to obey, but when they get older, you hope that character and love will motivate them to shun evil and do what's right. When Israel turned from the true and living God and began to worship idols, they were sinning against God's grace and love. The Lord hadn't chosen any other nation and given it His covenant, nor had He spoken to any other nation and given it His holy law. God had led His people and cared for them from the days of Abraham to the time of Moses, and He had done this for no other nation. Why? It wasn't because Israel deserved these blessings but because of God's everlasting love (Deut. 4:37; see 7:7–8, 13; 23:5).

God doesn't want His children obeying Him just to get blessings or to avoid chastening, but because they love Him from the heart. The word "heart" is mentioned more than forty times in Moses' speech, and the Shema (6:4–5) emphasizes love for the Lord. (See also 10:12; 11:1, 13, 22; 13:3; 19:9; 30:6, 16, 20.) When Moses gave the law to the older generation at Sinai, the emphasis was on the fear of the Lord (Ex. 19:10–25; 20:20), but his application of the law to the new generation magnifies God's love for Israel and the importance of Israel's loving the Lord. They were now to be a mature people who obeyed God from the heart. The Lord is a merciful God (Deut. 4:31), but we shouldn't tempt Him because He is also a jealous God (v. 24).

As evidence of God's love and mercy, Moses set apart three "cities of refuge" on the east side of the Jordan, to which people who accidentally killed somebody could flee and get justice and find protection (vv. 41–43). This subject will be dealt with in detail in 19:1–14.

GOD IS LORD OF ALL—OBEY HIM (4:44—5:33)

The archaeologist's spade has revealed that the book of Deuteronomy follows a literary pattern used in the ancient Near East for treaties between rulers and their vassal nations. With Israel, of course, the Lord had conquered their enemies and set the Jews free, and they were His special people, but as they entered their land, this freedom involved responsibilities. They were a covenant people, and Deuteronomy defines the terms of the covenant. Like the ancient vassal treaties, Deuteronomy has a preamble (1:1–5) and a review of the history behind the treaty (1:6—4:49). Then it lists the ruler's stipulations for the conduct of his subjects (chaps. 5—26) and what would happen if they disobeyed (chaps. 27—30). It closes with an explanation of how the treaty would operate in future generations (chaps. 31—34).

Moses began by calling Israel to hear God's covenant, learn it, and do whatever it commanded (5:1). As we have seen, "to hear" means much more than to listen casually to words that somebody is speaking. It means to listen attentively, to understand, to heed and obey. When God made this covenant, it included every generation of the nation of Israel from that day on and not just with the generation that gathered at Sinai. Moses was addressing a new generation and yet he said, "The LORD our God made a covenant with us in Horeb" (v. 2). Just as God's covenant with Abraham included the Jewish people of future generations, so did His covenant at Sinai, for God was their "dwelling place in all generations" (Ps. 90:1). Most of the people who had been at Sinai died during the wilderness wanderings, but the covenant of God stood fast.

Moses was the mediator between Jehovah and Israel because the people were afraid to hear the voice of God (Deut. 5:23–27; Ex. 20:18–21; see also Gal. 3:19). If we are believing and obedient people, hearing God's voice means blessing and encouragement, but if our hearts are not right with God, His voice could mean judgment.

The law of God (vv. 6–21; Ex. 20:1–17). The Lord opened the proclamation of His law by reminding the people that it was He who delivered them from the slavery of Egypt (Deut. 5:6; see Neh. 9:9–11; Ps. 77:14–15; 105:23–38; 136:10–15; Isa. 63:11–14). This great act of redemption should have been motive enough for the people to listen to God's law and obey it, just as the redemption we have in Christ should motivate us to obey Him. Each year at Passover, the Jews were reminded of God's great act of salvation, and each time the church celebrates the Lord's Supper, we're reminded that Christ died for us that we might be saved from our sins and belong to Him. The Lord wants us to obey Him, not as slaves cringing before a master, but as grateful children who love their heavenly Father and appreciate all He is to us and has done for us.

The first four commandments had to do with Israel's relationship to God personally: acknowledging that there is but one Lord (Deut. 5:6–7), abstaining from worshipping idols (vv. 8–10), honoring God's name (v. 11), and observing the Sabbath (vv. 12–15). The first commandment (vv. 6–7) is expressed in the Shema (6:4–5), and the second commandment (vv. 8–10) is the logical expression of the first. If there is but one true God, then the making and worshipping of idols is not only illogical, but it's a denial of Israel's confession of faith. Israel was "married" to Jehovah at Sinai, and idolatry was a breach of that marriage covenant and the equivalent of adultery. Keep in mind that in the East in that day, idolatry could involve sexual intercourse with temple prostitutes.

We have already noted that the Lord doesn't punish the children and grandchildren because of their ancestors' sins (Ezek. 18), but He can permit the sad consequences of those sins to affect future generations, physically, mentally, and spiritually. Children are prone to imitate their parents, and Eastern peoples lived in extended families, with three and four generations often in the same home. It's easy to see that the older members of the family had opportunities to influence the younger ones either for good or for evil. But the Lord also blesses successive generations of people who honor and obey Him. My great-grandfather prayed that there would be a preacher of the gospel in every generation of our family, and there has been. I minister today because of godly ancestors who trusted the Lord.

In the third commandment (Deut. 5:11), God's name represents God's character and reputation, and to honor His name means to make Him "look good" to the people around us. All parents want their children to bring honor to the family name. We pray, "Hallowed be thy name" (Matt. 6:9), and then we live and speak in such a way that we help to answer that prayer. Using God's name under oath to defend a dishonest statement, as well as cursing and swearing, are ways of dishonoring the Lord's name. Bearing that name and living like a Christian will honor God's good name before a watching world (1 Peter 4:12–16).

Nine of the Ten Commandments are repeated in the New Testament epistles for the church to obey; the exception is the fourth commandment (Deut. 5:12–15) about the Sabbath Day. Why? The Sabbath Day was a special sign between Israel and the Lord (Ex. 31:12–17; Neh. 9:13–15; Ezek. 20:12, 20) and wasn't given to any other nation (Ps. 147:19–20). The Sabbath had its beginning in creation (Gen. 2:1–3) and for that reason was a part of Israel's religious life even before the law was given at Sinai (Ex. 16:23, 25). But at Sinai, Sabbath observance became a part of God's covenant with Israel and was associated with their deliverance from Egypt (Deut. 5:15). Canaan would be Israel's place of rest (3:20; 12:10; 25:19), and the weekly Sabbath would give them a foretaste of that rest. Believers today have their rest in Christ (Matt. 11:28–30; Heb. 3—4) and look forward to eternal rest in heaven (Rev. 14:13). Unfortunately, Israel didn't honor the Sabbath Days or the Sabbatical year, and the Lord had to discipline them (2 Chron. 36:14–21; Ezek. 20; Isa. 58:13–14; Jer. 17:19–27).

Many well-meaning people call Sunday "the Christian Sabbath," but strictly speaking, this is a misnomer. Sunday is the first day of the week, the Lord's Day, and the Sabbath is Saturday, the seventh day of the week.

The Sabbath symbolizes the old covenant of law: You labored for six days and then you rested. The Lord's Day commemorates the new covenant of grace: It opens the week with rest in Christ and the works follow. Both the Sabbath and the Lord's Day emphasize the importance of devoting one day in seven to the Lord in worship and service. Every day belongs to the Lord, and it's unbiblical to make the observance of days a test of spirituality or orthodoxy (Col. 2:16–17; Rom. 14:1—15:7; Gal. 4:1–11).

The fifth commandment (Deut. 5:16) moves us from our relationship to the Lord to living out that relationship with other people, beginning in the home. Both the divine and human aspects of the law are important and must not be separated, because we're commanded to love the Lord and also love our neighbors (Mark 12:28–34). Piety begins at home with honoring one's father and mother, a law that was very important in Israel (Deut. 27:16; Ex. 21:15, 17; Lev. 19:3, 32; Prov. 1:8; 16:31; 20:20; 23:22; 30:17) and is still important in the church (Eph. 6:1–3; 1 Tim. 5:1–2). Too many people in today's society worship youth and resent the idea of getting old, and for this reason the aged are often neglected and abused and, in some nations, legally killed (euthanasia—"assisted suicide").

This leads logically to the sixth commandment (Deut. 5:17), which requires that we honor human life and not commit murder. God is the Giver of life and only He has the right to take it. Because we're made in God's image, murder is an attack against God (Gen. 1:26–27; 9:6). The Bible doesn't forbid self-defense (Ex. 22:2), but only the state has the right to take human life in cases of capital offense (Rom. 13). Jesus warned that murder often begins with anger (Matt. 5:21–26), and that while murder is far worse, anger is the moral equivalent of murder. It's worth noting that the law was given to Israel to restrain people and punish them for their crimes, and not to reform them. While the law can't change the human heart (Heb. 7:19), it can restrain and punish those who defy its authority and refuse to obey its precepts.

The seventh commandment (Deut. 5:18) calls for sexual purity and the honoring of marriage as God's appointed way for the proper use and enjoyment of human sexuality. In ancient Israel, adultery was considered a capital crime (22:22), while in today's society, it's hardly considered a sin, let alone a crime. God can forgive sexual sins (1 Cor. 6:9–11), but He doesn't promise to interfere with the painful consequences (2 Sam. 12:13–14; Prov. 6:20–35; Gal. 6:7–8; Heb. 13:4). It's disgusting the way the media glorify sex and turn fornication and adultery into entertainment.

God is concerned not only about the way we treat other people but also about the way we treat other people's property. The eighth commandment (Deut. 5:19) simply says, "Neither shalt thou steal." Brief and to the point, it covers a multitude of offenses: stealing property, stealing a person's good name (slander), cheating on an examination, and even stealing people (slavery, kidnapping). Ephesians 4:28 makes it clear that there are only three ways to get property: work for it, receive it as a gift, or steal it. Only the first two are acceptable to the Lord.

The ninth commandment (Deut. 5:20) forbids all forms of lying, whether on the witness stand in court or over the back fence (see 17:6–13). Truth is the cement that holds society together, and things fall apart when people don't keep their promises, whether contracts in business or vows at the marriage altar. This commandment also prohibits slander, which is lying about other people (Ex. 23:1; Prov 10:18; 12:17; 19:9; 24:28; Titus 3:1–2; James 4:11; 1 Peter 2:1). God's people should be known for speaking the truth in love (Eph. 4:15).

The focus of the tenth commandment (Deut. 5:21) is covetousness, the sinful desire in the heart for anything that rightfully we shouldn't have. This commandment and the first commandment (v. 7) deal with inward attitudes rather than outward actions, but breaking either of these two commandments could lead to breaking all the rest of them. Because of covetousness, people have robbed, committed adultery, lied, and even murdered. If we obey the first commandment and truly love God and worship only Him, then covetousness won't be a problem (Matt. 6:33; Eph. 5:3; Col. 3:5).

Christian believers who depend on the indwelling Holy Spirit (Gal. 5:22–26) and live by the law of love (Rom. 13:8–10) don't have to strive to obey these commandments, because the life of God will flow through them and enable them to fulfill the righteousness of God (8:1–17). The old nature knows no law, but the new nature needs no law. There's probably a law in your city that requires parents to care for their children, but how many parents think about that law? Parents care for their children because they love them, not because they're afraid of going to jail.

Because we've been born again into God's family and have received God's divine nature within, we are enabled by the Spirit to obey God's law and live godly lives (1 John 3:1–9).

The God of the law (vv. 22–33). The purpose of the law of God is to reveal the God of the law, and when you focus on Him, you find it a delight to obey His commands (Ps. 40:8). Moses closed his review of the Ten Commandments by reminding the new generation that at Sinai God revealed His glory and His greatness. The God of Israel is not to be trifled with because He is a holy God. Israel would never again go to Sinai and see the fire, the cloud, the darkness, and the lightning, and hear the awesome voice of God speak from the mountain, but they needed to remember the majesty of their God and the authority of His Word.

Many churches today have lost the biblical concept of the majesty and authority of God as expressed in His law. This deficiency has cheapened our worship, turned evangelism into religious salesmanship, and converted the Bible into a self-help book that's guaranteed to make you a success. A. W. Tozer was right when he said that "no religion has ever been greater than its idea of God." He also said, "The essence of idolatry is the entertainment of thoughts about God that are unworthy of Him."[6] If that's true, and I believe it is, then many evangelical Christians are guilty of idol worship.

In his appeal to Israel, Moses urged them to remember the majesty of God and respect the Word of God. He quoted Jehovah's own words, "Oh, that their hearts would be inclined to fear me and keep all my commands always" (Deut. 5:29 NIV). Obedience is always a matter of the heart, and if we love the Lord, we will keep His commandments (John 14:15, 21–24). There's no conflict between the greatness of God and the grace of God, His transcendence and His immanence, for we can love the Lord and fear the Lord with the same heart (Ps. 2:10–12; 34:8–9). The fear of the Lord is a major theme in Deuteronomy (6:2, 13, 24; 10:20; 14:23; 17:19; 31:12), but so is the love of God for us (7:7; 10:15; 23:5) as well as our love for Him (6:5; 10:12; 11:1, 13, 22; 19:9; 30:6, 16, 20). The immature believer with a shallow theology sees a contradiction here, but the mature believer rejoices in the balance revealed in the Word: "God is love" and "God is light" (1 John 4:8; 1:5).

Even though God's children live under grace and not under the Mosaic law (Rom. 6:14; Gal. 5:1), it's important for us to know the law of God so that we might better know the God of the law and please Him. Christ has fulfilled the types and symbols found in the law, so we no longer practice the Old Testament rituals as Israel did. Christ bore the curse of the law on the cross (Gal. 3:10–13) so that we need not fear judgment (Rom. 8:1). But the moral law still stands and God still judges sin. It's as wrong today to lie, steal, commit adultery, and murder as it was when Moses received the tables of the law at Mount Sinai. In fact, it's worse, because we have today the full revelation of God's will through Jesus Christ, and we sin against a flood of light.

"I will delight myself in thy statutes: I will not forget thy word" (Ps. 119:16).

QUESTIONS FOR PERSONAL REFLECTION
OR GROUP DISCUSSION

1. To "hear" God's Word also implies "to pay attention, to understand, to obey." Why do all of these meanings go together?

2. John says in 1 John 5:3 (NIV) that God's "commands are not burdensome." How do you experience God's commandments?

3. What does it mean to "fear" the Lord? Do you fear Him? Explain.

4. What is wisdom? How is wisdom different from human intelligence? What is the source of wisdom? What are some benefits of knowing and obeying God's wisdom?

5. What suggestions does Moses give for parents to influence their children in a godly direction? Which of these, if any, do you most need to work on?

6. G. Campbell Morgan said, "The church did the most for the world when the church was the least like the world." How is your church excelling at being a "separated people"? In what ways might your church have slipped into sameness with the world?

7. What should be our motivation to obey God? What motivates you to godly obedience?

8. When adults sin grievously before the Lord, how does this affect their children and grandchildren? Do you see any effects of sin passed down in your family? If so, what are they?

9. How do you understand the fourth commandment (Remember the Sabbath Day to keep it holy) in the church era?

10. Which of the commandments is the most difficult for you to keep? How can this struggle result in victory?

Chapter Three

THE SECRETS OF OBEDIENCE

(Deuteronomy 6—7)

Moses was a wise teacher of God's truth. First he reviewed what the Lord had done for Israel (Deut. 1—4) and reminded the people of God's mercy and goodness. Then he reaffirmed the basic principles of God's law (Deut. 5—6), what we know as the Ten Commandments (10:4). In chapters 6 and 7, Moses discussed motives for obedience and explained why the people should honor God's laws. He wanted the nation's obedience to be based on spiritual principles, not just personal opinions, and to be encouraged by the right motives. Only after Moses had laid this strong foundation did he apply God's commandments to specific areas of Israel's life.

God gave His law to build the people individually as well as the nation collectively. How could over two million people live together and work together, let alone fight the enemy together, unless they had rules and regulations to govern them? Israel's civic peace and general welfare depended on the people respecting the law and obeying it. Unfortunately, over the years, some of the religious leaders added so many traditions to God's law that the people felt like they were wearing a galling yoke (Acts 15:10; Gal. 5:1).

The law was also meant to reveal God and draw the people closer to Him. If Israel was to be a holy people and a kingdom of priests (Ex. 19:1–8), they needed a holy law to guide them. Certainly God was concerned about the external conduct of His people, but He was also concerned that their hearts be devoted to Him. When you read Psalm 119, you discover what the law of God meant to Jewish people who were spiritually minded and devoted to the Lord in their hearts. They saw God's righteous law, not as a heavy yoke, but as honey (v. 103), light (v. 105), a treasure (vv. 14, 72, 127, 162), freedom (v. 45), and a source of great joy (v. 14). They delighted in the law and meditated on it (vv. 15–16, 23–24, 47–48, 77–78; see 1:1–3). Yes, the Ten Commandments were engraved on tablets of stone, but the spiritual Jew also had the Word hidden in his heart (119:10–11).

One of the key themes in Deuteronomy 6—7 is motivation for obedience. These two chapters answer the question "Why should we obey God's Word in a world where most people ignore it or deliberately disobey it?" Moses explained four fundamental motives for obedience.

1. LOVE FOR THE LORD (6:1–9)

Moses has already emphasized God's love for Israel and the importance of Israel's love for God (4:32–43), and he will mention this topic several times before he concludes his address. If Israel obeyed the Lord, they would conquer the enemy, possess the land, multiply in the land, and enjoy a long life in the place of God's blessing (6:1–3). At least six times in this book, Moses called Canaan "a land of milk and honey" (v. 3; 11:9; 26:9, 15; 27:3; 31:20), a phrase that describes the richness and fruitfulness of the land. Milk was a staple food and honey a luxury, so "a land of milk and honey" would provide all that the people needed. There would be adequate pastures for their flocks and herds and sufficient plants in the fields for the bees to obtain pollen. How could the people not love and obey Jehovah when He blessed them so abundantly?[1]

Covenant (v. 3). There was always a danger that the new generation would become proud and think that God had blessed them because they were better than previous generations. Moses reminded them that all their blessings came from the Lord because of His covenant with their fathers, Abraham, Isaac, and Jacob. In fact, it was this truth that opened his address (1:8, 21, 35), and he would mention it again (6:10; 9:5, 27; 29:13; 30:20; 34:4; see also Ex. 6:8; 33:1). God's gracious promise to the patriarchs gave Israel ownership of the land, but it was their own obedience to the Lord that guaranteed their possession and enjoyment of the land.[2] It's unfortunate that after Israel had lived in the land, they took their blessings for granted, disobeyed God's law, and had to be punished for their rebellion. First they were chastened in the land (described in the book of Judges), and then they were removed from the land and taken captive to Babylon.

Believers today need to be reminded that all our blessings come to us because of God's eternal covenant with His Son (Heb. 13:20) and the new covenant, which Jesus made through His sacrificial death on the cross (Luke 22:20; 1 Cor. 11:25; Heb. 8—9). We aren't blessed because of what we are in ourselves but because of what we are in Christ (Eph. 1:3–14).

Confession (v. 4). As mentioned in chapter 2, the orthodox Jewish confession of faith is called "the Shema" after the Hebrew word that means "to hear." This confession is still recited each morning and evening by devout Jews all over the world, affirming "Jehovah, our Elohim, Jehovah is one." (See Matt. 22:37–38; Mark 12:29–30; Luke 10:27.) So important is this confession that Jewish boys in orthodox homes are required to memorize it as soon as they can speak. The nations around Israel worshipped many gods and goddesses, but Israel affirmed to all that there is but one true and living God, the God of Abraham, Isaac, and Jacob.

The Hebrew word translated "one" (*ehad*) can also mean "a unity" as well as "numerical oneness." It's used that way in Genesis 2:24, describing the oneness of Adam and Eve, and also in Exodus 26:6 and 11 to describe "unity" of the curtains in the tabernacle (see NIV). The word also carries the idea of "uniqueness." In contrast to the many pagan gods and goddesses, Jehovah is unique, for there is only one true God; He is God alone and not part of a pantheon; and He is a unity, which Christians interpret as leaving room for the Trinity (Matt. 28:19–20; 3:16–17). When Israel began to put Jehovah alongside the false gods of the Gentile nations, they denied their own confession of faith. The Gentiles could renounce their false gods and trust the true God, the God of Israel, but a devout Jew could never put Jehovah on the same level as the gods of the Gentiles.

Commandment (v. 5). Is it possible to command somebody to love? Isn't love a mysterious thing that just appears, a wonderful emotion that's either there or it isn't there? No, not according to Scripture. In the life of the believer, love is an act of the will: We choose to relate to God and to other persons in a loving way no matter how we may feel. Christian love simply means that we treat others the way God treats us. In His love, God is kind and forgiving toward us, so we seek to be kind and forgiving toward others (Eph. 4:32). God wills the very best for us, so we desire the very best for others, even if it demands sacrifice on our part. Love isn't simply an exotic feeling; love leads to action. "God so loved … that he gave" (John 3:16). The virtues of love that are listed in 1 Corinthians 13:4–7 describe how we treat people and not just how we feel about them.

To love God and worship and serve Him is the highest privilege we can have, so when the Lord commands us to love, He is inviting us to that which is the best. But our love for God must involve the totality of the inner person—"with all your heart … soul … and strength." It isn't necessary to define and distinguish these elements, as though they were three different internal human functions. In some Scriptures only two are named (Deut. 4:29; 10:12; Josh. 22:5), while in other parallel Scriptures there are four (Mark 12:30; Luke 10:27). The phrase simply means "all that is within you" (Ps. 103:1), a total devotion to the Lord. If the inner person is completely yielded to the Lord and open to His Word as ministered by His Spirit, then the feelings will follow. But even if they don't, we must still relate to other people as the Lord relates to us.

Communication (vv. 6–9). When we hear the Word of God and receive it into our hearts (1 Thess. 2:13), then the Holy Spirit can use the truth to transform us from within (2 Cor. 3:1–3; John 17:17). God "writes" the Word upon our hearts, and we become "living epistles" that others may read, and our lives can influence them to trust Christ. How we live is important because it backs up what we say. Moses admonished parents to discuss God's Word in the home, among the children, and to allow the Word to guide their minds and hands as they work throughout the day. The Word should even control who is permitted to go through the gate and come through the door into the house. The Jews took these commandments literally and wore portions of Scripture[3] in little containers called phylacteries on their foreheads and left arms (Matt. 23:5). They also attached a small container of Scripture, called a mezuzah, to the front door and on every door in the house. Each occupant touched the mezuzah reverently each time he or she passed through a door (Ps. 121:8). It was a sign that the house was to be a sanctuary for the Lord and a place where the Word was loved, obeyed, and taught.

We can't help but admire such respect for the Word of God, but it's likely that the emphasis of this commandment was obedience to God's Word in all that we think and do rather than the actual wearing of the Scriptures on the forehead and the arm. At least that seems to be the emphasis in Deuteronomy 11:18–21. However, we agree wholeheartedly that God's people ought to make their homes places where God dwells, where the Scriptures are honored, and we aren't ashamed of our faith. It isn't necessary to turn every room into a chapel, but a Bible on the table and a few Scripture texts on the wall at least bear witness that we belong to the Lord and desire to please Him.

2. GRATITUDE TO THE LORD (6:10–25)

Moses was equipping the new generation to enter and claim the Promised Land, and he knew that Canaan would be a place of temptation as well as a place of triumph. For one thing, when they conquered the nations in Canaan, the Israelites would inherit vast wealth and would be tempted to forget the Lord, who had made their victories possible. The second temptation would be for Israel to compromise with the pagan nations around them and not maintain their separated position as the people of the Lord. (Moses will deal with this second temptation in Deut. 7:1–16.)

Most people find it easier to handle adversity than prosperity (see Phil. 4:10–20), because adversity usually drives us closer to God as we seek His wisdom and help. When things are going well, we're prone to relax our spiritual disciplines, take our blessings for granted, and forget to "praise God from whom all blessings flow." The material things that we wait for and sacrifice for seem to mean much more to us than the gifts that fall in our laps without our help.

Moses named some of the material blessings the Lord would give the Israelites in the Promised Land: large prosperous cities, houses filled with different kinds of wealth, wells, vineyards, and olive groves, as well as the land itself. Whenever the Jews took water from the wells or fruit from the vines and trees, they should have looked up with gratitude to the Lord. Water is a precious commodity in the East, and the people didn't even have to toil to dig the wells! Nor did they have to plant the vineyards or the olive groves and then wait for the plants to grow and mature. God used these spoils of war to compensate the Jews for the wages they didn't receive when they were enslaved in Egypt, and at the same time He reminded them of His bounteous grace.

With privilege always comes responsibility, and Israel's responsibility was to fear Jehovah and obey Him (Deut. 6:13), the verse that Jesus quoted when He replied to Satan's third temptation (Matt. 4:10). When we cultivate a reverent and submissive heart, we will have an obedient will and won't even want to mention the names of false gods. Israel needed to remember that the Lord owned the land (Lev. 25:23) and that they were merely His "tenants." Their inheritance in the land was God's gift to His people, but if they disobeyed His covenant, they would forfeit the land and its blessings. The Lord is jealous over His people and will not share their love and worship with any false god (Deut. 5:8–10; 32:16–26).

Moses warned the people not to tempt (test) the Lord as the older generation had done at Massah (Ex. 17:1–7). We tempt the Lord when we openly and unbelievingly question His ability or defy His authority by what we say or do. After He delivered Israel from Egypt, the Lord deliberately led them through difficulties so He could teach them to trust Him. First they came to bitter water at Marah and complained about it instead of asking God to help them (15:22–26). Then they got hungry for the "fleshpots of Egypt" and murmured against the Lord, and the Lord provided the daily manna to sustain them (16:1–8). When they came to Rephidim, there was no water to drink, and once again they complained against the Lord instead of trusting the Lord (17:1–7). "Is the Lord among us or not?" was their question, meaning, "If He is among us, why doesn't He do something?"

Moses did what the people should have done: He turned to the Lord for help, and God supplied the water that they needed. But that place was given two special names: "Massah," which means "to test," and "Meribah," which means "contention, quarreling" (v. 7; see Ps. 95; Heb. 3:7–15). By their attitude and their words, Israel defied the Lord and proved that they neither loved Him nor trusted Him. Their bodies were in the camp of Israel, but their hearts were still in Egypt. If God had not been gracious and long-suffering, He could have judged them severely, but He knows that His people are only clay (Ps. 103:8–14).

The Lord tests our faith, not just in the great crises of life, but even more in the small unexpected events, such as a travel delay, an irritating interruption, a sudden sickness, or a lost wallet. The way we respond in these situations will indicate what's in our hearts, because what life does to us depends on what life finds in us. If we love and trust the Lord, we'll leave the matter with Him and do what He tells us, but if we question the Lord and rebel because we're not getting our own way, then we're in danger of tempting Him. One of the best protections against tempting the Lord is a grateful heart. If we're in the habit of thanking the Lord in everything, including the painful experiences of life, then the Holy Spirit will fill our hearts with love and praise instead of Satan filling us with bitter venom. How many "Massahs" and "Meribahs" are marked on the map of our journey of faith?

Of course, the greatest blessing for which Israel should have been thankful was their deliverance from Egypt (Deut. 6:20–25). In his farewell address, Moses frequently referred to this miracle, and in later years, so did the prophets. Had Israel remained in Egypt, there would have been no nation, no sanctuary, no priesthood, and no hope, but the Lord delivered them and brought them into their land and fulfilled His promises. Today, we have a Bible and a Savior because Moses led his people out of Egypt, an event that was celebrated annually at Passover. Jewish fathers were commanded to teach their children the meaning of Passover, and of the laws God had given Israel, so that the next generation would understand how to trust Jehovah, love Him, and obey His laws. When our children are ignorant of the past, they will have no hope for the future.

An attitude of gratitude is a wonderful weapon against unbelief, disobedience, a hard heart, and a bitter spirit. "Rejoice evermore. Pray without ceasing. In everything give thanks: for this is the will of God in Christ Jesus concerning you" (1 Thess. 5:16–18). Instead of complaining about what we don't have, let's be thankful for what we do have, because God always gives His best to those who leave the choice with Him.

3. SEPARATION UNTO THE LORD (7:1–16)

"A people dwelling alone," said the hireling prophet Balaam about Israel, "not reckoning itself among the nations" (Num. 23:9 NKJV). From the call of Abraham to the exodus from Egypt, the people of Israel were expected to be a separated people, not because they were better than any other nation but because they were different. They were God's chosen people. God commanded Abraham to leave Ur of the Chaldees and go to the land that He would show him (Gen. 11:31—12:4), and when Abraham left that land and went down to Egypt for help, God had to chasten him (vv. 10–20). Throughout her history, when Israel maintained a separated position by obeying God's laws and seeking to please Him, she succeeded in all that she did. But when she began to compromise with the other nations and to worship their gods, it led to failure and defeat.

Separation means safety (vv. 1–6). In Scripture, separation is not isolation, for if believers are isolated, how can they be "the salt of the earth" and "the light of the world" (Matt. 5:13–16) and influence others for the Lord? Believers can be separated from sin and to the Lord and still be involved in the normal challenges and activities of human life. Abraham was allied with some of his neighbors in Canaan and together they defeated the invaders and rescued the people of Sodom and Gomorrah (Gen. 14), yet Abraham never lived or worshipped as his neighbors did. Jesus was the "friend of publicans and sinners" (Matt. 11:19), and yet He was "holy, harmless, undefiled, separate from sinners" (Heb. 7:26). Jesus had contact with the real world and its people, but He wasn't contaminated from that contact. True biblical separation is contact without contamination. We're different from the world but not odd. When you're different, you attract people and have opportunities to share the good news of Christ, but when you're odd, you repel people and they slam the door on your witness.

God promised to drive out the pagan nations and deliver them into the hands of the Jewish army. With the Lord's help, Israel would defeat those nations and destroy them and everything connected with their religions.[4] Israel was to keep herself separate from these nations. The Lord would not permit intermarriage, political treaties, or any toleration of or interest in the pagan religion of the land. The reason was obvious: Any link with the godless Canaanite religion could lead Israel into alliances that would undermine their relationship with the Lord and invite His chastening. Israel is God's chosen people and treasured possession, and their separation from idolatry in Canaan was important to the nation's spiritual health and political future.

As an example of the kind of caution Israel had to exercise, the same God who allowed Israel to spoil the Egyptians warned them not even to covet or remove the precious metals that covered many of the Canaanite idols (Deut. 7:25). It was logical to destroy the idols, but why not keep the gold and silver? Since idolatry is associated with the demonic (1 Cor. 10:14–22), bringing idolatrous gold and silver into the camp of Israel would defile the camp and open the way for satanic attack. Of itself, neither the gold nor the silver was evil, but because it had been associated with demons, the precious metal took on a new character that made it useful to the enemy. Anyone who used that metal, even to make a beautiful thing, would be dealing with something that was associated with evil.

Separation means blessing (vv. 7–16). The Lord's choice of Abraham and Sarah was an act of sovereign grace. They were idol-worshippers in Ur of the Chaldees when "the God of glory" appeared (Acts 7:1–3; Josh. 24:1–3). They had no children and yet were promised descendants as numerous as the sands of the seashore and the stars of the heavens. They later had one son, Isaac, and he had two sons, Esau and Jacob, and from Jacob's twelve sons came the twelve tribes of Israel. When Jacob's family gathered in Egypt, there were seventy people (Gen. 46), but by the time they were delivered from Egypt, they had become a great nation. Why did this happen? Because God loved them and kept the promises that He made to their ancestors.

We must not overlook the parallel between Israel and the church. All who are born again through faith in Jesus Christ are "chosen … in him [Christ] before the foundation of the world" (Eph. 1:4). This salvation came to us "not by works of righteousness which we have done, but according to his mercy." One of my seminary professors once said, "Try to explain divine election and you may lose your mind, but try to explain it away and you will lose your soul." Like Israel, the church is God's chosen people and His treasured possession, a kingdom of priests and a holy nation (1 Peter 2:5, 9), and like Israel, we are called to be a light to the lost world (Matt. 5:14–16).

Privilege always brings responsibility, and Israel's responsibility was to obey God's commandments, for then He could bless them as He promised. God's covenant was a covenant of love, and He would show His love by blessing them if they obeyed and chastening them if they disobeyed. The Lord would bless them with children and grandchildren and increase their numbers greatly. He would also increase their crops and livestock so they would have enough to eat and a surplus to sell. Because of their obedience, Israel would escape the terrible diseases they saw in Egypt as well as the plagues that God sent to the land.

All these blessings on Israel would bring glory to the Lord. The other nations would see the fruitfulness of the land and the people and ask, "What is the reason for this?" The Jews would then reply, "This is the blessing of the Lord on His people!" It would give the Jews opportunities to share the truth about Jehovah with unbelievers and perhaps persuade them to trust the true and living God. Their national blessings would also give parents the opportunity to teach their children the importance of obeying God's Word.[5]

This section of the law opens with, "You shall conquer them [the nations] and utterly destroy them" (Deut. 7:2 NKJV), and it closes with the same admonition (v. 16).[6] Moses repeated this warning several times in his farewell speech, because he knew how easy it would be for Israel to compromise with the enemy, fraternize with them, and eventually imitate them. Most Christians today live in pluralistic societies in democratic nations and don't have the authority to annihilate everybody who worships a false God, nor should they want that authority. Our task is to love those we disagree with and seek to win them to faith in Christ. But at the same time, we must maintain a separated position and not be contaminated by the ideas or activities of the lost world (Ps. 1:1).

The key passage in the New Testament on separation is 2 Corinthians 6:14—7:1. In it, Paul points out that there are both negative and positive elements in biblical separation. Because of what we are in Christ—righteousness, light, the temple of God—we have nothing in common spiritually with unbelievers whom he describes as unrighteousness, darkness, and worshippers of idols. Separation is simply living up to what we are in Christ. If we separate ourselves from sin, God will be able to deal with us as obedient children. He will commune with us and bless us. "Let us cleanse ourselves" is the negative part of godly living, but "perfecting holiness in the fear of God" is the positive part, and the two go together (2 Cor. 7:1).

We aren't supposed to isolate ourselves from the world (but see 1 Cor. 5:9–13) because the world needs our witness and service. We cooperate with different people at different times for different reasons, but we're careful not to compromise our witness for Christ. We do some things because it's for the good of humanity and other things because we're citizens or employees. But whatever we do, we seek to do it to the glory of God.

4. Promises from the Lord (7:17–26)

The first motive Moses mentioned for Israel's obedience was love for the Lord (Deut. 6:1–9), because love is the greatest motive in life. "If you love

Me, keep My commandments" (John 14:15 NKJV). The second motive is gratitude (Deut. 6:10–25), for showing gratitude is one way of expressing love. We must never forget what the Lord has done for us. The third motive is separation from sin and unto the Lord (7:1–16), for we want to live up to all that God has called us to be. He's called us to be a holy nation, a chosen people, a people to bring glory to His name, and we can't fulfill any of those honorable callings if we don't separate ourselves from what is wicked and cleave to the Lord.

But these three motives all depend on faith in the promises of God, for "without faith it is impossible to please [God]" (Heb. 11:6). Israel wasn't operating on what the world calls "blind faith" because they had God's covenant promises to encourage them and the long record of God's care to assure them. God's people don't live on explanations; they live on promises. At the end of his life, Joshua reminded the people, "And you know in all your hearts and in all your souls that not one thing has failed of all the good things which the LORD your God spoke concerning you" (Josh. 23:14 NKJV).

God was faithful in the past (vv. 17–19). The older generation didn't believe that victory was possible in Canaan (Num. 13—14), so they rebelled against God and eventually died in the wilderness. But the new generation should have had no problem believing God's promises after all that He had done for them. The Lord defeated Pharaoh and humiliated all the gods and goddesses of Egypt. The Lord also helped Israel defeat the Midianites; Sihon, king of Heshbon; and Og, king of Bashan. He enabled the tribes of Reuben, Gad, and Manasseh to settle their families east of the Jordan while the men of those tribes prepared to march into Canaan and take the land. Ever since Israel had arrived in the area of the Jordan, not one nation had been able to stand against God's people, because God's people trusted the Lord. The same God who gave victory in Egypt and in the territory east of the Jordan could also give victory in the land of Canaan.

God would go before Israel (vv. 20–21). The terror of the Lord went before Israel and brought fear to the hearts of the people of Canaan (Josh. 2:11; Ex. 15:16). The news about the defeat of Egypt, the opening of the Red Sea, and the slaughter of the nations east of the Jordan couldn't help but paralyze even the strongest in the land. Bible students don't agree on what is meant by "the hornet" in Deuteronomy 7:20 (Ex. 23:27–30; Josh. 24:12), but it's likely that it was the familiar stinging insect that swarmed into the land and attacked the people. The Canaanites were a superstitious people who saw omens in every unusual happening, and they may have interpreted this strange occurrence as an announcement of defeat. Insects are sometimes used as metaphors for nations (Isa. 7:18), and some students understand "hornets" to refer to invading nations that God sent into Canaan prior to Israel's arrival. These local wars would weaken the Canaanite military defenses and prepare the way for Israel's invasion. Whatever the interpretation, and the literal one makes good sense, two facts are clear: God goes before His people and opens the way for victory, and He can use even small insects to accomplish His purposes.

The assurance that the Lord was with His people as they invaded the land (Deut. 7:21) should have encouraged the Israelites to be brave and obedient. Forty years before, when the older generation rebelled at Kadesh-barnea (Num. 13—14), Caleb and Joshua used the promise of the presence of the Lord as an argument for courage and obedience: "The LORD is with us: fear them not" (14:9). The distinctive thing about the nation of Israel was that the Lord was with them (Ex. 33:12–17). The assurance of God's presence goes all the way back to Isaac (Gen. 26:24) and Jacob (28:15) and was often repeated to Israel when they needed encouragement (Isa. 41:10; 43:5; Jer. 46:28; Hag. 1:13; 2:4), and this wonderful assurance has been given to the church today (Matt. 28:18–20; Heb. 13:5–6).

The British expositor G. Campbell Morgan told of visiting some elderly sisters when he was a young pastor and reading Matthew 28:18–20 as part of his ministry to them. The phrase "Lo, I am with you always" struck Morgan with power and he said, "Isn't that a wonderful promise!" One of the women replied, "Young man, that isn't a promise—it's a reality!" How true! "The LORD of hosts is with us; the God of Jacob is our refuge" (Ps. 46:7, 11).

God had a timetable for the conquest (vv. 22–23). Obeying the Lord means doing the right thing in the right way at the right time for the right reason, which is to the glory of God. "Do not be like the horse or like the mule," warned David (Ps. 32:9 NIV), because the horse wants to bolt ahead and the mule wants to lag behind and balk. God has a time for everything (Eccl. 3:1–8), and when Jesus ministered here on earth, He followed a divine schedule (John 11:9; 2:4; 7:6, 8, 30; 8:20; 12:23; 13:1; 17:1). Happy is the believer who can honestly say, "My times are in thy hand" (Ps. 31:15).

As they gradually made their way through the land of Canaan, winning one victory after another, the Jewish people would grow in their faith and learn better how to trust the Lord. But by following God's timetable, they would take better care of the land (Ex. 23:28–30) and prevent the wild beasts from multiplying rapidly and becoming a threat. According to the record in the book of Joshua, it took Israel about seven years to get control of the whole land. First Joshua cut straight across Canaan and divided the land (Josh. 1—8); then he conquered the nations in the south (Josh. 9—10) and then those in the north (Josh. 11). But this still left "mopping up" operations for the individual tribes, some of whom never did eliminate the enemy from their territory (13:1; Judg. 1—2). These pockets of paganism brought great temptation and trouble to the Jews and led to divine discipline.

God expected the nation to obey Him (vv. 23–26). Faith without works is dead (James 2:14–20) because true faith always leads to obedience. "By faith Abraham ... obeyed" (Heb. 11:8). People may talk about faith, analyze faith, and seek to explain it, but until they do what God commands, they will never understand what faith is all about. The people of Israel had to obey God's clear command to wipe out the heathen nations and their religion. Everything in the land was to be devoted to God, and nobody had a right to claim it. The detestable things were to be completely devoted to destruction so they wouldn't become snares to the Jews. Anybody who stole a devoted thing from God and took it home would also be devoted to destruction, which is what happened to Achan (Josh. 6—7).

But it wasn't enough for the Jews simply to obey the command to destroy what God had condemned; they must obey from their hearts. They were to "utterly detest" and "utterly abhor" the abominable things they encountered in Canaan (Deut. 7:26). No doubt Achan helped to destroy many abominable things when Israel conquered Jericho, but he decided that some silver and gold and beautiful garments weren't really abominable, so he took them (Josh. 7:20–23). He would rather have the spoils of war than enjoy the blessings of obeying the Word (Ps. 119:14, 72, 127, 162), and it cost him dearly. King Saul made this same mistake and lost his crown (1 Sam. 15).

As we grow in grace, we learn to love and enjoy what pleases God and to despise and reject what displeases Him. It's not just a matter of our will obeying God's commands; it's also a matter of developing a heart that enjoys obeying God (Eph. 6:6). It's possible to do God's will in such a way that others get the blessing but we don't! This was true of two of God's prophets, Moses and Jonah. Moses arrogantly smote the rock and God provided water, but Moses lost the privilege of entering the Promised Land (Num. 20). Jonah eventually obeyed the Lord's will but he didn't do it from his heart, and became a bitter person (Jonah 4). This brings us back to the first motive Moses discussed—love for the Lord (Deut. 6:1–9). Love makes obedience a blessing and not a burden.

It's good for God's people to pause occasionally and ask, "Why are we doing what we're doing?" Is it to please ourselves or others, or to impress the world? Are we doing the will of God because we want Him to bless us? Or are we "doing the will of God from the heart" (Eph. 6:6) because we love Him? To obey God just to avoid punishment and receive blessing is a selfish motive that follows the philosophy of Satan (Job 1—2), but if we obey God out of love, it pleases His heart and He will give us what is best and what glorifies Him the most.

Like Israel of old, the church today must move forward by faith, conquer the enemy, and claim new territory for the Lord (Eph. 6:10–18; 2 Cor. 2:14–17). But unlike Israel, we use spiritual weapons, not human weapons, as by faith we overcome the walls of resistance that Satan has put into the minds of sinners (John 18:36; 2 Cor. 10:1–6; Eph. 6:17; Heb. 4:12). The apostolic church had no buildings, budgets (Acts 3:6), academic degrees (4:13), or political influence but depended on the Word of God and prayer (6:4), and God gave them great victory. Can He not do the same for His people today? Jesus has overcome the world and the Devil (John 12:31; 16:33; Eph. 1:19–21; Col. 1:13; 2:15); therefore, we fight from victory and not just for victory. "If God be for us, who can be against us?" (Rom. 8:31).

QUESTIONS FOR PERSONAL REFLECTION
OR GROUP DISCUSSION

1. What motivates you to obey God?

2. Why does genuine love for God lead naturally to obeying God?

3. What differences lie between the ownership of the land and the possession and enjoyment of the land? How does this apply to the Christian life?

4. How is it possible to be commanded to love? What does this command require of us?

5. What are some reasons for you to be grateful to the Lord?

6. How can people "tempt" the Lord? Why would someone do this? What would keep a person from doing this?

7. How does the Lord test our faith? Why does the Lord do this testing?

8. What did the commanded separation from other nations do for Israel when they obeyed? What is true biblical separation?

9. How could all the blessings on Israel bring glory to the Lord? How can this also be true for your blessings?

10. How does the promise of the presence of the Lord make a difference in your life?

11. How can we be, as Wiersbe says, "developing a heart that enjoys obeying God"?

Chapter Four

Nov 3

SEE WHAT YOU ARE

(Deuteronomy 8—11)

Oliver Cromwell told the artist painting his portrait that he refused to pay even a farthing for the painting unless it truly looked like him, including "pimples, warts, and everything as you see me."[1] Apparently the Lord Protector of the Commonwealth of England, Scotland, and Ireland was as courageous sitting for a portrait as he was leading an army on the battlefield. Most of us aren't that brave. We're uncomfortable looking at unretouched proofs of our photographs, and we'd certainly willingly pay for a painting that improved our appearance.

In this part of his farewell address, Moses painted the people of Israel as they really were, "warts and all." It was important for their spiritual lives that Moses do this, for one of the first steps toward maturity is accepting reality and doing something about it. But let's not point the finger at Israel and fail to look at ourselves, for the pictures that Moses painted apply to us today. We need to see ourselves as God sees us and then, by His grace, seek to become all that we can become in Jesus Christ.

CHILDREN IN THE WILDERNESS (8:1–5)

The three essentials for Israel's conquest and enjoyment of the Promised Land were: listening to God's Word, remembering it, and obeying it. They are still the essentials for a successful and satisfying Christian life today.

As we walk through this world, we can't succeed without God's guidance, protection, and provision, and it also helps to have a good memory. Four times in these chapters Moses commands us to remember (v. 2, 18; 9:7, 27), and four more times he admonishes us to forget not (8:11, 14, 19; 9:7). The apostle Peter devoted his second letter to the ministry of reminding God's people to remember what the apostles had taught them (2 Peter 1:12–18; 3:1–2). Moses pointed out four ministries God performed for Israel and that He performs for us today as He seeks to mature us and prepare us for what He has planned for us.

God tests us (vv. 1–2). God knows what's in the hearts of His children, but His children don't always know—or want to know. "And all the churches shall know that I am He who searches the minds and the hearts" (Rev. 2:23 NKJV). Life is a school (Ps. 90:12), and we often don't know what the lesson was until we failed the examination! People sometimes say, "Well, I know my own heart," but the frightening fact is that we don't know our own hearts. "The heart is deceitful above all things and beyond cure. Who can understand it?" (Jer. 17:9 NIV).

How we respond to the tests of life reveals what's really in our hearts, especially when those tests involve the everyday experience of life. The people of Israel were frequently hungry and thirsty and weary from the journey, and it was on those occasions that they became fretful and critical. The Devil tempts us to bring out the worst in us, but God tests us to bring out the best in us. When God allows a difficult circumstance to test us, we will either trust Him and become more mature, or we will tempt Him and become more miserable. The difference? Believing the promises of God and relying on the Lord to care for us and bring us through for His glory and our good.

God teaches us (v. 3). Each morning during their wilderness journey, God sent the Jewish people "angels' food" (Ps. 78:21–25) to teach them to depend on Him for what they needed. But the manna was much more than daily physical sustenance; it was a type of the coming Messiah who is "the bread of life" (John 6:35).[2] When Satan tempted Him to turn stones into bread (Matt. 4:1–4), Jesus quoted Deuteronomy 8:3 and indicated that the Word of God is also the bread of God, for we "feed on" Jesus Christ when we "feed on" the Word of God. God was teaching the Jews to look to Him for "daily bread" (Matt. 6:11) and to begin each day meditating on the Word of God. Those who obeyed God in the daily responsibility of gathering manna would be inclined to obey the rest of His commandments. Our relationship to the Word of God (manna) indicates our relationship to the God of the Word.

God cares for us (v. 4; 29:5). Not only did God feed the Jews "miracle bread" each morning, but He also kept their clothes from wearing out and their feet from swelling. The three pressing questions of life for most people are "What shall we eat? What shall we drink? What shall we wear?" (Matt. 6:25–34), and the Lord met all these needs for His people for forty years. "Casting all your care upon Him, for He cares for you" (1 Peter 5:7 NKJV). "For your heavenly Father knows that you need all these things" (Matt. 6:32 NKJV). God doesn't miraculously deliver bread, water, and clothing to our front doors each day, but He does give us jobs and the ability to earn money (Deut. 8:18) so we can purchase what we need.[3] The same Lord who provided Israel's needs without human means can provide our needs by using human means.

God disciplines us (v. 5). God saw the children of Israel as His own children whom He greatly loved. "Israel is my son, even my firstborn" (Ex. 4:22; see Hos. 11:1). After years of slavery in Egypt, the Jews had to learn what freedom was and how to use it responsibly. We commonly think of "discipline" only as punishment for disobedience, but much more is involved. Discipline is "child training," the preparation of the child for responsible adulthood. A judge justly punishes a convicted criminal in order to protect society and uphold the law, but a father lovingly disciplines a child to help that child mature.[4] Discipline is evidence of God's love and of our membership in God's family (Heb. 12:5–8; Prov. 3:11–12).

When you think of the Lord's discipline of His children, don't envision an angry parent punishing a child. Rather, see a loving Father challenging His children to exercise their muscles (physical and mental) so they will mature and be able to live like dependable adults. When we're being disciplined, the secret of growth is to humble ourselves and submit to God's will (Deut. 8:2–3; Heb. 12:9–10). To resist God's chastening is to harden our hearts and resist the Father's will. Like an athlete in training, we must exercise ourselves and use each trial as an opportunity for growth.

CONQUERORS IN THE LAND (8:6–20)

After being set free from Egypt, Israel's destination wasn't the wilderness; it was the Promised Land, the place of their inheritance. "And he [God] brought us out from thence [Egypt] that he might bring us in" (6:23). So with the Christian life: Being born again and redeemed from sin are only the beginning of our walk with Christ, a great beginning, to be sure, but only a beginning. If like Israel at Kadesh-barnea we rebel in unbelief, then we will wander through life and never enjoy what God planned for us (Eph. 2:10; Heb. 3—4). But if we surrender to the Lord and obey His will, He will enable us to be "more than conquerors" (Rom. 8:37) as we claim our inheritance in Christ and serve Him.

Enjoying God's blessing (vv. 6–9). The "key" that opened the door to the Promised Land was simple: Obey God's commandments, walk in His ways, and reverence Him (v. 6). If the people of Israel disobeyed God's Word, walked in their own way, and showed no fear of the Lord, this would invite the judgment of God on the nation. But why would Israel not want to enter and enjoy the Promised Land, the good land that God had prepared for them? It was a land that offered them all that they could want or need to lead a happy life.

Since water is a precious commodity in the East, Moses mentions it first: streams, pools, and springs flowing in the hills and valleys. Later he will mention God's promise to send the rains each year (11:14), the early rain in autumn and the latter rain in spring. With God's blessing, an abundance of water would make possible an abundance of crops, and the Israelites would harvest grain, grapes, figs, and olives, and they would also find honey. There would be plenty of pasture for flocks and herds, and copper and iron were buried in the rocks and the hills. Indeed, it was a land of milk and honey, a land where nothing was lacking. All of this typifies for believers today the spiritual wealth we have in Christ: the riches of His grace (Eph. 1:7; 2:7), the riches of His glory (1:18; 3:16), the riches of His mercy (2:4), and "the unsearchable riches of Christ" (3:8). We are complete in Christ (Col. 2:10) in whom "all fullness dwells" (1:19), and therefore we have everything we shall ever need for living a full Christian life to the glory of God. God has a wonderful life planned for each of His children (Eph. 2:10), and He provides all we need to fulfill that plan.

Forgetting God's goodness (vv. 10–18). There's peril in prosperity and comfort, for we may become so wrapped up in the blessings that we forget the one who gave us the blessings. For this reason, Moses admonished the Jews to praise God after they had eaten their meals so they wouldn't forget the Giver of every good and perfect gift (v. 10; James 1:17). When I was a lad, my Uncle Simon—my Swedish "preacher uncle"—occasionally visited our home, and I recall that he not only gave thanks at the beginning of the meal, but he always closed the meal with a prayer of thanksgiving. I didn't know until years later that he was obeying Deuteronomy 8:10. It's natural to give thanks for food when we're hungry, but it's also wise to give thanks after we're full.

Moses spelled out the dangers involved in forgetting that God is the source of every blessing that we enjoy. If we forget God, then success has a way of making us proud (v. 14), and we forget what we were before the

Lord called us. The Jews had been slaves in Egypt, and now they would be living in fine houses, watching their flocks and herds increase, gathering gold and silver, and forgetting what the Lord had done for them. They had been nomads in the wilderness, and now they would be settled down in a rich land, enjoying peace and prosperity with their children and grandchildren. How easy it would be for Israel to become proud, to forget how helpless they were before the Lord rescued them, and to think that their success was due to their own strength and wisdom—and that they deserved it! "But remember the LORD your God, for it is he who gives you the ability to produce wealth" (Deut. 8:18 NIV).

Rejecting God's authority (vv. 19–20). The climax of this spiritual declension is that the "wealthy Israelites" would turn from the Lord, the true and living God, and start worshipping the false gods of their neighbors. Idolatry begins in the heart when gratitude to the Giver is replaced by greediness for the gifts. "Because that, when they knew God, they glorified him not as God, neither were thankful" (Rom. 1:21). An ungrateful heart can quickly become a haven for all sorts of sinful attitudes and appetites that cater to the flesh. What would the Lord do? He would treat His own people's idolatry the way He treated the idolatry of the nations that they dispossessed, and He would destroy Israel and their false gods. Before Moses finished his speech, he outlined the terms of God's covenant with Israel and the chastening God would send if the people persisted in worshipping idols.

Prosperity—ingratitude—idolatry: three steps toward ruin. But these aren't ancient sins, for they're present in hearts, homes, businesses, and churches today.

REBELS AGAINST THE LORD (9:1—10:11)

For the fifth time in his address, Moses says, "Hear, O Israel!" (See 4:1; 5:1; 6:3–4.) He was giving them the Word of God, and when God's speaks to

His people, they must listen. The word "hear" is used over fifty times in Deuteronomy, for God's people live by faith, and "faith cometh by hearing, and hearing by the word of God" (Rom. 10:17). The Jews couldn't see their God, but they could hear Him, while their pagan neighbors could see their gods but couldn't hear them (Ps. 115:5). In this section, Moses reminded the people that their conduct since leaving Egypt had been anything but exemplary, in spite of His long-suffering and grace.

The grace of God (9:1–6). The phrase "this day" doesn't mean the very day on which Moses was speaking, for Israel didn't enter the land of Canaan until over forty days later (Deut. 1:3; 34:8; Josh. 4:19). The word "day" refers to a period of time during which God is doing a special work, such as the day of creation, which was six days (Gen. 2:4), or the "day of the LORD," when God will judge the world (Joel 2). God reminded Israel of the unbelief of the previous generation at Kadesh-barnea, when they saw the obstacles in Canaan but forgot the power of their God (Deut. 9:1–2; Num. 13—14). God assured His people that there was no need to fear the future because He would go before them to help them defeat their enemies. He wouldn't do it instead of them, for they had to do their part and fight the battles, nor would He do it in spite of them, for they had to be obedient and respect His laws, but He would work in them and through them to conquer the nations in the land (Phil. 2:12–13; Prov. 21:31).

Once again, Moses reminded the nation that the land was a gift from the Lord, not a reward for their righteousness. God had graciously covenanted with Abraham to give him and his descendants the land of Canaan (Gen. 12:1–3; 13:14–17; 15:7–21), and He would keep His promise. The people in the land were wicked and ripe for judgment, and even though Israel wasn't a perfect people, God would use them to bring that judgment. The emphasis is on the grace of God and not the goodness of God's people, and this emphasis is needed today (Titus 2:11—3:7). When we forget the grace of God, we become proud and start thinking that we deserve all that

God has done for us, and then God has to remind us of His goodness and our sinfulness, and that reminder might be very painful. That's the theme of the next part of Moses' message.

The discipline of God (9:7—10:11). Moses was addressing a new generation, but they needed to hear this part of the message and realize that they were sinners just like their ancestors. The theme is expressed bluntly in 9:24, "You have been rebellious against the LORD from the day that I [the Lord] knew you [chose you]" (NKJV). God called Abraham and led him to the Promised Land, but then he fled to Egypt to escape a famine (Gen. 12:10ff.). No sooner were the Jews delivered from Egypt than they began to complain about the way God led them and fed them (Ex. 15:22ff.). The scenery in the drama of the life of faith may change, but the actors and the script are pretty much the same: God blesses, we enjoy the blessings, then we rebel against His disciplines and miss the blessing He planned for us.

In his review of Israel's history of rebellion, Moses started with their worship of the golden calf at Mount Sinai (Deut. 9:7–21, 25—10:11; Ex. 32) and then simply mentioned the places where they rebelled on the journey from Sinai to Kadesh-barnea (Deut. 9:22). After that, he declared the nation's unbelief and rebellion at Kadesh-barnea (vv. 23–24), followed by a second reminder of the episode of the golden calf (9:25—10:11). Moses didn't follow a strict chronological account of all the events in Israel's history but emphasized their two greatest sins: the worship of the golden calf at Sinai and the refusal to enter the land at Kadesh-barnea.

Israel committed a very great sin when they worshipped the golden calf (Ex. 32—34). Behind them was the history of their deliverance from Egypt, a demonstration of the grace and power of the Lord, and yet they rebelled against their Redeemer! Israel was the people of God, redeemed by His hand, and yet they manufactured a new god! Before them was Mount Sinai, where they had seen God's glory and holiness demonstrated and from which they had received the law of the Lord. In that law, God commanded them to worship Him alone and not to make idols and worship them. They had accepted that law and twice promised to obey it (Ex. 24:3, 7), and yet they broke the first and second commandments by making and worshipping an idol, and the seventh commandment by engaging in lustful revelry as a part of their "worship."

Impatience and unbelief prompted Israel's great sin at Mount Sinai, for Moses had been on the mountain with the Lord for forty days and nights (vv. 1–18). Aaron should have opposed their request for a new god, but instead he compromised and went along with their demands, hoping it would bring peace to the camp. Imagine the first high priest making an idol! Moses had given his brother authority to act in his absence (v. 14), and Aaron could have rallied the tribal leaders and urged the Israelites to obey the Lord; but he wanted to please the people and avoid conflict. Centuries later, Pontius Pilate would make the same mistake when he obeyed the crowd that wanted Jesus to be crucified (Mark 15:15).

Never underestimate the importance of spiritual leadership that encourages obedience to the Word of God. Aaron failed God, who had appointed him as high priest; he failed his brother, who was depending on him to guide the nation; and he failed the people, who desperately needed strong spiritual leadership. When Moses confronted him, Aaron tried to excuse his way out of his sin by blaming the people! All he did was take their golden jewelry and throw it into the fire, and out came a calf! (See Ex. 32:22–24.) Moses spent another forty days and nights on the mountain, interceding for Aaron and the people. God was ready to slay Aaron, wipe out the nation, and begin a new nation with Moses, but Moses prayed for Aaron and the people and refused God's offer to make him the father of a new nation. Moses faced this same test at Kadesh-barnea and again put the glory of God and the good of the people ahead of personal promotion (Num. 14:12ff.). Moses was more concerned with the glory of God and His reputation before the pagan nations, for he knew that the fear of God had to go before Israel if they were to conquer the land and claim their inheritance.

We can't help but admire Moses as the leader of God's people. He spent forty days on the mountain, learning how to lead the people in their worship of God, and then he spent another forty days fasting and praying, interceding for a nation that complained, resisted his leadership, and rebelled against the Lord. But leaders are tested just as followers are tested, and Moses passed the test. He showed that his great concern wasn't his own fame or position but the glory of God and the good of the people. In fact, he was willing to die for the people rather than see God destroy them (Ex. 32:31–34). A true shepherd lays down his life for the sheep (John 10:11).

After reviewing Israel's great sin at Sinai, Moses mentioned Israel's repeated rebellions on the way to Kadesh-barnea (Deut. 9:23). At Taberah, the people complained about their "hardships," and God sent fire that consumed some of the people on the outskirts of the camp (Num. 11:1–3).[5] Then the people who complained to Moses begged him to pray for them, and God listened to Moses and stopped the judgment. "Taberah" means "burning," and the name should remind all of us that it's a sin to complain (Phil. 2:14–15; 1 Cor. 10:10). At Massah, the Jews complained because they were thirsty, so Moses struck the rock and God provided water abundantly (Ex. 17:1–7). "Massah" means "testing" and is joined with "Meribah" which means "quarreling." "Kibroth Hattaavah" means "graves of lust" and refers to the time Israel became weary of the manna and craved meat to eat (Num. 11:4ff.). God sent flocks of quail over the camp of Israel, and all the people had to do was knock the birds down, dress them, cook them, and eat them. It was the old "Egyptian appetite" asserting itself again, the flesh rebelling against the Spirit. While the people were eating the meat, God's judgment fell and He sent a plague to the camp. "So he gave them what they asked for, but he sent a plague along with it" (Ps. 106:15 NLT).

Sometimes God's greatest judgment is to let us have our own way (Rom. 1:22–28).

Finally, Moses rehearsed Israel's great failure at Kadesh-barnea (Deut. 9:23–24; Num. 13—14). During the march from Egypt to Kadesh, the Jews had seen the hand of God at work day after day, meeting their every need, but at Kadesh, they felt that God wasn't great enough to give them victory over the nations in Canaan. They had "an evil heart of unbelief" (Heb. 3:12), which is actually rebellion against the Lord. Unbelief is a sin of the will; it's tempting the Lord and saying, "I will not trust the Lord and do what He commands me to do!" The ten unbelieving spies walked by sight, not by faith, and saw only the problems in the land. Moses, Aaron, Caleb, and Joshua walked by faith and believed that God could defeat any enemy and overcome every obstacle.

This review of Israel's sins is quite an indictment, but God never forsook the people of Israel and often forgave them when He should have judged them. "He has not dealt with us according to our sins, nor punished us according to our iniquities" (Ps. 103:10 NKJV; see Ezra 9:13). God is always faithful to His promises; when we don't allow Him to rule, He will overrule and still accomplish His purposes. However, we will miss the blessings that He planned for us.

Every believer and every Christian ministry, whether it be a local church or a parachurch ministry, must trust God to meet their needs a day at a time. If we complain along the way, we're only giving evidence that we don't trust God but think we know more than He does about what's best for us. When we come to those "Kadesh-barnea" places in life, when we must claim what God has planned for us and move forward by faith, we must not rebel against God and refuse to trust and obey. If we do, we may find ourselves wandering through life, failing to accomplish what God has planned for us. Claiming our inheritance in Christ is one of the major themes of the book of Hebrews, and the writer uses Israel as the main illustration (Heb. 3—4).

SERVANTS OF THE LORD (10:12—11:32)

"And now, Israel" (10:12) forms a transition as Moses moves into the closing section of this part of his address, a section in which he reminds the people why they should obey the Lord their God. This was not a new topic, but it was an important topic, and Moses wanted them to get the message and not forget it: Loving obedience to the Lord is the key to every blessing. Jesus often repeated truths He had already shared, and Paul wrote to the Philippians, "For me to write the same things to you is not tedious, but for you it is safe" (Phil. 3:1 NKJV). Not everybody listening gets the message the first time, and some who do might forget it. The Jewish people didn't carry pocket Bibles and had to depend on their memories, so repetition was important.

Obey because of God's commandments (10:12–13). The sequence of these five imperatives is significant: fear, walk, love, serve, and keep. The fear of the Lord is that reverential awe that we owe Him simply because He is the Lord. Both in the Old Testament and the New, the life of faith is compared to a walk (Eph. 4:1, 17; 5:2, 8, 15). It starts with a step of faith in trusting Christ and yielding ourselves to Him, but this leads to a daily fellowship with Him as we walk together in the way that He has planned. The Christian walk implies progress, and it also implies balance: faith and works, character and conduct, worship and service, solitude and fellowship, separation from the world and ministry and witness to the world. Obeying Him is "for [our] own good" (Deut. 10:13 NIV), for when we obey Him, we share His fellowship, enjoy His blessings, and avoid the sad consequences of disobedience.

The central element in these five imperatives is love, a word that Moses uses six times in this section (Deut. 10:12, 15, 19; 11:1, 13, 22). Is it possible both to fear and love the Lord at the same time? Yes, it is, for the reverence we show Him is a loving respect that comes from the heart. Moses used the word "heart" five times in this section of his address (10:12, 16; 11:13,

16, 18), so he made it clear that God wants more than external obedience. He wants us to do the will of God from the heart (Eph. 6:6), a loving obedience that brings joy to our Father in heaven. Love is the fulfillment of the law (Rom. 13:10), so if we love God, serving Him and keeping His commandments will not be a burden or a battle. These five elements are like the sections of a telescope that belong together and work together.

Obey because of God's character (10:14–22). A balanced fear of the Lord and love for the Lord is the result of a growing understanding of the attributes of God, and these attributes are described in the Scriptures. He is the Creator (Deut. 10:14); "all things were created by him, and for him" (Col. 1:16). While living in Egypt, the Jewish people saw the power of the Creator as He sent fire and hail, darkness, frogs and lice, and even death, proving that He was in control of all things. He opened the Red Sea to allow Israel to escape, and then He closed the waters so the Egyptian army couldn't escape. He gave water from the rock and bread from heaven. When the Creator of the universe is your Father, why should you worry?

As we look at creation, we can easily see that there is a God who is powerful and wise, for only a powerful Being could create something out of nothing, and only a wise Being could make it as intricate and marvelous as it is and keep it working harmoniously. Whether you gaze through a telescope or peer through a microscope, you will agree with Isaac Watts:

> Lord, how Thy wonders are displayed
> Where e'er I turn my eye,
> If I survey the ground I tread
> Or gaze upon the sky![6]

Creation doesn't clearly reveal the love and grace of God, but we do see these attributes of God in the covenants He has made with His people (Deut. 10:15–16). God chose Israel because He loved them, and because of that love, He covenanted to be their God and bless them. The seal of that covenant was circumcision, given first to Abraham (Gen. 17:9–14) and commanded to be practiced on all his male descendants. So important was circumcision to the Jews that they spoke of the Gentiles as "the uncircumcised" or "the uncircumcision" (Judg. 14:3; 1 Sam. 17:26, 36; Acts 11:3; Eph. 2:11). But Israel so magnified the physical ritual that they forgot the spiritual reality, that circumcision marked them as God's people with spiritual privileges and responsibilities. Circumcision wasn't a guarantee that every Jewish man was going to heaven (Matt. 3:7–12). Unless there was a change in the heart, wrought by God in response to faith, the person didn't belong to the Lord in a vital way. That's why Moses exhorted them to let God "operate" on their hearts and do a lasting spiritual work (see Deut. 30:6), a message that was repeated by the prophets (Jer. 4:4; Ezek. 44:7, 9) and the apostle Paul (Rom. 4:9–12; see Acts 7:51).

Unfortunately, this same spiritual blindness is with us today, for many people believe that baptism, confirmation, church membership, or participation in the Lord's Supper automatically guarantees their salvation. As meaningful as those things are, the Christian's assurance and seal of salvation isn't a physical ceremony but a spiritual work of the Holy Spirit in the heart (Phil. 3:1–10; Col. 2:9–12). Jewish circumcision removed but a small part of the flesh, but the Holy Spirit has put off the whole "body of the sins of the flesh" and made us new creatures in Christ (Col. 2:11). Old Testament Jews knew they were in the covenant because of a physical operation; New Testament Christians know they're in the covenant because of the presence of the Holy Spirit within (Eph. 1:13; 4:30; Rom. 8:9, 16).

The God we worship and serve is also holy and just. "God is light, and in him is no darkness at all" (1 John 1:5). After they had crossed the Red Sea, the Israelites sang, "Who is like unto thee, O LORD, among the gods? Who is like thee, glorious in holiness, fearful in praises, doing wonders?" (Ex. 15:11; see also Ps. 22:3; Isa. 6:3). The love of God is so emphasized today that we tend to forget that it is a holy love and that "our God is a consuming fire" (Heb. 12:29). Because God is holy, all that He does is just, for it is impossible for God to sin. People may accuse God of being unjust because circumstances didn't work out as they expected, but a holy God cannot do anything unjust. He is impartial in His dealings and cannot be bribed by our promises or our good works. God has a special concern for the helpless, especially the widows, the orphans, and the homeless aliens (Deut. 27:19; Ex. 22:21–24; 23:9; Lev. 19:33; Ps. 94:6; Isa. 10:2). God cared for the Jews when they were aliens in Egypt, and He expected them to care for other aliens when Israel was settled in their own land.

Obey because of God's care (10:21—11:7). The phrase "what he did" or its equivalent is used six times in this paragraph, because the emphasis is on the mighty acts of God on behalf of His people Israel, "his greatness, his mighty hand, and his outstretched arm" (v. 2). What did God do for Israel? To begin with, when they were slaves in Egypt, He cared for them and multiplied them greatly. Jacob and his family journeyed to Egypt to join Joseph (Gen. 46), and seventy people became a mighty nation of perhaps two million people.[7] God certainly kept His promise to Abraham to multiply his descendants as the stars of the heavens and the dust of the earth (13:14–16; 15:5; 22:17; 26:4).

While the Jews were in Egypt, they saw the mighty power of God unleashed against Pharaoh and the nation as God sent one judgment after another that finally led to Israel's release. God's power not only ruined the land and destroyed Pharaoh's army, but it demonstrated that Jehovah was the true God and that all the gods and goddesses of Egypt were but dumb and powerless idols. Once Israel settled in the land, they would annually celebrate Passover and remember what the Lord had done for them.

Moses also reminded the new generation that God cared for them during their wilderness wanderings, but he mentioned only one specific event, God's judgment of Dathan and Abiram (Deut. 11:5–6; Num. 16; Jude 11). Korah, a Levite, enlisted Dathan and Abiram and 250 leaders in Israel to stand with him in challenging the authority of Moses, because Korah wanted the Levites to have the privilege of serving as priests. This was against the will of God, so Moses and Aaron turned the matter over to the Lord. God opened the earth, which swallowed up the three rebels, and He sent fire to destroy the 250 tribal leaders.[8] It was important for the new generation to learn to respect God's leaders and obey His commandments concerning the priesthood. Even today, arrogant people who want to promote themselves and be "important" in the church had better beware of God's disciplines and judgments (Acts 5:1–11; 1 Cor. 3:9–23; Heb. 13:17; 3 John 9–12).

Obey because of God's covenant promises (11:8–25). The key word in this section is "land," used at least a dozen times, referring to the land of Canaan, which God promised to Abraham and his descendants when He entered into a covenant relationship with him (Gen. 13:14–17; 15:7–21; 17:8; 28:13; Ex. 3:8). Canaan was not only the Promised Land because God promised it to Israel, but it was also "the land of promises" because in that land God would fulfill many of the promises relating to His great gift of salvation for the whole world. The land of Israel would be the stage on which the great drama of redemption would be enacted. There the Savior would be born and live, and there He would die for the sins of the world. He would be raised from the dead and ascend to heaven and to His born-again people in that land He would send the gift of the Holy Spirit. From that land, His people would spread out across the world and share the message of salvation.

If Israel wanted to possess the land, remain in it, and enjoy it, they had to obey the commandments of the Lord, because He owns the land of Israel (Lev. 25:2, 23, 38). Only He could open the Jordan River so Israel could enter the land, and only He could give the Jews victory over the nations already living in the land. Those nations were stronger than Israel, and the people were living in walled cities. But even after Israel entered and conquered the land, they wouldn't remain in the land to enjoy it if they failed to listen to God's Word and obey it. The same principle applies to believers today: In Christ we have "all spiritual blessings" (Eph. 1:3), but we can't possess them or enjoy them unless we believe God's promises and obey His commands.

The Promised Land was "a land of milk and honey," but if the rain didn't come at its appointed seasons, nothing would grow and the people would starve, and only God could send the rain. Baal was the Canaanite storm god, and often in their history, the Jews turned to this false god for help, and God had to chasten them. Elijah's dramatic encounter on Mount Carmel with the priests of Baal proved that the Lord Jehovah was the true and living God (1 Kings 18:16ff.). Unlike the land of Egypt, which depended on irrigation from the Nile River,[9] the land of Israel received the life-giving rains from heaven, sent by the Lord. Often in Jewish history, God shut up the heavens and disciplined His people until they confessed their sins and returned to Him (Deut. 28:23–24; 2 Chron. 7:12–14). God would watch over and care for the land and its inhabitants (Deut. 11:12). If the nation of Israel feared God, loved Him, and obeyed Him, He would send the crops in their seasons and feed the people and the flocks and herds. God wasn't "buying" their obedience; He was rewarding their faith and teaching them the joys of knowing and serving Him.

The problem wasn't with God or the land; it was in the hearts of the people. "Take heed to yourselves, that your heart be not deceived" (v. 16). If the people turned aside from worshipping Jehovah, His anger would be kindled and He would have to discipline them. Since their idolatry polluted the land, God would have to remove them from the land and cleanse it, and this He did when He sent the Jews into captivity in Babylon. The greatest deterrent to idolatry was the Word of God (vv. 18–21; see 6:6–9), the treasure that God had given to Israel and to no other nation. That Word was supposed to govern their lives and be the topic of their conversation. As we have seen, the Jews took this commandment literally and made phylacteries for their arms and heads and mezuzahs for their houses, but they failed to receive the Word into their hearts. Christians today face the same danger. It's much easier to wear a gold cross on our person than to bear Christ's cross in daily life, and to hang Scripture texts on the walls of our homes than to hide God's Word in our hearts. If we love the Lord and cleave to Him, we will want to know His Word and obey it in every area of our lives.

How do we claim God's blessings? By stepping out by faith (11:24–25). This is what God commanded Abraham to do (Gen. 13:17) as well as Joshua (Josh. 1:3). It was this promise that Caleb claimed when he asked for his inheritance in the Promised Land (14:6–15), and it's the promise all believers must claim if they expect to enjoy the blessings God has for them. You don't "claim the land" by studying the map and dreaming of conquest. You claim the land by stepping out by faith, believing God's Word, and depending on His faithfulness. J. Hudson Taylor, founder of the China Inland Mission, now the Overseas Missionary Fellowship, said: "Not by striving after faith, but by resting in the Faithful One."[10]

Obey because of God's chastening (11:26–32). The upshot of the whole matter was that the nation had to make a choice whether to obey God and enjoy His blessing or disobey Him and experience His chastening. They could enjoy the land, endure chastening in the land (the book of Judges), or be evicted from the land (the Babylonian captivity). You would think that the choice would be an easy one, for who would want to be chastened by the Lord? But just as children defy their parents' commands, knowing full well that their disobedience will bring punishment, so God's people deliberately disobey God and defy His will. They have no fear of God and really think they will escape His chastening hand! This is what the Bible calls "tempting God."

Moses had two horizons in mind when he gave this warning. The first was the nation before him that day (Deut. 11:26–28) and the second was the nation after they had entered the land (vv. 29–30). Their future victories depended on their present decision, the determination in their hearts to love the Lord and obey His Word. They would soon be on a battlefield and only the help of the Lord could give them victory over the enemy. The offer was a simple one: If they obeyed the Lord, He would bless them; if they disobeyed, He would chasten them.

After the Jews entered the land and began to conquer it, they were to conduct a special ceremony at Shechem, which is located between Mount Gerizim and Mount Ebal. (The details are given in Deut. 27—28 and the fulfillment in Josh. 8:30–35.) At Mount Ebal, Joshua was to write the words of the law on some large plastered stones and also build an altar. Mount Ebal was to be "the mount of curses" and Mount Gerizim "the mount of blessings." The tribes on Mount Gerizim would be Simeon, Levi, Judah, Isaachar, Joseph (Ephraim and Manasseh), and Benjamin, and the remaining tribes would gather on Mount Ebal. In the valley between the two mountains Joshua, the priests and Levites, and the tribal officers would stand with the ark of the covenant, and from that location the Levites would loudly address the people and recite the curses and the blessings. After each curse was spoken, the people on Mount Ebal would shout, "Amen," meaning, "So be it—we agree!" After each blessing was read, the tribes on Mount Gerizim would shout, "Amen!"

The priests would offer on the altar on Mount Ebal[11] burnt offerings, symbolizing dedication to God, and peace offerings, symbolizing fellowship with God, and they would eat "before the Lord" and enjoy a covenant meal. This important ceremony would be a reaffirmation of the covenant which Israel accepted at Mount Sinai and heard a second time in the Plains of Moab in Moses' farewell address.

Spiritually speaking, believers today live between two mounts: Mount Calvary, where Jesus died for us, and the Mount of Olives, to which Jesus will one day return (Zech. 14:4; Acts 1:11–12). But God hasn't written the old covenant law on stones and warned us about curses; rather, He has written His new covenant on our hearts and blessed us in Jesus Christ (2 Cor. 3:1–3; Heb. 8; Eph. 1:3). "There is therefore now no condemnation to them which are in Christ Jesus" (Rom. 8:1). However, the fact that Christians are under grace and not under law doesn't mean that we have a license to sin (6:1–14). God's dispensations change but His principles never change, and one of those principles is that God blesses us when we obey and chastens us when we disobey. As we walk in the power of the Holy Spirit, we overcome the appetites of the flesh, and God's righteousness is fulfilled in us (8:4) and we never hear the voices from Mount Ebal.

QUESTIONS FOR PERSONAL REFLECTION —
OR GROUP DISCUSSION

1. Which of these is hardest for you: listening to God's Word, remembering it, or obeying it? (Or none of the above.) Why?

2. How do our responses to the tests of life reveal something about us? What recent test in your life revealed something about you?

3. What do you think your life would be like now if God had never tested you? *As you go through problems, you better understand how others feel*

4. What could the Israelites have learned through the giving of manna? What blocked their full learning? *To fully trust in God*

5. How has God cared for you? How would you like Him to care for you? *Has led to me to new friends*

6. What is the purpose of God's discipline? Who and how does God discipline? *He Teach us to to trust + obey.*

7. What are some of the spiritual riches that we have in Christ? How does this knowledge affect your living?

   God loves us / Forgives us.
   always with us /

8. What danger is there in forgetting the Giver of the good gifts? How can you be more thankful to God for your many gifts?

   We get anquer, think we can
   do change on our own

9. Where does idolatry start? What or who tempts you toward idolatry?

   When we want what we do not need.

10. When people walk by sight and not by faith, what are they really saying and doing?

    That they do not trust God

Chapter Five

WORSHIP HIM IN TRUTH

(Deuteronomy 12—13; 18:9–22)

Moses was a wise instructor. He devoted the first part of his address (Deut. 1—5) to reviewing the past and helping the new generation appreciate all that God had done for them. Then he told the people how they should respond to the goodness of God and why they should obey Jehovah (Deut. 6—11). In other words, Moses was helping his people develop hearts of love for the Lord, because if they loved Him, they would obey Him. Moses repeated God's covenant promises to the nation but also balanced the promises with the warnings of what would happen if they disobeyed. More than anything else, Moses wanted the Israelites to mature in faith and love so they could enter the land, conquer the enemy, and enjoy their inheritance to the glory of God.

In Deuteronomy 12—26, Moses built on this foundation and applied the law to Israel's new situation in the Promised Land. The Jews had been slaves in Egypt and nomads in the wilderness, but now they would become conquerors and tenants in God's land (Lev. 25:23 NIV). He set before them the responsibilities they had to fulfill if they were to live like God's chosen people and be faithful residents in the land, enjoying God's blessing.

PURGING THE LAND (12:1–3)

The statement in verse 1 was both an assurance and a commandment. The assurance was that Israel would enter the land and overcome the enemy, and the commandment was that, having entered the land, they must purge it of all idolatry.[1] Israel's conquest of the nations east of the Jordan was a prototype of their cleansing of the land of Canaan (Num. 21; 31). This wasn't a new commandment, for Moses had mentioned it before (Deut. 7:1–6, 23–26; Num. 33:50–56), and he would mention it again.

The religions of the Canaanite peoples were both false and filthy. They worshipped a multitude of gods and goddesses, chiefly Baal, the storm god, and Asherah, his consort. The wooden "Asherah poles" ("groves," KJV) were sex symbols, and the people made use of temple prostitutes as they sought to worship their gods. Since the major goal of the Canaanite religion was fertility for themselves and for their crops, they established places of worship on the mountains and hills ("the high places") so as to get closer to the gods. They also worshipped under the large trees, which were also symbols of fertility. Their immoral religious practices were a form of magic with which they hoped to please the gods and influence the powers of nature to give them bountiful crops.

But Moses pointed out that anything idolatrous remaining in the land was dangerous because it might become a tool for the Devil to use in tempting Israel. The admonition "Neither give place to the devil" (Eph. 4:27) warns us that, whenever we disobey the Lord and cherish that which He wants us to destroy, we provide Satan with a foothold in our lives. Israel was even to wipe out the names of the pagan deities, because their names might be used in occult practices to cast spells.

We live in a world that has abandoned absolutes and promoted "plurality." As long as it "helps you," one religion is just as good as another religion, and it isn't "politically correct" to claim that Jesus Christ is the only Savior of the world (Acts 4:12; John 4:19–24). But Moses made it clear that God rejected the Canaanite religions and wanted all evidence of their pagan practices removed from the land. The land belonged to the Lord, and He had every right to purge it. His first commandment is, "Thou shalt have none other gods before me" (Deut. 5:7). Israel did not purge the land and were disciplined for their disobedience. "They did not destroy the nations, concerning whom the LORD commanded them: but were mingled among the heathen, and learned their works. And they served their idols: which were a snare unto them" (Ps. 106:34–36).

WORSHIPPING THE LORD (12:4–14)

"You must not worship the LORD your God in their way" (v. 4 NIV) is a simple statement that carries a powerful message. As the people of God, we must worship the Lord the way He commands and not imitate the religious practices of others. The Jewish faith and the Christian faith came by revelation, not by man's invention or Satan's instruction (1 Tim. 4:1; 2 Tim. 3:5–7). The most important activity of the church is the worship of God because everything truly spiritual that the church does flows out of worship. How tragic it is when congregations imitate the world and turn Christian worship into entertainment and the sanctuary of God into a theater. "To the law and to the testimony! If they do not speak according to this word, it is because there is no light in them" (Isa. 8:20 NKJV).

Israel worshipped the true and living God, while the pagans in the land worshipped dead idols that represented false gods. The Canaanites had many shrines, but Israel would have one central place of worship. There is a definite contrast in the text between "all the places" in Deuteronomy 12:2 and "the place" in verses 5, 11, 14, 18, 21 and 26:2. The Canaanites built many altars, but Israel was to have but one altar. The Canaanites sacrificed whatever they pleased to their gods and goddesses, including their own children, but the Lord would instruct the Jews what sacrifices to bring, and He made it clear that they were never to sacrifice their children.

One place where God dwells (vv. 5, 8–11a). In the book of Genesis, we're told that God walked with His people, such as Enoch (5:24), Noah (6:9), and Abraham (17:1); but at Mount Sinai, God announced to Moses that He wanted to dwell with His people (Ex. 25:8). He instructed them to make Him a tabernacle, and for this holy project the people of Israel contributed their wealth (35:4—36:6). When Moses dedicated the tabernacle, God came down in glory and moved into the Holy of Holies, making the mercy seat on the ark His holy throne (40:34–38; Ps. 80:1; 99:1 NIV). We sometimes speak of "the Shekinah glory" of God in the camp of Israel, which is from a Hebrew word that means "to dwell."

The Canaanite nations had plenty of temples and shrines, but only Israel had the glorious presence of the true and living God dwelling with them (Rom. 9:4). The fact that there was only one central sanctuary for Israel signified that there was but one true God, one authorized worship and priesthood, and one holy nation. The tabernacle, and later the temple, unified the twelve tribes spiritually and politically.

It's interesting to trace the history of God's tabernacle. The Israelites carried the tabernacle into Canaan and placed it at Shiloh (Josh. 18:1; 19:51; Jer. 7:12). During the days of Samuel, it was at Mizpeh (1 Sam. 7:6) and then at Nob (21:1–6). Because of Israel's sins against the Lord, the glory of God departed from the tabernacle (4:21–22). During the time of David, the ark was on Mount Zion while the tabernacle itself was at Gibeon (1 Chron. 16:1, 37–42; 1 Kings 3:4). God revealed to David that his son Solomon would succeed him on the throne and build a temple for His glory on Mount Zion, and when Solomon dedicated the temple, the glory of the Lord came to dwell there (8:10–11). When Babylon captured Judah, the prophet Ezekiel saw the glory of God leave the temple (Ezek. 8:1–4; 9:3; 10:4, 18; 11:22–23), but he also saw it return and dwell in the kingdom temple (43:1–3).

When Jesus came to earth to "tabernacle among us," the glory of God returned (John 1:14), but sinful men nailed the Lord of glory to the cross. He arose from the dead and returned to heaven to receive back the glory that He had laid aside in His humiliation (17:1, 5). Now each person who trusts Christ becomes a temple of God and has the Spirit dwelling within (1 Cor. 6:19–20). But each local assembly of believers is also a temple of God (vv. 10–17), and Christ is building His church universal as a dwelling place for the Spirit (Matt. 16:18; Eph. 2:19–22). Someday, all of God's people will dwell in the heavenly city that will be lighted by the glory of God (Rev. 21:23).

One altar for sacrifices (vv. 6–7, 12–14). Canaanite worship permitted the people to offer whatever sacrifices they pleased at whatever place they chose, but for Israel there was to be but one altar. The Jews were allowed to kill and eat livestock and wild game at any place (vv. 15, 21–22), but these animals were not to be offered as sacrifices when they were killed. The only place where sacrifices were accepted was at the altar of God's sanctuary, and the only people who could offer them were the Lord's appointed priests.[2] The Lord didn't want His people inventing their own religious system by imitating the practices of the pagan nations. During the decadent days of the judges, that's exactly what some of the people did (Judg. 17—18).

The burnt offering (Lev. 1) symbolized total dedication to the Lord, for all of it was consumed on the altar. Paul may have had this image in mind when he commanded us to present ourselves wholly to the Lord to do His will (Rom. 12:1–2). The peace offering or fellowship offering (Lev. 3) spoke of communion with God, and the worshipper shared the meat with his family and with the priests. They had a joyful meal as they celebrated the goodness of the Lord (Deut. 12:12, 18; 26:11). While worship is certainly a serious thing, it need not be grim and somber. True worship not only draws believers closer to God, but it also draws God's people closer to each other.

The tabernacle was not only a place where the Jews brought their sacrifices, but it was also where they brought their tithes and offerings. The tithe was 10 percent of what their land had produced, and this was shared with the priests and Levites. The priests also received a certain amount of meat from some of the sacrifices, and this was how they and their families were supported. Moses frequently reminded the people to support the Levites by faithfully bringing tithes and offerings to the sanctuary (12:12, 18–19; 14:27, 29; 16:11, 14). God promised to bless His people abundantly if they would faithfully bring their tithes and offerings to His sanctuary (Mal. 3:6–12; see also 1 Kings 7:51; Neh. 13:12).

RESPECTING LIFE (12:15–16, 20–28)

These verses focus on the Jews' treatment of the blood of animals that were either sacrificed at the altar or eaten at home, a theme Moses discussed in Leviticus 17:1–16. The Lord introduced this theme after Noah and his family came out of the ark, for it was then that He permitted mankind to eat meat (Gen. 9:1–7; and see 1:29; 2:9, 16). In the Genesis legislation, God prohibited the shedding of human blood and the eating of animal blood, whether the animal was domestic or wild. He also established what we today call "capital punishment." Since humans are made in the image of God and derive their life from God, to murder someone is to attack God and to rob that person of God's gift of life. God decreed that murderers should be punished by losing their own lives, and the right to enforce this law belonged to the officers of the state (Rom. 13). By giving this law, the Lord was actually establishing human government on the earth. It's worth noting that if an animal killed a person, that animal was to be slain (Ex. 21:28–32).

Long before science discovered the significance of blood, the Lord declared that life was in the blood and that the blood should be respected and not treated like common food.[3] If a Jew slaughtered an animal at home, he was to drain out all the blood on the ground before the meat could be cooked and eaten. If he brought an animal to be sacrificed at the sanctuary, the priest would drain the blood beside the altar. If the ritual called for it, the priest would catch in a basin only enough blood to sprinkle on or about the altar. By following this procedure, the Jews not only showed respect for God's gift of life, even to animals, but they also showed respect for the animal that gave its life for the worshipper. The Jews didn't eat meat frequently because it was too costly to slay livestock, so when they did slaughter an animal, they were to do it with respect. They could take an animal to the sanctuary and offer it as a peace offering and then enjoy eating the meat as part of a special feast (Lev. 3; 7:11–38).

This emphasis on the shedding of blood is at the heart of the message of the gospel. We aren't saved from our sins by the life of Christ or the example of Christ, but by the sacrificial death of Christ, "in whom we have redemption through his blood" (Eph. 1:7; Col. 1:14). The blood of Christ is precious to us (1 Peter 1:19) because of who shed it—the spotless Lamb of God—but also because of what it accomplishes for those who trust Him: justification (Rom. 5:9), cleansing (Rev. 1:5; 1 John 1:7), eternal salvation (Heb. 9:11–28), access to God (10:19–20), and reconciliation (Eph. 2:13), to name but a few of the blessings we have through Christ's blood.

BRINGING TITHES AND OFFERINGS (12:17–19)

The practice of bringing 10 percent of the produce to the Lord antedates the law, for Abraham tithed (Gen. 14:17–20; Heb. 7:4) and so did Jacob (Gen. 28:22). In most places in the world today, God's people bring money rather than produce. The New Testament plan for giving is found in 2 Corinthians 8—9, and though tithing isn't mentioned, generous giving from the heart is encouraged. If believers under law could give the Lord 10 percent of their income, that's certainly a good place for believers who live under the new covenant to start their giving. However, we shouldn't stop with 10 percent but should give systematically as the Lord has prospered us (1 Cor. 16:1–2).

The priests and Levites had no inheritance in the land of Israel, for the Lord was their inheritance (Num. 18:20; Deut. 10:8–9; Josh. 13:14, 33; 14:13; 18:7), so they trusted God for His provision through the people. God assigned to the priests portions from various sacrifices (Lev. 6:14—7:38) as well as the firstfruits of the harvests and the first-born animals (Num. 18:8–20). The Levites received the people's tithes and in turn gave a tithe of that to the priests (vv. 20–32). The people also brought an extra tithe every three years, which was shared with the poor. People who lived too far from the sanctuary were permitted to sell the produce and with the money buy a substitute sacrifice when they arrived (Deut. 14:24–26), and if they didn't do so, they were fined.

It's a basic principle in Scripture that those who serve the Lord and His people should have the support of God's people. "The laborer is worthy of his hire" (Luke 10:7) and "those who preach the gospel should live from the gospel" (1 Cor. 9:14 NKJV). Believers who receive spiritual blessings from teachers and preachers should share material blessings with them (1 Tim. 5:17–18). Paul saw the supporting gifts of God's people as spiritual sacrifices dedicated to the Lord (Phil. 4:10–19). If all of God's people practiced the kind of giving described in 2 Corinthians 8—9, there would be no church debts, God's servants would be provided for, and the work of the Lord would prosper around the world.

AVOIDING CONTAMINATION (12:29—13:18)

Moses pointed out four approaches the Enemy could use to trap the Israelites into practicing idolatry, and he warned his people to avoid following them.

(1) Human curiosity (vv. 29–32). The inhabitants of Canaan had grossly defiled their land by their personal conduct and their abominable

religious practices, which included sacrificing their children to the false gods, usually Molech "the abomination of the Ammonites" (Deut. 12:31; 1 Kings 11:5, 33). This despicable practice was forbidden to the people of Israel (Deut. 18:10; Lev. 18:21; 20:2–5), but in later years, both kings and commoners in Israel abandoned God's law and sacrificed their children (2 Kings 17:16–17). Godly King Josiah defiled the place in the Valley of Hinnom where this detestable ceremony had been practiced in Judah (23:10), but King Manasseh brought it back (2 Chron. 33:6).

The British essayist Samuel Johnson called curiosity "one of the permanent and certain characteristics of a vigorous intellect," and certainly our children and grandchildren learn because they're curious about life and the world they live in. Someone defined a child as "an island of curiosity surrounded by a sea of question marks." However, there are some areas of human knowledge that are dangerous to investigate, for God wants His people to be "wise in what is good and innocent in what is evil" (Rom. 16:19 NASB). We don't have to experience sin to learn how deadly it is. Inquisitive Israelites who investigated the despicable religious practices of the Canaanites were in danger of tempting themselves and giving Satan opportunity to move in.

As we mature in the faith and become grounded in the Word, we can carefully study the philosophies and ideas that are held by various religious groups, but only so that we might better share the gospel with them. Missionaries must know the religious mind-set of the peoples to whom God sends them so they can communicate effectively with them. This is also true when we study the so-called "classics" that are often filled with moral filth and attacks against the Christian faith. "Beware of the atmosphere of the classics," wrote Robert Murray M'Cheyne to a friend. "True, we ought to know them; but only as chemists handle poisons—to discover their qualities, not to infect their blood with them."[4] With God's help, it's possible for Christian students to practice contact without contamination, but they had better "watch and pray" lest they are tempted and fall into sin.

(2) Temptation from the prophets (13:1–5).[5] God raised up prophets in Israel during those times when the people needed to be called back to the faithful worship of the Lord. It has often been said that prophets weren't just "foretellers"; they were primarily forth-tellers who declared the Word of the Lord in the name of the Lord. The faithful prophet spoke in God's name and gave only God's message for God's glory and for the good of God's people.

The key phrase in Deuteronomy 13 is, "Let us go after other gods" (vv. 2, 6, 13). In this paragraph, Moses describes a prophet who predicted an event and it occurred, which was the test of a true prophet (18:21–22). But then the prophet invited the people to join him in worshipping other gods. Why would a prophet deliver a true message followed by an invitation to worship false gods? For the same reasons formerly orthodox religious leaders in the church will abandon their calling and get involved in cults or even organize their own cults: pride, the desire to have a following and exercise authority, and the desire to make money. The Israelites knew that God's law prohibited the worship of idols, but there are always unstable people who will blindly follow a "successful religious leader" without testing their decision by God's truth.

Moses made it clear that the Word of God was true no matter how many miracles or signs a prophet might perform. We don't test the message by supernatural events; we test the message by God's Word. Satan can perform miracles (2 Thess. 2:9; Rev. 12:9) and not everybody who addresses Jesus as "Lord" and performs miracles is a genuine child of God or servant of God (Matt. 7:21–23). God sometimes allows these things to happen in order to test His people to see if they will obey His Word. Even if this man had been originally called of God, when he asked the people to disobey God's law, he ceased to be a true servant of the

Lord. Because he enticed the people to rebel against the Lord, he was to be put to death.

"So you shall put away [purge] the evil from your midst" (Deut. 13:5 NKJV). This statement is found at least eight more times in the book of Deuteronomy (17:7, 12; 19:19; 21:21; 22:21–22, 24; 24:7), and Paul quoted it in 1 Corinthians 5:13 with reference to discipline in the local church. We don't stone guilty people in our churches, but we should expel from the fellowship any who openly live in sin and refuse to repent and obey the Word of God. Why? For the same reason the idolater was removed (by death) from the nation of Israel: Sin is like yeast and when it's not purged, it will spread and infect others (1 Cor. 5:6–8; Gal. 5:9). Just as a surgeon removes cancerous tissue from a patient's body to keep it from spreading, so the local body of believers must experience surgery, no matter how painful, to maintain the spiritual health of the church.

Since the accuser was to throw the first stone, it would encourage him to give serious consideration to the facts and not impetuously accuse an innocent person. (See 1 Kings 21.) The method of execution was stoning so that all the people could participate and cast their votes against the worship of idols. Either one person's sin affects the whole nation (Josh. 7), or the whole nation must deal with that one person's sin.

It's remarkable how many otherwise intelligent people study their horoscopes and consult professional "psychics" who claim to have the power to see into the future. If people really had that ability, they could make a great deal of money on the stock market or at the racetrack and wouldn't have to earn a living reading palms, gazing at the stars, or consulting crystal balls. Later in his address, Moses will name specific occult practices that are forbidden to God's people, and one of them is consulting Satan in order to know the future (Deut. 18:9–13). Jesus warned about false prophets and the apostles warned about false teachers (Matt. 7:15–20; 2 Cor. 11:3–4, 11–13; 1 Tim. 1:6–7; 2 Peter 2).

(3) Temptation from friends and relatives (vv. 6–11). It would not be difficult to expose and execute a false prophet, but what about a relative or close friend who tempts you to worship a false god? And what if the temptation is secret and the worship of the idol is also secret? As long as you maintained your public image as a worshipper of Jehovah, you might get away with being a secret Baal worshipper. But to this suggestion, Moses gave a resounding, "No!" Even if man's own wife enticed him to worship idols—King Solomon comes to mind (1 Kings 11:1–13)—the husband was not to shield her but was to take her to the authorities and even participate in her execution. The Jews were to love the Lord their God even more than they loved their own mates or family. Jesus laid down a similar condition for discipleship (Luke 14:25–27). Moses taught that this kind of capital sentence would put the fear of the Lord into the rest of the nation, and they would think twice before turning to idols (Deut. 13:11; see 17:13; 21:21). The lesson for the church is "Those who are sinning rebuke in the presence of all, that the rest also may fear" (1 Tim. 5:20 NKJV).

During my years of pastoral ministry, I was occasionally contacted by heartbroken ministers who were unable to deal with flagrant sinners in the church because the offenders had relatives on the board or in the congregation. How sad it is when the testimony of a church is totally destroyed because of people who put their family ahead of God and His Word. "Peace at any price" isn't the biblical way to deal with problems, for "the wisdom that is from above is first pure, then peaceable" (James 3:17). Unity that is based on hypocrisy will never last. On the other hand, I have seen godly people stand with the congregation in disciplining their own relatives who had brought disgrace to the name of Christ and the church.

(4) Temptation from a multitude (vv. 12–18). "You shall not follow a crowd to do evil" (Ex. 23:2 NKJV). If a person has committed wickedness, the fact that hundreds of people approve of it doesn't change its character. It is God who defines what sin is and how we should deal with it. God governs His people by decree, not by consensus. How could an entire town in Israel turn away from the Lord and start worshipping false gods? By failing to deal with the first person in the town who turned to false gods. The leaders didn't obey God's law and purge the evil from the town, so the sin easily spread from person to person and eventually infected everybody. When you remember that the land belonged to the Lord (Lev. 25:23), that He graciously allowed the Jews to live there, and that He alone had the right to lay down the rules, you can see that the idolatrous town was guilty of very serious sin.

It was important that the matter be investigated thoroughly and accurately. "He who answers a matter before he hears it, it is folly and shame to him" (Prov. 18:13 NKJV). If the accusation was found to be true, the wealth and possessions of the people were to be burned in the town square as a burnt offering to the Lord. The people were to be slain, and the city itself was to be destroyed and nothing was to be salvaged from it. It was to be left a "heap," which is the translation of the Hebrew word *tel*, which is a mound composed of layers of ruins. The heap of ruins would be a constant witness to warn the Jews not to worship idols.

But could the nation of Israel afford to lose a town and all its inhabitants? Yes, because God would multiply His people and bless them for obeying His Word and honoring His name. Why not rebuild the town and start all over? Because God said it was to remain a heap of ruins forever and never be rebuilt. Human calculation would say that this was a great loss, but divine wisdom says it is a great gain, for a festering sore had been removed from the nation.

Unfortunately, Israel didn't obey these laws, and idolatry multiplied in the nation during the reign of Solomon and after the kingdom divided. When Jeroboam became ruler of the northern kingdom of Israel, he made idolatry official by setting up two golden calves for the people to worship, one at Dan and the other at Bethel. In this way, he encouraged the people not to go to Jerusalem to worship (1 Kings 12:25ff.). Because of their idolatry, Israel fell to Assyria in 722 BC and Judah fell to Babylon in 606–586 BC. God would rather that the nation be scattered and the holy sanctuary be destroyed than that His people worship false gods. The people forgot that it was the Lord Jehovah who delivered them from Egypt and gave them their land (Deut. 13:5, 10).

HONORING GOD'S WORD (18:9–22)

If people don't know the true and living God and don't have His Word to guide them, they have to find substitutes to help them make decisions and face up to the demands of life. Instead of worshipping the true and living God, the people in Canaan worshipped dead idols (Ps. 115), and for the Word of God they substituted superstitious practices that linked them to Satan and his demonic forces. No matter what the experts in "comparative religions" might say, pagan idolatrous religion is Satan worship (1 Cor. 10:14–22; Rev. 9:20). The explosion of the occult that we've seen in recent years is evidence that people are seeking in the wrong direction for the spiritual help they need. Visit any large secular bookstore and you'll find shelves of books devoted to Satan, demons, black magic, and allied themes. People who refuse to love the truth must end up believing lies (2 Thess. 2:7–12), and only Jesus Christ can deliver them from the bondage that these occult practices bring to their lives.

The abominations of Satan (vv. 9–13). God forbids His people to have anything to do with occult practices. Moses had already mentioned some of these "abominations" (Deut. 18:9, 12; "detestable practices," NIV) and warned Israel not to meddle with them (Ex. 22:18; Lev. 17:7; 19:26, 31; 20:6, 27), so this wasn't an entirely new theme, but here he went into greater detail. The false prophet Balaam discovered that no sorcery could work against Israel (Num. 23:23), but the Jews could ensnare themselves if they investigated these dangerous practices and got themselves involved.

One reason God commanded Israel to wipe out the nations in Canaan was because of their evil occult practices (Deut. 18:14), and why should the conqueror follow the religion that brought judgment to the conquered?

Lest we conclude that these warnings about the occult don't apply to Christians in this "enlightened age," we need to be reminded that idolatry and witchcraft are listed among the sins of the flesh in Galatians 5:19–21, and that the book of Revelation teaches that occult practices will be very widespread in the end times (9:20–21; 18:2). In fact, those who engage in such things are among the ones destined for the lake of fire (21:8; 22:14–15).

In Deuteronomy 18:10–11, Moses listed the practices that were forbidden by God, beginning with sacrificing children, a subject we've already discussed (12:31). If you want to worship Satan, you have to pay the price he demands. He will give you what you want if you give him what he wants. He offered Jesus the kingdoms of the world in return for one act of worship (Matt. 4:8–10), and he sneered at Job and claimed that he worshipped God only because the Lord rewarded him (Job 1—2). There are poems, novels, and plays in ancient and modern literature telling about people who sold themselves to Satan, received their rewards, and then regretted they had ever entered into the bargain. Perhaps the most famous is Goethe's *Tragedy of Dr. Faustus.*

The second forbidden practice is divination, which is seeking to get secret knowledge, especially about future events. Divination was widely practiced in the ancient world in various ways, including interpreting omens, consulting the stars, inspecting various animal organs, using divining rods, interpreting dreams, watching the movement of the water, and contacting the dead (1 Sam. 28). In some way, the sacrificing of children was also involved in divination. Mediums, necromancers, and spiritists consulted the dead with the hopes of learning forbidden things about the future.

The diviner wants to know the future, but the sorcerer wants to control people and the future by using various forms of magic, witchcraft, and spells. By being in league with the demons and casting spells, magicians and witches seek to influence people and events to achieve their own selfish purposes. People in today's "scientific world" may scoff at these things, but any evangelical missionary can tell you of the demonic influence that has held many backward peoples in bondage and fear. Certainly demonic forces are at work in the "modern" Western world today, but they operate with greater subtlety and aren't always easily detected. Those who would deny the influence of demons in the church today will have to explain the prevalence of demonism when Christ was here on earth and His victory over demons. They must also consider our Lord's commission to His disciples (Mark 3:14–25; Luke 9:1) and their experience ministering to the demonized (10:17). And what about the ministry of Paul (Acts 19:11) and what Paul wrote about demons to believers in the churches (1 Cor. 10:20–21; Rom. 8:37–39; Eph. 6:10–18)?[6]

If any Jew ever considered getting personally acquainted with these wicked practices, he would have to consider Moses' closing admonition, "You must be blameless before the LORD your God" (Deut. 18:13 NIV). "Blameless" implies, not sinless perfection, but a heart totally devoted to the Lord. It speaks of integrity and an undivided heart, what David meant when he wrote, "I will walk within my house with a perfect heart" (Ps. 101:2 NKJV). The Jewish "Shema" declared, "Love the LORD your God with all your heart and with all your soul and with all your strength" (Deut. 6:5 NIV).

The revelation of the true God (vv. 14–19). Israel didn't need to experiment with new religions because the Lord had revealed Himself and His Word to them through Moses, His chosen prophet. Once you have the real thing, why go in search of substitutes? Israel could have said to the nations in Canaan what Jesus said to the Samaritan woman at Jacob's well, "You worship what you do not know; we know what we worship, for salvation is of the Jews" (John 4:22 NKJV). In this statement, Jesus rejected all other religions except Old Testament Judaism and New Testament Christianity, and Christianity came out of Judaism and fulfilled it.

Moses promised the people that God would raise up other prophets as the nation needed them, and the people were to give heed to their messages and obey it, for their messages would be the Word of God. Moses reminded the people that at Sinai they had requested that he give them God's message, because they were afraid to hear God's voice (Ex. 20:18–21). Not all the prophets wrote down their messages for future generations to read and study, but Moses did and so did Isaiah, Jeremiah, Ezekiel, Daniel, and the twelve men we call "the minor prophets." These prophets not only rebuked Israel for sin and encouraged them in holy living, but they pointed to the coming of the Messiah who would be the Savior of the world. During His walk with the two Emmaus disciples, Jesus began at "Moses and all the Prophets" and "expounded to them in all the Scriptures the things concerning Himself" (Luke 24:27 NKJV).

Over the centuries, Jewish scholars interpreted Deuteronomy 18:15 to refer to a special prophet who would appear before Messiah came to establish His kingdom. From Malachi 4:5, the Jews knew that Elijah would return at the end of the age, and they wondered if it was John the Baptist, who dressed and ministered so much like Elijah (Luke 3:1–9; Matt. 3:4). John denied it and also denied that he was the prophet that Moses promised (John 1:19–21). In one sense, John was an "Elijah" who prepared the way for Christ (Matt. 11:14; 17:12; Luke 1:13–17), but John did not identify himself as the fulfillment of Malachi 4:5. (On Moses' writing about the Christ, see John 1:19–28, 45; 5:46; 6:14; 7:40.)

Moses was doing more than promise the whole line of prophets that the Lord would send; he was also announcing the coming of the Prophet, the Lord Jesus Christ. At least that's the way Peter explained it in Acts 3:22–26. Our Lord has three offices, that of Prophet, Priest, and King.

When He ministered here on earth, He declared God's Word as Prophet, and by the inspiration of His Spirit has caused it to be written down for our learning. He intercedes for His people as the High Priest in heaven, and He also sits on the throne and reigns as King, working out His purposes in this world (1 Cor. 15:25; Eph. 1:18–23). One day He will return and reign on earth as King of Kings (Rev. 19:11ff.).

It's a serious thing to hear God's Word and not respect it and obey it, for it is the Word of the living God, the God of truth. The written Scriptures are a priceless treasure; they teach us what we need to know about God, the way of salvation, and how to live godly lives and please Him. There is no substitute for the Word of God. Peter was right: "Lord, to whom shall we go? You have the words of eternal life" (John 6:68 NIV).

The identification of true prophets (vv. 20–22). Moses promised that there would be prophets sent by God to Israel to teach them what they needed to know, but the logical question people would ask was, "How can we distinguish a true prophet from a false prophet?" Moses had already told them that everything a prophet says and does must be tested by the Word of God (Deut. 13:1–5), and he repeated that warning. "But the prophet who presumes to speak a word in My name, which I have not commanded him to speak, or who speaks in the name of other gods, that prophet shall die" (18:20 NKJV). This test was valid even if the prophet's prediction came true or if he performed signs and wonders. But the ultimate test is that God's true prophets are always 100 percent accurate (v. 22). Modern day "prophets" boast of being 75 percent accurate, or maybe 80 percent, but that admission only brands them as false prophets. A prophet sent by God is never wrong; what he predicts will come to pass.

Believers today must exercise spiritual discernment because "many false prophets are gone out into the world" (1 John 4:1–6). John makes it clear that the first test of a true minister of the Word is the confession that Jesus Christ came in the flesh and is indeed the Son of God. When you listen to a teacher who is truly God's servant, the Spirit dwelling in your heart will respond to the Word being taught (1 John 2:18–27). The message will be true to the Scriptures and will exalt Jesus Christ.[7]

Moses has been focusing on the true worship of the Lord, a subject that's very important to the church today. I have traveled enough in this world to know that you meet different styles of worship in different countries and among different peoples. My wife and I have attended formal worship services in cathedrals as well as informal meetings in homes and even out-of-doors, and our hearts have been blessed. The important thing is not the culture or the setting but that we worship the Lord "in spirit and in truth" (John 4:24). True worship comes from within, from a heart totally yielded to the Lord, and true worship is controlled by the Holy Spirit and the Word of God (Eph. 5:18–21; Col. 3:16–20). Our subjective feelings must be monitored by Scripture and motivated by the Spirit, otherwise we may be engaging in false worship. False worship is dangerous because it may open the door to demonic influences. Satan is a counterfeiter (2 Cor. 11:13–15) who knows how to lead undiscerning people away from Christ and the truth. They think they're filled with the Spirit when they're really fooled by the spirits.

"Little children, keep yourselves from idols" (1 John 5:21).

QUESTIONS FOR PERSONAL REFLECTION
OR GROUP DISCUSSION

1. What are some common idols people worship in our society?

   money, sports, good looks, power,

2. Why was it so important that Israel purge the land of all idolatry?

   Idolary was dangerous because it might become a tool for the Devil

3. Israel was instructed to worship God in a certain way. What guidelines or commands do we have for our worship of God today?

   Tithes, offerings   10 Commandments   Communion

4. Why is blood viewed as special and deserving of regulations and respect? What is the role of the blood of Christ? *The Blood of Christ is precious to us because of who shed it and because of what it accomplishes for those who trust in him.*

5. What commands or regulations about giving are for believers today? How do you decide when, to whom, and how much to give?

   Generous giving from the heart is encouraged I decide who to give to by who it helps

6. How might the enemy use human curiosity to trap people into practicing idolatry today?

7. What temptations might lure someone with a fruitful ministry away from the Lord? How can a person withstand that temptation?

8. What is the true purpose of church discipline? In what circumstances would church discipline be appropriate?

9. What does it mean for you to love the Lord your God more than your earthly family?

10. When Moses admonished the people to "be blameless before the Lord your God," what did he mean by "blameless"?

Confess are sins.

11. How can you grow in practicing true worship?

Chapter Six

FOOD AND FESTIVALS

(Deuteronomy 14:1—16:17)

Worship is not a "business arrangement" with God by which we agree to praise Him if He will agree to bless us. (See Job 1:6–12.) Our primary purpose in worshipping God is to please and glorify Him, but one of the spiritual by-products of true worship is that we become more like Christ (2 Cor. 3:18). Moses didn't know that he had a shining face (Ex. 34:29), and we don't always recognize the transformation the Lord makes in our hearts and lives because we spend time with Him. However, they are there just the same, and others see them and glorify God. Worship is our highest priority and our greatest privilege.

In these chapters, Moses further explains Israel's worship and focuses on the kind of people they—and we—should be as the people who belong to the true and living God.

A HOLY PEOPLE (14:1–21)

We must never take for granted that we are "the children of the LORD [our] God" and "a holy people to the LORD [our] God" (vv. 1–2 NKJV). These are privileges that we don't deserve and that we could never earn, and we enjoy them only because of God's love and grace. The Lord announced to Pharaoh, "Israel is my son, even my firstborn" (Ex. 4:22; see Jer. 31:9), and because Pharaoh wouldn't listen and obey, Egypt lost all their firstborn.

At Sinai, before He gave the law, the Lord announced to Israel, "And you shall be to Me a kingdom of priests and a holy nation" (Ex. 19:6 NKJV). Because of their unique relationship to the Lord as His chosen people and special treasure, the Israelites were responsible to obey Him and truly be a holy people. Their relationship to the Lord was the most important factor in their national life, for without the Lord, Israel would be like all the other nations. As a holy people, they had to learn to distinguish the things that differed.

The holy and the unholy (vv. 1–2). The Hebrew word translated "holy" means "that which is set apart and marked off, that which is different and wholly other." Our English word "holy" comes from an Old English word meaning "to be whole, to be healthy." What health and wholeness are to the body, holiness is to the inner person. As a holy people, the Jews were set apart from all the other nations because the holy presence of the Lord was with them and they had received God's holy law (Deut. 23:14; Rom. 9:4). Because they were a holy people, they were not to imitate the wicked practices of their neighbors, such as cutting their bodies or shaving their foreheads in mourning (1 Kings 18:28; Jer. 16:6; 41:5). This reminds us of Romans 12:2 (NKJV), "And do not be conformed to this world, but be transformed by the renewing of your mind."

This section opens and closes with the same reminder: "Thou art a holy people unto the LORD" (Deut. 14:2, 21). In the book of Leviticus, the Lord told the people, "Be holy, for I am holy" (11:44–45; see 19:2; 20:7, 26; 21:8), an admonition that Peter quoted in his first epistle for the church to obey today (1:15–16). The local church is a holy temple (1 Cor. 3:17) and a holy priesthood (1 Peter 2:5), and therefore believers should separate themselves from the defilement of the world and seek to perfect holiness in the fear of God (2 Cor. 6:14—7:1). It's depressing to read statistical surveys and discover that, when it comes to morality, professed Christians don't believe or live much differently from unconverted people. And yet God's people are supposed to be "set apart, marked off, different" so we can "advertise" the glorious virtues of the Lord (1 Peter 2:9).

The clean and the unclean (vv. 3–21). The people of Israel were to "demonstrate the difference" even by what they ate. We've already seen that the Jews were not permitted to eat meat with blood in it (12:16, 23; 15:23), and now Moses reminded them of the creatures they were permitted to eat (see Lev. 11:1–23).

The distinction between "clean and unclean" sacrifices was known in the days of Noah (Gen. 7:1–10) and therefore must have been told to our first parents when God taught them to worship. In the Jewish law, the words "clean" and "unclean" have nothing to do with the intrinsic nature or value of the creatures themselves. This was a designation given by the Lord for reasons not always explained. Some students believe that the Jews enjoyed better health because they avoided certain foods,[1] but both Jesus and the apostles declared all foods clean (Mark 7:14–23; Acts 10:9–25; Rom. 14:1—15:13), the so-called "healthful" foods as well as the "unhealthful." Fasting is an accepted spiritual discipline, when connected with prayer, but "food does not commend us to God; for neither if we eat are we the better, nor if we do not eat are we the worse" (1 Cor. 8:8 NKJV). Believers who think they're more spiritual than others because of what they eat or don't eat need to ponder Colossians 2:16–23.

It's likely that God declared some creatures "unclean" as a means of teaching His people to exercise discernment and to behave like a holy people in the everyday activities of life, such as eating. The same principle applies to believers today: "Therefore, whether you eat or drink, or whatever you do, do all to the glory of God" (1 Cor. 10:31 NKJV). When we give thanks and ask God's blessing before we eat a meal, we're not only acknowledging His faithfulness and goodness in supplying daily bread, but we're also telling Him that we want to honor Him in what we eat and the way we eat it. The Jew who wanted to glorify God would refuse to eat anything that the Lord had forbidden.

Another factor in the dietary laws may have been that the prohibited creatures were in some way associated with the pagan worship that Israel was to avoid. The admonition about boiling a kid in its mother's milk (Deut. 14:21; Ex. 23:19; 34:26) may fall into that category. Some scholars think this was a pagan "fertility rite" and that the milk was sprinkled on the fields to encourage bountiful crops, but we have no archaeological evidence to back up this interpretation. We do know that this strange law explains why orthodox Jews do not have milk and meat together at a meal.

The list includes land animals (Deut. 14:4–8), water creatures (vv. 9–10), fowl (vv. 11–18), and flying insects (vv. 19–20). The water creatures and birds that are scavengers were prohibited, perhaps because those who ate them might pick up parasites and become ill. We remember that John the Baptist's diet was locusts and wild honey (Lev. 11:20–23; Matt. 3:4). Finally, we must admit that we don't know what some of these creatures were and can't identify them with creatures we know today. For example, the hare (Deut. 14:7) certainly isn't the same as our "rabbit" even though the NIV gives that translation. The rabbit doesn't chew the cud, although the movements of his jaw and nostrils may look like that's what he's doing.

The final admonition to refrain from eating creatures found dead (v. 21) involved the important rule that Jews were not to eat blood, and there was likely blood in the carcass. Another consideration was that Jews were not to touch dead bodies because this made them unclean (Lev. 11:24–25; 22:8). If a Jew found a dead animal, he could give it to a resident alien in the land or sell it to a visitor, because neither of them would be under the jurisdiction of the Jewish law. There are some things that the people of the world can do that Christians can't do and should not even want to do, because Christians belong to the Lord and want to obey Him. As the familiar adage says, "Others may—you cannot." God has every right to tell us what we can have around us (Deut. 12:1–3) and what we can put within us.

A GENEROUS PEOPLE (14:22–29)

When we studied Deuteronomy 12, we learned that God commanded His people to give 10 percent of their produce (grain, fruits, vegetables, and animals) to Him as an act of worship and an expression of gratitude for His blessing. Every year, each family had to go to the sanctuary with their tithes, enjoy a feast there, and share the tithe with the Levites, who, in turn, would share it with the priests (Num. 18:20–32). Moses repeated this commandment, because when it comes to giving to the Lord, some people need more than one reminder (2 Cor. 8:10–11; 9:1–5).

The people of Israel were to be generous with tithes and offerings because the Lord had been generous with them. Each time they brought their tithes and gifts to the sanctuary and enjoyed a thanksgiving feast, it would teach them to fear the Lord (Deut. 14:23), because if the Lord hadn't blessed them, they would have nothing to eat and nothing to give. As David said, everything we give to God first comes from His hand and it all belongs to Him (1 Chron. 29:16). When we cease to fear God and fail to appreciate His bountiful provision, we become proud and start to take His blessings for granted. Then the Lord has to discipline us to remind us that He is the Giver of every gift.

Every third year, the people were to give the Lord a second tithe, which remained in their towns and was used to feed the Levites and the needy people in the land, especially the widows and orphans. The Levites served at the sanctuary but were scattered throughout Israel. If the people of Israel demonstrated concern for the needs of others, God would bless their labors and enable them to give even more (Deut. 14:29). Our Lord promised, "Give, and it will be given to you: good measure, pressed down, shaken together, and running over will be put into your bosom" (Luke 6:38 NKJV). "He who sows sparingly will also reap sparingly, and he who sows bountifully will also reap bountifully" (2 Cor. 9:6 NKJV).

As Christians enjoying the blessings of God's grace, we ought to do far more than the Jews who lived in the dispensation of the Mosaic law. The New Testament doesn't command us how much we should give, but it does urge us to give in proportion to the blessings we have received from the Lord (1 Cor. 16:1–2; 2 Cor. 8—9). The calculating Christian will always be the loser; the generous Christian will enjoy the blessing of God. However, Christian industrialist R. G. LeTourneau used to warn, "If you give because it pays, it won't pay." Our motive must always be to please God and glorify Him.

A Trusting People (15:1–18)

Those who think that it takes a great deal of faith to give God a tithe of their income will probably be shocked when they read this section of the law. Just as every seventh day of the week was set apart for God as the Sabbath Day, so every seventh year was to be set apart as a Sabbath Year. During that year, the Jews were not to cultivate the land but allow it to rest. The people would have to trust God to produce the grain, vegetables, and fruits they needed for themselves and for their flocks and herds and farm animals. (See Lev. 25:1–7.) Every fiftieth year was a "Year of Jubilee" (v. 8ff.) when the land lay fallow for another year! It would really take faith on the part of the people to trust God for what they needed for two long years!

The poor debtor (vv. 1–11). But the Sabbath Year involved much more than rest for the land (Ex. 23:10–11). It also meant canceling debts (Deut. 15:1–11) and setting free the servants who had served for six years (vv. 12–18). Bible students don't agree on whether the entire debt was cancelled or just the interest on the loan for that year (31:10).[2] "He shall not require payment from his fellow Israelite or brother" (Deut. 15:2 NIV). However, they could collect interest from foreigners. Since people weren't getting any income from their land, they wouldn't be able to pay their debts easily. But what was a test of faith for some would be an answer to prayer for the poor and the needy. They were permitted to eat freely from the fields and orchards and were given an extra year to raise money to pay their debts.

The seeming contradiction between verse 4 ("there shall be no poor among you") and verse 11 ("the poor shall never cease out of the land") is resolved by paying attention to the context. During the Sabbath Year, the lenders were obligated to remit the debt (or the interest owed) by their poor Jewish brothers, unless there were no Jewish poor people who owed them money, and there would be no poor if the people obeyed God's laws. Any Jewish borrower who was not poor was expected to pay his debts during the seventh year, and the lenders could collect from foreigners in the land. If a Jewish borrower could afford to pay and didn't, he would be exploiting the person who loaned him the money and defeating one of the purposes of the Sabbath Year.

The Sabbath Year and the Year of Jubilee were part of God's wise plan to balance the economic scales in the nation so that the rich could not exploit the poor or the poor take advantage of the rich. However, the Lord knew that there would always be poor people in the land (Matt. 26:11; Mark 14:7; John 12:8) because Israel would not consistently obey these laws. The nation of Israel would have been the most prosperous nation on earth if they had followed the instructions God gave them, but they rejected His will and adopted the methods of the nations around them. They did not observe the Sabbath Year every seventh year or the Year of Jubilee every fiftieth year (Lev. 26:32–45), and for this failure they paid a great price. Their seventy years captivity in Babylon gave their land the

Sabbath rest that it missed during those years of disobedience (2 Chron. 36:14–21).

The Sabbath Year was a test of faith, but it was also a test of love (Deut. 15:7–11). Suppose a poor Jew needed a loan and the Sabbath Year was only two years away. The borrower would then receive an extra year for paying back the loan and the loaner would lose the interest for one year! If the loaner looked at the loan strictly as a business proposition, he would turn it down, but that's the very attitude the Lord wanted to correct. It wasn't a business proposition; it was a ministry to a brother. If the wealthier Israelite closed his heart and his hand to the needy man, he would hurt his brother and grieve the Lord, who had given him all the wealth he had. Therefore, he was to open both his heart and his hand to help his brother, and the Lord would see to it that he was compensated for his generosity. See Proverbs 14:21, 31; 19:17; 21:13; 28:27; Ephesians 4:28; 1 Timothy 6:17–19; 1 John 3:14–18.

The indentured servant (vv. 12–15, 18). Jewish debtors unable to repay their loans could become indentured servants in the household of the man to whom they were indebted and in that way work off the debt. The Jews were not allowed to enslave their fellow Jews, although they could have slaves from other nations (Lev. 25:39–43). Male servants were to be released after six years of service, whether the seventh year was the Sabbath Year or not. This law assumes that the man's six years of service without a salary had adequately repaid the loan. But once again, the Lord commanded generosity, for the masters were to send their servants away bearing gifts that would help them start life over again, including livestock, grain, and wine. After all, when the Jews left Egypt, they received expensive gifts in return for their years of enslavement (Ex. 11:2; 12:35–36), so why shouldn't a Jewish brother be rewarded for six years of faithful labor to a fellow Jew?

The willing servant (vv. 16–18; Ex. 21:1–6). During those six years of service, the debtor might come to love the host family and want to stay with them. Or he might have gotten married during that time, have a family, and want to remain with them. If that was the debtor's choice, he would be taken to the judges where his decision would be officially recognized. Then his master would bore a hole in his ear to mark him as a willing servant for life. A female servant could make the same choice, but see Exodus 21:7–11 for special provisions.

Certainly there's a spiritual message here for God's people today. We should love our Lord so much that we should want to serve Him willingly and gladly all our lives. We must never look upon our service as "slavery" but as privilege. "I love my master ... and do not want to go free" is a wonderful confession of faith and love (Ex. 21:5 NIV). Granted, the servant's love for his wife and children entered into the picture, but even those blessings came because of his master's kindness, and the master was caring for them as well as his servant. What we all need is the open ear to hear God's will (Ps. 40:6–8; Isa. 50:4–5) and a pierced ear that announces we love Him and are ready to obey His every command.

The emphasis in this section is on faith that produces generosity. If we are "hardhearted or tightfisted" (Deut. 15:7 NIV), it's evidence that we don't really believe that God keeps His promises and provides for those who give to the needy. Jesus became poor that He might make us rich (2 Cor. 8:9), and He blesses us that we might be a blessing to others.

A CELEBRATING PEOPLE (15:19—16:8; EX. 12—13; LEV. 23)

The Lord gave Israel a unique calendar to help His people remember who they were and to encourage them to review all He had done for them. In following this calendar of special events year by year, the Jews would find cause for great celebration. But this calendar also belongs to believers today, because it illustrates what Christ has done for His church and what He will do when He comes again. As the Jewish people followed this calendar year by year, they had every reason for great celebration because of the Lord's mercies to their ancestors and to them. As we study this calendar, we should give thanks and rejoice that we have so great a salvation and such a great Savior.

On the seventh day of the week, the Jews celebrated the Sabbath. God gave them the Sabbath as a sign that they were His special covenant people and belonged to the Creator of the universe (Ex. 31:12–17). There's no record in Scripture that God ever gave the Sabbath to any other people and commanded them to observe it. (See Col. 2:16–17.) Every seventh year was a Sabbath Year (Deut. 15:1–11), and every fiftieth year was the Year of Jubilee (Lev. 25:8–55).

The Jewish civil year began with "Rosh Hashanah," the Feast of Trumpets on the first day of the seventh month (our September–October), but the religious calendar began with Passover on the fourteenth day of the first month (our March–April; see Ex. 12:1–2). The week that followed was called "the Feast of Unleavened Bread." On the day following the Sabbath after Passover, which would be a Sunday, the priest waved the first sheaves of the barley harvest before the Lord, and this was known as the Feast of Firstfruits. Fifty days later, they celebrated Pentecost, and from the fifteenth to twenty-first day of the seventh month (our September–October), they celebrated the Feast of Weeks, also called the Feast of Tabernacles.

Moses emphasized only three of these seven special occasions because they were the feasts that every Jewish male would be obligated to celebrate at the central sanctuary every year (Deut. 16:16–17; Ex. 23:14–17; 34:22–24). That chosen place would be the tabernacle or temple in Jerusalem.

Passover and Unleavened Bread (15:19—16:8; Ex. 12—13). Moses discusses three topics related to the Passover: the sanctifying of the firstborn animals (Deut. 15:19–23), the sacrificing of the Passover lamb (16:1–3, 5–7), and the observing of the Feast of Unleavened Bread (vv. 4, 8). At the first Passover in Egypt, God killed all the firstborn in the land, both humans and animals, except those Jews who were in their houses and protected by the blood on the doorposts (Ex. 12:12–13). From that time on, God claimed for Himself all the firstborn sons and animals in Israel, and they all had to be redeemed with a sacrifice (13:1–3, 11–13; Lev. 12; Num. 18:14–19; Luke 2:21–24). If the animal wasn't redeemed, it had to be killed. Whenever a Jewish father had to redeem a firstborn animal, it gave him an opportunity to explain Passover to his children.

Passover was "Independence Day" for the nation of Israel, for on that night the Lord not only gave them freedom from slavery but also demonstrated His great power over the gods and armies of Egypt. Israel celebrated Passover a year later at Sinai (Num. 9:1–14), but after their rebellion at Kadesh-barnea (Num. 13—14), the nation didn't celebrate Passover again until the new generation had entered the Promised Land (Josh. 5:10–11). Once they were settled in the land, the men had to obey the command to go to the sanctuary to observe Passover, and they could take their families with them. Parents were instructed to use the occasion of Passover to instruct their children about Israel's deliverance from Egypt (Ex. 12:25–28).

The New Testament interpretation and application of Passover identifies the lamb with Jesus Christ, the Lamb of God, who gave His life for the sins of the world (John 1:29; 1 Cor. 5:7; 1 Peter 1:19; Rev. 5:12). Outside the city of Jerusalem, Jesus died on the cross at the time when the Passover lambs were being slain by the priests at the Jewish temple. The blood shed by many lambs in Egypt delivered a nation on that first Passover night, but the blood of one Lamb, slain on the cross, will deliver from judgment any lost sinner who will trust Jesus Christ. The blood of the many Jewish sacrifices could cover sin but never take it away, which explains why these sacrifices were repeated, but the blood of Christ has settled the matter of salvation once and for all (Heb. 10:1–18). It wasn't the life of the lamb that saved Israel from bondage but the death of the lamb and the application of the blood by faith. Christ is our perfect example in all things (1 Peter 2:21–25; 1 John 2:6), but trying to follow His example cannot save us, because He did no sin. First we need Jesus as our Savior, and then we can follow in His steps.

The Feast of Unleavened Bread followed Passover and lasted for a week (Deut. 16:3–4, 8). During those days, no yeast was allowed in any Jewish home. At the first Passover, the Jews didn't have time for the bread dough to rise and therefore ate unleavened bread with the roasted lamb and the bitter herbs (Ex. 12:1–12; 13:2–10). But more was involved here than just shortness of time and readiness for a quick exit. In Scripture, yeast often symbolizes evil of one kind or another, because yeast is a substance that, though small and seemingly insignificant, rapidly grows and "infects" the whole lump of dough. Yeast represents the sins that belong to the old life (1 Cor. 5:7), such as malice and wickedness (v. 8) and hypocrisy (Luke 12:10); it also represents unbelief (Matt. 16:6), compromise (Mark 8:15), and false doctrine (Gal. 5:9).

The nation of Israel wasn't rescued from Egypt by cleaning their houses and getting rid of yeast. They were delivered by the power of God because of the blood that had been sprinkled on the doorposts of their houses. Sinners aren't redeemed by getting rid of their bad habits and "cleaning up" their lives, but by trusting in the Lord Jesus Christ, who died for them on the cross. However, one of the characteristics of a true child of God is a changed life. "Let everyone who names the name of Christ depart from iniquity" (2 Tim. 2:19 NKJV). "Let us cleanse ourselves from all filthiness of the flesh and spirit, perfecting holiness in the fear of God" (2 Cor. 7:1). Anyone who professes to belong to Christ who doesn't seek to conquer sin and become more Christlike in daily conduct is making a false profession (1 John 3:1–10).

In 1 Corinthians 5:8, Paul compared the life of the local church to "keeping the feast" of Passover. The church doesn't "keep the feast" literally because it has been fulfilled in Christ our Passover Lamb, who was sacrificed for us (v. 7). But like the Jews on Passover night in Egypt, we are a pilgrim people, ready to be called out, and we must not be encumbered by sin. The Jews ate the Passover feast as families, and each local church is a family of God, feasting on Jesus Christ through the Word and waiting for Him to call His people out of this world. Like Israel of old, we must remind ourselves that we were once slaves of sin, in bondage to the world (Eph. 2:1–3), and God delivered us by sending His Son as the sacrifice for our sins. When we observe the Lord's Supper (Eucharist), we remember His death and look forward to His return.[3]

Pentecost (vv. 9–12; Lev. 23:15–22). The word "pentecost" means "fiftieth" and comes from the Greek translation of the Old Testament, the Septuagint. This feast was celebrated fifty days after Firstfruits, which means that it also occurred on the first day of the week. For the Jews, it was a joyful time of celebrating the wheat harvest, but for the Christian, it commemorates the coming of the Holy Spirit and the "birthday of the church" (Acts 2). Jesus promised that He and the Father would send the Spirit to believers (John 14:16–17), but the Spirit couldn't come until first Christ died, was raised from the dead, and was glorified in heaven (7:37–38).

Beginning at creation (Gen. 1:1–2), the Holy Spirit is found at work throughout the Old Testament, usually empowering men and women to do mighty acts to the glory of God. During Old Testament times, the Spirit was a temporary visitor who came upon people, but since His coming in Acts 2, the Spirit permanently indwells all who belong to Christ (John 14:16–17). He gives spiritual gifts to the church (1 Cor. 12) and empowers God's people to bear witness of Jesus Christ (Acts 1:8). Without the ministry and power of the Holy Spirit, believers can't live for God or serve Him effectively.

On the Feast of Firstfruits, the priest waved a sheaf of grain, but on the Feast of Pentecost, he presented two loaves of bread baked with yeast

(Lev. 23:17, 20). When the Spirit came at Pentecost, He baptized all believers into Christ (Acts 1:4–5; 1 Cor. 12:13), so we no longer have single sheaves of grain but the grain made into flour and formed into loaves. The flour was made from the "firstfruits sheaves" from the wheat harvest. The presence of leaven in the loaves indicates that the church on earth isn't yet a pure church and never will be until Christ takes it to heaven.

The Feast of Pentecost ushered in the harvest season (Lev. 23:22), and the Jews were commanded to share what they had and feast joyfully before the Lord (Deut. 16:11). When the Spirit came upon the believers at Pentecost, it was the beginning of a great harvest season for the church. Peter's message at Pentecost brought 3,000 people to Christ (Acts 2:41), and shortly after that, his ministry added 2,000 more (4:4). The book of Acts is the inspired record of the growth of the church as the Holy Spirit empowered witnesses to share the gospel in the harvest field, wherever the Lord sent them.

Dr. A. W. Tozer once said, "If God were to take the Holy Spirit out of this world, much of what the church is doing would go right on, and nobody would know the difference." What an indictment that our churches depend on everything except the power of the Holy Spirit! The early church had none of the things that we deem essential—budgets, buildings, academic degrees, and even political "connections"—but they did have the power of the Holy Spirit and saw multitudes turn to Christ.

Tabernacles (vv. 13–15). Like the Feast of Unleavened Bread, the Feast of Tabernacles lasted seven days. It took place in the autumn (our September–October) and was also called the Feast of Weeks, the Feast of Booths, and the Feast of Ingathering. It celebrated the completion of the harvest that had begun with barley harvest at the Feast of Firstfruits, continued with the wheat harvest at Pentecost, and now the harvest of fruits, grapes, figs, and olives. After the harvest, the farmers would plow their fields and sow their grain, and then the winter rains would begin. During this feast, the Jewish people lived in booths made of tree branches, a reminder of the years their ancestors lived in temporary dwellings as they wandered in the wilderness. It was a week of joyful celebration that began with a holy convocation and closed with a solemn assembly (Lev. 23:33–44).

Certainly God wants His people to be thankful and to rejoice at the good gifts He showers down upon us. After Israel moved into the Promised Land, He wanted them to remember that life had not always been that easy, that their ancestors lived in tents and booths after they left Egypt. All of us know that no younger generation wants to hear the "old people" talk about the difficulties of "the good old days," but the Lord wrote the memory of Israel's past into Passover and Tabernacles, the first and last feasts of the year. While the church must not live in the past, the church must not forget the past and what the Lord has done for His people down through the ages. We're prone to take our blessings for granted and forget the faithfulness of the Lord.

Two of the churches I pastored celebrated significant anniversaries while I was serving them, and during those special years we took time in our worship services to remember the goodness of the Lord and thank Him for all He had done. It was helpful for the younger members to learn about the sacrifices people had made in the past, and it was good for the older members to receive a new challenge for the future. After all, the church isn't a parking lot; it's a launching pad!

As God's people, we have many reasons to celebrate the greatness and goodness of the Lord. We've been redeemed by the blood of Christ (Passover), we're indwelt and empowered by the Spirit (Pentecost), and we're generously supported by the Lord in our pilgrim journey (Tabernacles). Our time here on earth is brief and temporary, but one day we shall enter heaven, where Jesus is now preparing places for us.

"Oh, magnify the LORD with me, and let us exalt his name together" (Ps. 34:3).

QUESTIONS FOR PERSONAL REFLECTION
OR GROUP DISCUSSION

1. Wiersbe says our primary purpose in worshipping God should be to please and glorify God. What does "glorify" mean? How do your own worship times stand up to this standard?

2. What are Christians "set apart" or "marked off" for? What distinguishes you from non-Christians around you? What defilement(s) do you separate yourself from?

3. Why did God declare some creatures unclean for Israel? What is "unclean" for Christians?

4. What is the New Testament approach to how and how much we give?

5. How would you describe your own giving in terms of motive, attitude, and amount of sacrifice?

6. In what way was the Sabbath Year a test of love? When this year has your love been tested?

7. What was the purpose of God's calendar for the Israelites? What calendar or other aids could you use for this same purpose?

8. What are the similarities and the differences between the Passover lambs and Jesus, the Lamb of God?

9. What is the role of the Holy Spirit? How does He do this in your life?

10. What would change in your life and church if the Holy Spirit were to be removed?

Chapter Seven

JUDGES, KINGS, PRIESTS, AND ORDINARY PEOPLE

(Deuteronomy 16:18—18:8; 26:1–19)

As Moses continued to prepare the new generation for life in the Promised Land, he not only instructed them about their past history and their obligations in worship, but he also explained to them the kind of government God wanted them to organize. When their ancestors were in Egypt, the Jews had minimal organization involving only elders (Ex. 3:18), and during the wilderness journey, Moses had tribal officers who assisted him in solving the problems the people brought them (18:13ff.). Each tribe in Israel also had a leader (Num. 1:5–16; 7:10–83), and there were seventy elders who assisted Moses in the spiritual oversight of the nation (11:10ff.).

This basic organization was adequate to govern a nomadic people following a gifted leader, but it wouldn't suffice once the nation moved into the Promised Land. For one thing, Moses would no longer be with them to give them messages directly from the mouth of God. Furthermore, each of the twelve tribes would be living in its own assigned territory, and Reuben, Gad, and Manasseh would be located on the other side of the

Jordan River. How would they deal with tribal differences? Who would protect the people and enforce God's laws? God in His grace gave them the kind of government that would meet their needs.

Christians too often undervalue the importance of government to the peace, safety, and progress of society. Without human government, even with all its shortcomings, society would be in shambles, and no nation could adequately improve or defend itself. "The powers that be are ordained of God" (Rom. 13:1) doesn't mean that God is to blame for the appointment or election of each individual public official or the decisions they make once they're in office. It means that the authority for government comes from God and that those who serve in public offices are ministers of the Lord and accountable to Him (v. 4). "Let all things be done decently and in order" (1 Cor. 14:40) applies not only to the public worship services of the church but also to the public service of civic officials. God's people are commanded to pray for those in authority (1 Tim. 2:1–6), but too often we're guilty of criticizing them instead of interceding for them.

Moses pointed out the basic offices and obligations of the government God wanted Israel to establish in the land.

COMPETENT JUDGES (16:18—17:13)

The repetition of the word *gates* (16:5, 11, 14, 18; 17:2, 5, 8) indicates that the basic unit of government in Israel was the local town council. It was made up of judges and officers who, with the elders, conducted business at the city gates (Ruth 4:1–12). The judges and officers were probably appointed or elected by the male landowning citizens of the town, but we aren't given the details. The word translated "officers" (KJV) means "writers, secretaries" and refers to the men who kept the official records and genealogies, advised the judges, and carried out their decisions. God was the supreme Legislator in the land, because He gave the laws; the local judges formed the judicial branch of the government; and their officers constituted the executive branch.

Godly character (16:19–20). The most important thing about the judges and officers was that they be men of character, because only just men could honestly execute just judgment.[1] The judges were not to twist the law and "distort justice," nor were they to "respect persons," which in the Hebrew is literally "regard faces." The important thing was to determine what the accused person did and not to major on who the accused person was. The Lord warned the judges not to favor their friends by acquitting the guilty, reducing the sentences, or tampering with the legal process, nor were the judges to accept bribes. "Justice" is usually pictured as a woman carrying scales and wearing a blindfold. "It is not good to show partiality to the wicked, or to overthrow the righteous in judgment" (Prov. 18:5 NKJV).

The decisions of the judges affected not only the individuals on trial but the entire nation. If the judges freed the guilty at the expense of the innocent, the land would be defiled and God would eventually remove the nation from the land. Unfortunately, that's exactly what happened during the years that preceded the fall of Israel and Judah. The courts became corrupt and allowed the rich to rob the poor and needy, and the wealthy soon owned great estates and controlled the economy.[2] Because the leaders didn't obey the laws about the Sabbath Year and the Year of Jubilee, the economy got out of balance and the land was stolen from its rightful owners. God couldn't permit such flagrant disobedience to His law, so He punished His people severely by sending them into captivity.

Leadership in the local church must be given only to those who are qualified (Acts 6:1–7; 1 Tim. 3; Titus 1:5–9). "Everything rises or falls with leadership," says Dr. Lee Roberson, and he is right. How tragic it is when churches choose unqualified and untried people to "fill" offices instead of to "use" those offices for the building of the church and the glory of God (1 Tim. 3:10). In the leadership of the local church, spiritual character is far more important than a person's popularity, personality, talent, or occupation.

Devotion to God (16:21—17:7). Idolatry was the great enemy of the spiritual life of the Jewish nation, and the judges had to be alert enough to detect it and courageous enough to deal with it. The "groves" were areas dedicated to the worship of Baal's consort, Ashtoreth, and among their idols were wooden poles that symbolized the male member. Note that the idolaters tried to locate their worship centers as close to God's altar as possible (16:21; NIV, "beside the altar"). The idolaters wanted to encourage people to worship both Jehovah and Ashtoreth, and eventually Ashtoreth would win out. If the judges were devoted to God, they would carefully investigate such practices, get the facts, condemn the guilty, and remove the idols from the land. They had to put Jehovah first.[3]

It can't be emphasized too much that the religion of the Canaanite nations was unspeakably filthy and mingled blind superstition with gross immorality. Human nature being what it is, the Jews would be attracted to gods they could see and ceremonies that appealed to their sensual appetites. This explains why God commanded the Jews to wipe out every vestige of Canaanite religion from the land (7:1–11), for He knew that the hearts of the people were too often set on doing evil in spite of His holy laws and His warnings.

The wisdom of God (17:8–13). Many times, the local judges and courts would have to consider cases that were complicated and perplexing and too difficult for them to settle, cases involving bloodshed, accusations, lawsuits, and various kinds of assault. To assist the local officials, the Lord would establish a central "court" at His sanctuary where the priests and Levites would share their wisdom and explain the law of God. In Israel, God's law was national law, and the best ones to interpret and apply the law were the priests and Levites.

This "sanctuary court" was not a court of appeals where a convicted person could seek a second trial, nor was it an advisory committee whose decisions could be accepted or rejected. It was a court that tried cases carefully and whose decisions were authoritative and binding. Anybody who showed contempt for the authority of the courts or the decisions that they rendered was actually showing contempt for God and His law. Such rebels were guilty of a capital crime and were subject to the death penalty. God would not have rebellious citizens in His nation or permit people to resist His law presumptuously. No sacrifices were provided in the law for people who committed "high-handed" and deliberate sins (Num. 15:30–36).

When Woodrow Wilson was president of the United States, he said, "There are a good many problems before the American people today, and before me as president, but I expect to find the solution of those problems just in the proportion that I am faithful in the study of the Word of God."[4] Statesman Daniel Webster said, "If we abide by the principles taught in the Bible, our country will go on prospering and to prosper; but if we and our posterity neglect its instruction and authority, no man can tell how sudden a catastrophe may overwhelm us and bury our glory in profound obscurity."[5] Living as we do in a democratic pluralistic society, we can't expect the government to make the Bible its official guidebook, but it would help the nation if professed Christians and Christian churches would major on preaching, teaching, and obeying the Word of God.

GODLY KINGS (17:14–20)

Elected leaders, not hereditary rulers, govern democratic nations today, but in ancient times, kings and emperors ruled nations and empires with despotic authority. But Israel was different from the other nations, for the law of the Lord was the "cement" that united the twelve tribes. The Levites, who were scattered throughout the land, taught the people God's law, and the priests and judges saw to it that the law was enforced justly. The

Israelites had to bring their tithes and sacrifices to the central sanctuary, and three times each year all the adult males assembled there to celebrate the goodness of the Lord. Jehovah was King in Israel (Ex. 15:18; Judg. 8:23) and He sat "enthroned between the cherubim" (Ps. 80:1 NIV) in the Holy of Holies.

Desiring a king (v. 14). But the Lord knew that the day would come when Israel would ask for a king because they wanted to be like the other nations (1 Sam. 8). During the time of the judges, the political and spiritual unity of the twelve tribes deteriorated greatly (Judg. 17:6; 21:25), and Israel was in constant danger of invasion by their enemies (1 Sam. 9:16; 12:12). Instead of trusting God, the people wanted a king who would build an army and lead the nation to victory. Unfortunately, the spiritual leadership in Israel had decayed, and Samuel's sons weren't following the ways of the Lord (8:1–5). But the main cause for Israel's cry for a king was their desire to be like the other nations. Yet Israel's great distinction was that they were not like the other nations! They were God's chosen people, a kingdom of priests, and God's special treasure (Ex. 19:5–6). "Lo, the people shall dwell alone, and shall not be reckoned among the nations" (Num. 23:9).

Imitating the world instead of trusting the Lord has always been the great temptation of God's people, and each time they've succumbed, they've suffered. During their wilderness journey, Israel compared everything that happened with what they had experienced in Egypt, and at Kadesh-barnea they even wanted to choose a leader and go back to Egypt (14:1–5)! But the church today is equally guilty of unbelief. When church leaders adopt the methods and measurements of the world, then the church has taken a giant step toward becoming like the world and losing its divine distinctives. Instead of trusting the Word of God and prayer (Acts 6:4), we depend on following the world's wisdom, imitating the world's methods, and catering to the world's appetites, giving people what they want instead of what they need. Believers today need to take to heart

God's reminder to Israel: "I am the LORD your God, who has separated you from the peoples" (Lev. 20:24 NKJV).

Qualifications for a king (vv. 15–17). The king was not to be elected by the people; he was to be chosen by God. Israel's first king was Saul (1 Sam. 9—10), but God never intended Saul to establish a royal dynasty in Israel. Saul was from the tribe of Benjamin, but Judah was the royal tribe (Gen. 49:8–10), and the Messiah would come from Judah. Actually, Saul was given to the people to chasten them because they rejected the Lord (1 Sam. 8:7), for God's greatest judgment is to give His people what they want and let them suffer for it.

Not only must the king be chosen by God, but the king must be from Israel and not be a foreigner. Whenever God wanted to chasten His people, He would set a foreign ruler over them and let the people experience the contrast between the goodness of God and the oppressiveness of the idolatrous Gentiles. Israel's king must also put his full trust in the Lord and not depend on horses and armies (Deut. 17:16), foreign alliances based on marriage (v. 17a), or material wealth (v. 17b). King Solomon violated all three of these regulations, and it led him and the nation into sin. He married an Egyptian princess (1 Kings 3:1), the first of many political alliances he made by taking foreign wives (11:1–6). He went back to Egypt not only for a wife but also for horses for his army, and built "chariot cities" in Israel where he stabled his horses and chariots (10:26, 28–29). As for his wealth, it was fabulous and impossible to calculate (vv. 14–25, 27).[6]

Wisdom for the king (vv. 18–20). The most important qualification for the king was a personal knowledge of the law of God (Deut. 17:18–20). He was to write out his own copy of the law, using the official copy provided by the priests (31:9, 24–26), read it regularly, and take it to heart. (See God's command to Joshua in Josh. 1:7–8.) His study of the law would not only help him to rule the people justly, but it would also reveal to him the character of God and encourage him to fear Him and love Him more (Prov. 4). The king's submission to God and His law would keep him from getting proud and abusing the authority the Lord had given him.[7] For him to think that he was better than his brethren and privileged to live above God's law would indicate that he wasn't fit to lead the nation.

FAITHFUL SPIRITUAL LEADERS (18:1–8)

The church of Jesus Christ *is* a priesthood (1 Peter 2:5, 9), but the nation of Israel *had* a priesthood. All the priests and Levites were descendants of Levi, Jacob's third son by Leah. Levi had three sons—Gershon, Kohath, and Merari—and Aaron and Moses were from the family of Kohath (Ex. 6:16–25). Only the descendants of Aaron were called "priests" and were allowed to serve at the altar and in the sanctuary proper. The Levites, who were descendants of Gershon and Merari, assisted the priests in the many ministries connected with the altar and the sanctuary. Neither the priests nor the Levites were given any inheritance in the land of Israel (Deut. 10:8–9; 12:12, 18–19) but lived from the tithes, offerings, and sacrifices that were brought to the sanctuary.

The priests (vv. 3–5). The priests were to receive specified parts from the sacrifices, except for the burnt offering, which was totally consumed on the altar. They would burn a handful of the meal offering on the altar and keep the rest for themselves, and various parts of the animal sacrifices were given to them as their due (Lev. 6:8—7:38). They were also given the firstfruits of the grain, oil, wine, and wool. This Old Testament practice carries over into the New Testament ministry. "Do you not know that those who minister the holy things eat of the things of the temple, and those who serve at the altar partake of the offerings of the altar? Even so the Lord has commanded that those who preach the gospel should live from the gospel" (1 Cor. 9:13–14 NKJV). The Lord's command is found in Luke 10:7 and is quoted in 1 Timothy 5:18.

If the people didn't support the priests as God commanded, then the priests would have to find their support elsewhere, and this would take them away from the ministry at the sanctuary. But only the priests could offer the sacrifices, care for the lamps and the table of bread, and burn the incense on the golden altar. Without the presence of the priests, the ministry at the sanctuary would come to a halt, and the people would be without intercession and spiritual help.

The Levites (vv. 6–8). The Levites lived in forty-eight cities scattered throughout the nation of Israel (Josh. 21). We assume that there was a definite schedule that governed their participation at the sanctuary, such as there was in the days of David (1 Chron. 23—26), with each Levite assigned to a task and a time. The priests and Levites could purchase land if they wanted to (1 Kings 2:26; Jer. 32:7; Acts 4:36–37) and even get an income from the land, but their major interest had to be serving at the sanctuary and helping the people know God and obey His Word. If a Levite sold or leased his property and came to the sanctuary because of his love for the Lord and His house, he must be permitted to serve there and to share in the gifts that the people brought. The fact that he earned money by leasing or selling his land did not change this policy.

In the time of Nehemiah, the people didn't faithfully bring their tithes and offerings to the temple, and some of the Levites had to return to their lands in order to live (Neh. 13:10–14). Nehemiah urged the people to obey the Word and support their spiritual leaders, and they brought their tithes and offerings to be distributed to the Levites. It's tragic the way professed Christians fail to support their churches by faithfully bringing their tithes and offerings, yet expect their churches to help them when they have needs.

OBEDIENT PEOPLE (26:1–19)

It isn't enough for a nation to have gifted and godly leaders; it must also have godly citizens who obey the law of the Lord. Confucius said, "The strength of a nation is derived from the integrity of its homes." But homes are made up of individuals, so it's the strength of the individual that helps to make the home what it ought to be. "Whatever makes men good Christians," said Daniel Webster, "makes them good citizens." The three public confessions recorded in this chapter help us to understand what kind of citizens we ought to be as the followers of Jesus Christ.

(1) Confession of God's goodness (vv. 1–11). This ceremony was to be used the first time any Jew brought his firstfruits offering to the Lord. It should not be confused with the annual firstfruits offering (16:4; Ex. 23:19; 34:26; Lev. 23:10–17; Num. 15:18–20; 18:12–13). Not only was this special ceremony a confession of God's goodness to Israel and to this worshipper, but it was also a declaration that the man had now claimed his inheritance in the land. He had worked the land and received a harvest, and he brought the first and the best to give to the Lord. The basket of fruit sitting by the altar was a witness to the faithfulness of the Lord to His people. The entire ceremony was an Old Testament version of Matthew 6:33.

The confession begins with Israel's entrance into the land of Canaan (Deut. 26:3), and this would remind the worshipper of the miracle of the crossing of the Jordan (Josh. 3). The God who opened the Red Sea for the nation to get out of Egypt also opened the Jordan River so they could go in and claim their inheritance. "He brought us out … that he might bring us in" (Deut. 6:23). The only reason the Jews didn't enter the land sooner was because the older generation rebelled against the Lord at Kadesh and refused to trust Him for victory (Num. 13—14). The worshipper was reminded that the secret of Israel's great success was faith in the promises of God. Years later, Joshua would say, "There failed nought of any good thing which the LORD had spoken unto the house of Israel; all came to pass" (Josh. 21:45; see 23:14; 1 Kings 8:56).

Then the worshipper would speak about Jacob, the father of the twelve tribes of Israel (Deut. 26:5), who left home and went to Haran in northwest Mesopotamia (Hos. 12:12; Gen. 25:20) to find himself a wife. After twenty years in the household of his father-in-law, Laban, Jacob obeyed God's commandment and returned to his own land and settled down with his twelve sons and their families. Indeed, Jacob had been a "fugitive" and a "pilgrim" all those years, but the Lord had watched over him and blessed him. Jacob's twelve sons were to become the founders of the twelve tribes of Israel, and through Israel God would bless the whole world (Gen. 12:1–3).

How would God transform one man's family into a great nation? By taking them down to Egypt where they were put through the "iron furnace" of suffering (Deut. 26:5–7; 4:20; 1 Kings 8:51; Gen. 46). Seventy people traveled to Egypt where Joseph had prepared homes for them, and years later, on Passover night, probably two million Jews marched triumphantly out of Egypt. The more the enemy persecuted the Jews, the more the Jews had multiplied (Ex. 1). Suffering and trial are often God's tools for bringing blessing to His people, though at the time we may not understand it. The more the Enemy persecuted the early church, the more they scattered and multiplied (Acts 5:41—6:1; 8:1–4).

The confession mentions nothing about Israel's complaining on their journey or their failure at Kadesh-barnea. This is a confession of faith, not unbelief. "So the LORD brought us out of Egypt … He has brought us to this place and has given us this land" (Deut. 26:8–9 NKJV). The man calls Canaan "a land that flows with milk and honey," which is what God often called it. God gave His people a wonderful land that would meet their every need. During Israel's years of wandering and rebellion, some of the Jews called Egypt "a land that flows with milk and honey" (Num. 16:13). It's tragic when people are so unspiritual that the things of the world are more inviting than the things of the Lord.

In response to the goodness and grace of the Lord, the worshipper presented to God the first and the best of his labors, for there would have been no harvest apart from the blessing of the Lord. But in presenting the firstfruits, the worshipper was actually giving the entire harvest to the Lord. Stewardship doesn't mean that we give God a part and then use the rest as we please. True stewardship means that we give God what belongs to Him as an acknowledgment that all that we have is His. We then use all that is left wisely for His glory. To bring the Lord 10 percent and then waste the 90 percent that remains is not stewardship. It's foolishness.

The Lord "gives us richly all things to enjoy" (1 Tim. 6:17 NKJV), which explains why Moses admonished the Jews to rejoice in every good thing that the Lord gave to them (Deut. 26:11). While at the sanctuary, they could bring a thank offering to the Lord and enjoy a feast of good things, all to the glory of God. But note the mention of the Levite and the stranger, those with whom we need to share the gifts of the Lord (12:12, 18; 16:11, 14). This introduces the second confession.

(2) Confession of honesty and generosity (vv. 12–15). This scene would take place two years later, when the Jews were supposed to bring the extra tithe to the local officers (14:28–29). The previous ceremony occurred only once, after the first harvest in the land, but this ceremony was repeated every third year. The seventh year would be the Sabbath Year, and then the cycle started again. This confession was tantamount to a summary renewal of the covenant that Israel made at Sinai, their promise to obey the Lord and His promise to bless their obedience.

The tithe of the third year was kept in the towns and used locally to feed the Levites, strangers, orphans, and widows. In giving this tithe, the worshipper was to confess to the Lord that he had been honest in setting aside the tithe and using it as the Lord commanded. He was not to take the tithe for his own personal use and certainly not to use it for any sinful purpose. He had been careful not to defile the tithe by touching it while unclean because of a death in the family. In other words, the setting aside of this tithe for others was a serious matter and had to be done with dignity and obedience. The ceremony would end with the prayer of 26:15, asking God to bless the whole nation and not just the individual worshipper.

Both the first and the second confession express appreciation for the land "flowing with milk and honey" (vv. 9, 15). It's a good thing when God's people appreciate all that the Lord gives them. During their forty years of wandering, the older generation had frequently wanted to go back to Egypt and enjoy the food they had eaten there, but this backward look only got them into trouble. When it comes to the circumstances of life, we all need to follow Paul's example: "I have learned in whatever state I am, to be content" (Phil. 4:11 NKJV). One of the best ways to learn contentment is to share with others the blessings God gives to us.

(3) Confession of obedience (vv. 16–19). The first two confessions looked forward to the time when Israel would be settled in their land and reaping the harvests. This confession brings us back to the plains of Moab where Moses was equipping the younger generation to enter the land. "This day" (vv. 16–18) and "today" were words Moses used frequently as he addressed the people (2:25; 4:26, 39; 6:6; 7:11; 8:1, 18; 10:13; etc.). It was indeed a solemn time when Moses reiterated the law and reviewed the nation's history. The future of the nation depended on the people receiving, understanding, and obeying the Word of God that Moses was sharing with them.

The constant danger was that the people not receive God's Word into their hearts but only hear it with their ears and then forget it. Like the Jewish people in Jesus' day, they had ears but could not hear (Matt. 13:13–15). A mere casual acquaintance with the Word isn't sufficient. If God's Word is to nurture us and change us so that God can bless us (Ps. 1:1–3), we must devote ourselves to it, heart and soul. God had claimed Israel for His own people and promised to bless them if they obeyed Him (Deut. 26:18), and Israel had declared that Jehovah was their God and that they would obey Him (v. 17). There was no doubt that God would keep His promises, but would Israel keep their promises?

God had great things planned for Israel, just as He has great things planned for each of His children (Eph. 2:10; 1 Cor. 2:6–10). If the people kept their covenant promises to the Lord, He would bless them and make them a blessing, but if they disobeyed Him, He would have to chasten them. "But My people would not heed My voice, and Israel would have none of Me. So I gave them over to their own stubborn heart, to walk in their own counsels. Oh, that My people would listen to Me, that Israel would walk in My ways! I would soon subdue their enemies, and turn My hand against their adversaries. ... He would have fed them also with the finest of wheat; and with honey from the rock I would have satisfied you" (Ps. 81:11–14, 16 NKJV).

God is faithful to us, but how much we miss when we're not faithful to Him!

QUESTIONS FOR PERSONAL REFLECTION
OR GROUP DISCUSSION

peace, safety & progress of society

1. What is the role of government? What does it mean that "the powers that be are ordained of God" (Rom. 13:1)? *Authority for government comes from God*

2. Why was godly character so important for judges and officers? In elections today, how important would you rank character compared with experience or training? *1. Only just men could honestly execute just judgement. Character is the most important*

3. What qualifies a person for leadership in a local church? Wiersbe says spiritual character is most important for church leadership. What is spiritual character?

4. Why did the Jews keep turning back to idolatry? What was the lure? What do you think is the allure today of false gods like money or success? *They wanted something they could see.*

5. Israel desired a political king so they could be like the other nations. In what area are you tempted to imitate the world instead of trust in the Lord? In what areas have you stopped imitating the world?

Do not dress like the world. Am content with what I have.

6. What would help keep a person in authority from getting proud and abusing that authority? *Term lemits*

7. What character traits and activities would you expect of a godly citizen? *Honest, faitful, truthful, hard working, just, humble*

8. What could you offer to God as a firstfruits offering? *time, joy, lith*

9. Why do you suppose sharing what we have with those in need is a great way to learn contentment?

10. When is it most difficult for you to be content? In what ways are you more content now than you used to be? To what do you attribute that change?

Chapter Eight

MANSLAUGHTER, WAR, AND MURDER

(Deuteronomy 19:1—21:14)

The people of Israel were greatly blessed. They had the Lord God for their King, a wonderful land for their home, and a holy law for their guide, and yet they faced some of the same problems that society faces today. Sinful human nature being what it is, nations will always have to deal with "man's inhumanity to man," because the heart of every problem is still the problem of the heart. Laws are necessary to bring order to society, to restrain evil, and to help control behavior, but laws can never change the human heart. Only the grace of God can do that. If this section of Scripture emphasizes anything, it's that God holds human life precious and wants us to treat people fairly, for they are made in the image of God (Gen. 9:1–7). God's desire for all nations is, "Let justice run down like water, and righteousness like a mighty stream" (Amos 5:24 NKJV). And His standard for us individually is Micah 6:8 (NKJV): "He has shown you, O man, what is good; and what does the LORD require of you but to do justly, to love mercy, and to walk humbly with your God?"

JUSTICE IN THE LAND (19:1–21)

The Quaker poet John Greenleaf Whittier called justice "the hope of all who suffer, the dread of all who wrong." That's the ideal, but it isn't always achieved in real life. Without justice, society would fall apart, anarchy would take over, and it wouldn't be safe for people to leave their homes. Israel didn't have the elaborate police system we have today, so locating and punishing guilty criminals depended primarily on the elders and the judges. By singling out the "cities of refuge," the Lord promoted justice in the land.

The cities (vv. 1–3, 7–10). Moses here reviews what he had taught Israel in Numbers 35; in fact, he had already set up the three cities of refuge east of the Jordan (Deut. 4:42–43). It would be Joshua's responsibility to set up the other three cities west of the Jordan after Israel had conquered the land (Josh. 20). Those east of the Jordan were Golan, Ramoth, and Bezer, and on the west, they would be Kedesh, Shechem, and Hebron. If you consult a map of the Holy Land, you will see that these cities were so located that they were easily accessible to those who needed protection. The roads leading to these cities were to be kept in good repair and be clearly marked. Rabbinical tradition states that there were signs at all the crossroads pointing the way to the nearest city of refuge. The Lord wanted to make it easy for the innocent manslayer to escape the vengeance of angry people.

The Lord also made arrangements for the nation to add three more cities of refuge if the borders of their land were expanded. He had promised Israel a large land (Gen. 15:18; Ex. 23:31), and if they had obeyed His law, He would have kept His promise. It was only during the reign of David that this much territory was actually held by Israel, and then they lost it when things fell apart during Solomon's reign. If we don't obey God's will and claim God's promises, we can never receive all that God wants us to have.

The manslayer (vv. 4–6). Modern law still follows Moses in making a distinction between murder and manslaughter (Ex. 21:12–14; Lev. 24:17). The person who unintentionally killed someone could flee to the nearest city of refuge and present his case to the elders there. If he didn't flee, a member of the victim's family might chase him down and become "the avenger of blood" and kill him. Israel had no system for locating and arresting suspected criminals; it was left to the family of the victim to see that justice was done. The "avenger of blood" wasn't given authority to act as judge, jury, and executioner; he was only to hand the accused over to the proper officers. But if this relative was angry, he might take the law in his own hands and kill an innocent man. By fleeing to the city of refuge, the manslayer was safe until the facts of the case could be examined and a verdict declared. If found innocent, the manslayer was allowed to live safely in the city of refuge until the death of the high priest. Even though he was innocent, he still paid a price for accidentally killing another human being. If he left the city of refuge, his life was in danger and the elders couldn't protect him.

These cities of refuge illustrate our salvation in Jesus Christ to whom we have "fled for refuge to lay hold upon the hope set before us" (Heb. 6:18), but they do so by contrast. The man who fled in Israel did so because he wasn't guilty of murder, but we flee because we are guilty and deserve to be judged. Nobody has to investigate our case because we know we have sinned and deserve God's punishment. In the case of the cities of refuge, the innocent man was allowed to live, but in our case, Jesus Christ the innocent One was condemned to die. The Israelite had to remain in the city of refuge, for if he left it he might die at the hand of the avenger. The salvation we have in Christ isn't conditioned on our obedience but depends wholly on His grace and promises. "And I give them eternal life, and they shall never perish; neither shall anyone snatch them out of My hand" (John 10:28 NKJV). "There is therefore now no condemnation to them which are in Christ Jesus" (Rom. 8:1). The Israelite manslayer could legally leave the city of refuge after the death of the high priest, but our High Priest in heaven will never die and ever lives to make intercession for us (Heb. 7:25).

The murderer (vv. 11–13). But perhaps a man who had murdered his enemy would flee to a city of refuge and lie to the elders, telling them that he was innocent. It was up to the elders in his home city to set the record straight by sending notice to the city of refuge and bringing the man back to his native city. The elders in the city of refuge would extradite the accused so he could be properly tried and, if found guilty, executed. God expected each citizen to be concerned about seeing that justice was done in the land. It would be easy for the officers in the murderer's home city to let the elders in the city of refuge worry about the case, but that wouldn't promote justice or prevent the defilement of the land. In the nation of Israel, shedding innocent blood defiled the land, and one way to cleanse the land was to punish the offender. "Do not pollute the land where you are. Bloodshed pollutes the land, and atonement cannot be made for the land on which blood has been shed, except by the blood of the one who shed it" (Num. 35:33 NIV).

Murder was one of several capital crimes in Israel. Others were idolatry and sorcery (Lev. 20:1–6), blasphemy (24:10–16), violating the Sabbath (Num. 15:32–36), willful and repeated disobedience to parents (Deut. 21:18–21; Ex. 21:15, 17), kidnapping (v. 16), bestiality (22:19), homosexuality (Lev. 20:13), adultery, and the rape of an engaged maiden (Deut. 22:22–27). We don't have this many capital crimes today, but Israel was a theocracy and her laws were God's laws. To break the law was to sin against the Lord and defile the land, and the people needed to understand the seriousness of such actions. In 1972, the United States Supreme Court declared capital punishment unconstitutional but then reinstated it in 1976. Capital punishment may not restrain every would-be murderer from taking a life, but it does magnify the preciousness of human life as well as honor the law.

The thief (v. 14). After Israel conquered the land of Canaan, each tribe was assigned its territory and their borders accurately described. Joshua, Eleazar the high priest, and the heads of the twelve tribes cast lots and made the assignments (Josh. 14:1–2). Within the tribes, each family and clan would make its own claim and mark it out with boundary stones. In that day, officials didn't draw detailed real estate maps, what we today call "plats." Everybody was expected to honor the landmarks (boundary stones), because to move the stones meant to steal land from your neighbors and their descendants (Prov. 22:28). Unscrupulous officials could easily exploit poor widows and orphans and take away their land and their income (15:25; 23:10–11). Since God owned the land and the people were His tenants, moving the stones also meant stealing from God, and He would punish them (Hos. 5:10). No wonder this crime was included among the curses announced from Mount Ebal (Deut. 27:17).

The punishment of the murderer reminded people that human life is precious, and the punishment of the thief reminded them that personal property must be respected. "Thou shalt not steal" (Ex. 20:15) covers much more territory than just forbidding a thief to enter a house and take what isn't his. Extortion is also stealing, and God condemns officials who make unjust laws so they can rob the poor and the helpless (Ezek. 22:29). Slanderers and false witnesses rob people of their good name (Deut. 19:16–19; Matt. 15:19–20), and a good reputation is more difficult to restore than stolen merchandise.

The liar (vv. 15–21). Every system of justice depends on people knowing the truth and speaking the truth. To bear false witness is to break God's commandment (Ex. 20:16) and to undermine the foundation of the legal system. The person who swears to tell the truth and then tells lies is committing perjury, which itself is a serious crime. The Jewish law required two or three witnesses to establish the guilt of an accused person (Deut. 17:6; Num. 35:30), and both Jesus (Matt. 18:16) and Paul (2 Cor. 13:1;

1 Tim. 5:19) applied this principle to local church discipline. The fact that two or three persons bear witness doesn't guarantee that they are telling the truth (1 Kings 21:1–14), but Moses warned that false witnesses would be punished with the same punishment they wanted for the accused.

However, there could be situations where only one witness stands up to accuse a person and he is a false witness. What then? Both the accused and the single witness would have to go to the central court at the sanctuary and present the case to the priests and the judges there (Deut. 17:8–13). If the court discovers that the single witness is not telling the truth, he would receive the same sentence that would have been given to the accused if he had been guilty. This law would make liars think twice before falsely accusing an innocent person. Having to go to the priestly court would be deterrent enough, for the Lord could convey His truth to the priests and judges and expose the wickedness of the accuser. But knowing that they might receive the punishment they wanted for the accused would also make them hesitate, especially if it were a capital crime. "A false witness will not go unpunished, and he who speaks lies will not escape" (Prov. 19:5, 9 NKJV).

We sometimes hear that fear of punishment doesn't deter people from breaking the law, but Deuteronomy 19:20 says otherwise: "And those who remain [the rest of the people] shall hear and fear, and hereafter they shall not again commit such evil among you" (NKJV). Every law on the books has probably been violated many times and not all violators have been arrested and tried. But that doesn't prove that the prosecution of those who have been caught hasn't done society good and prevented more crime. Some legal experts argue that capital punishment hasn't stopped people from committing capital crimes, but how do they know? The speed laws haven't stopped careless people from driving beyond the speed limit, but the fact that they have radar detectors in their cars suggests that they don't want to meet the police! And think of how dangerous the highways would be if there were no speed laws!

Moses closed this section by reminding the people that in every case, the punishment must fit the crime (Deut. 19:21; see Ex. 21:23–25). This is known as the *lex talionis,* which is Latin for "the law of retaliation." People who call this principle "barbaric" probably don't understand what it means. The sentence must be neither too strict nor too easy but must be suited to what the law demands and what the convicted criminal deserves. Honest judges don't give a murderer the same sentence they give the man who poisoned his neighbor's cat, nor is a shoplifter given the same punishment as a kidnapper. This judicial principle emphasized fairness and humane treatment at a time in history when punishments were terribly brutal. In eighteenth-century England, there were over two hundred capital crimes, and a person could be hanged for picking pockets. Children who broke the law were frequently treated as adults and imprisoned for minor offenses.

When our Lord referred to the *lex talionis* in the Sermon on the Mount (Matt. 5:38–42), He wasn't talking about the official judicial system but how believers should deal with personal offenses and injuries. He didn't rescind the Old Testament law, because He came to fulfill it (vv. 17–20); rather, He prohibited His followers from "paying back in kind" those who offend them or take advantage of them. If our courts followed our Lord's commands found in verses 38–42, the country would be in the hands of the criminals! Jesus exhorted us not to practice personal revenge but to leave such matters in the hand of God (Rom. 12:17–21). We're to imitate the Master and return good for evil, love for hatred, and sacrifice for selfishness (1 Peter 2:11–25).

WAR IN THE LAND (20:1–9, 16–18)

The Jews weren't entering Canaan as sightseers but as soldiers prepared for battle and expecting God to give them victory. It's important to note that God gave the nation two different military approaches, one for the cities *in* the land of Canaan (vv. 1–9, 16–18) and the other for cities *outside* Canaan (vv. 10–15). After Israel had conquered the land and was settled down in their inheritance, they might have to attack a distant city, because there were always enemies to deal with, and they could always accept the challenge of claiming God's promise and enlarging the land (19:8–9).

The Lord's assurance (v. 1). Moses didn't minimize either the size or the strength of the enemy, for he knew that the nations living in Canaan had horses, chariots, large armies, and fortified cities. The spies who had investigated the land thirty-eight years before had seen all these obstacles and dangers (Num. 13) but had failed to see how small these matters were when compared with the greatness of their God. Moses reminded the people that the Lord had successfully brought them from the land of Egypt to the plains of Moab and defeated every enemy that had attacked them. In fact, the territory Israel now inhabited belonged to the Jews and not to the enemy, because the Lord had given His people great victory over the nations east of the Jordan. Just as the Lord had defeated Pharaoh and his army in Egypt, so He would defeat the nations in Canaan.

In the early days of the Great Depression, President Franklin D. Roosevelt said in his inaugural address, "The only thing we have to fear is fear itself." There is a fear that mobilizes a person, as when you hear the fire alarm go off, but there is also a fear that paralyzes a person, and that's the fear that Moses was addressing. When we fear the Lord and trust Him, we need not fear the enemy. Israel had nothing to fear, for the God who drowned the army of Egypt would defeat the armies of Canaan.

The priest's encouragement (vv. 2–4). This was not the high priest but one of the other priests who was assigned to address the army. We shouldn't be surprised to hear a priest encouraging the army, because the wars in Canaan were holy wars, God's judgment against wicked nations that had rebelled against Him and sinned against a flood of light. The Lord had given these nations ample time to repent and turn to Him, but they refused to obey. Israel's miraculous deliverance from Egypt and crossing of the Jordan River were proof enough that Almighty God was with them and judgment was coming (Josh. 2). The Jews were God's people, fighting God's battles, and it was fitting that they hear from God's servant, a priest.[1]

The Lord's "Fear not" is what every believer needs to hear when confronting the enemies of the faith. It's the message the Lord gave to Abraham after helping him defeat the kings (Gen. 15:1) and to Jacob when he left home to go to Egypt (46:3). Moses gave that message to the Jews as they stood at the Red Sea (Ex. 14:13), and the prophet Isaiah repeated it several times to encourage the Jewish remnant (Isa. 41:10, 13–14; 43:1, 5; 44:2, 8). You find the phrase seven times in the gospel of Luke (1:13, 30; 2:10; 5:10; 8:50; 12:7, 32). When we walk by faith and keep our eyes on the Lord (Heb. 12:1–3), He will give us the peace we need (Phil. 4:4–9). You are heading for victory when you know that the Lord is with you and fighting for you.

The officers' encouragement (vv. 5–9). The priest encouraged the soldiers to face the enemy without fear, but the officers told them to go back home if they had any unfinished business. No officer wants to lead distracted soldiers whose minds and hearts are elsewhere, for "a double-minded man is unstable in all his ways" (James 1:8). Paul may have had this scene in mind when he wrote 2 Timothy 2:4, "No one engaged in warfare entangles himself with the affairs of this life, that he may please him who enlisted him as a soldier" (NKJV).

The officers announced three different occasions for granting temporary deferment, and the first was to allow the soldier to dedicate a new house to the Lord and start living in it (Deut. 20:5). The word translated "dedicate" (KJV) also means "to initiate," that is, to start living in the house with his family and enjoying it. The family needed the man much more than the battlefield did, so he was deferred for a year. The second occasion was to harvest a new vineyard whose fruit the soldier hadn't yet tasted. According to Leviticus 19:23–25, an owner of an orchard had to wait until the fifth year before he could eat the fruit of the trees, but this law probably wasn't applied to vineyards. Five years would be a rather long deferment. The third occasion was perhaps the most important, and that was to permit the engaged soldier to go home and get married. According to Deuteronomy 24:5, he was deferred a year.

These three exceptions suggest to us that God is more interested in our enjoying the common blessings of life—homes, harvests, and honeymoons—than devoting ourselves only to the battles of life. He didn't want any of the Jewish men to use their military responsibilities as an excuse to neglect their families, their vineyards, and their fiancées. Certainly military service was important, but the Lord was more concerned that the men have the right priorities in life. What good was accomplished for the Jewish people if their army defeated the enemy on the field but things were falling apart back home?

The priests asked the soldiers to look up and trust the Lord, and the officers asked them to look back and consider any unfinished business that would hinder them from doing their best. But the officers presented another challenge and asked the soldiers to look within and see if they were too afraid to go into battle. Gideon lost 22,000 men when he issued this challenge (Judg. 7:1–3). Fear and faith can't coexist successfully in the same heart (Matt. 8:26; Luke 8:25). Furthermore, fear is contagious and could discourage the other soldiers. It was fear and unbelief that caused Israel's great failure at Kadesh (Num. 13—14).

Once the ranks had been thinned out, the officers would appoint captains, so each man had to be ready to serve. At this time, Israel didn't have what we would call a "standing army" with an organized system of permanent officers. The major officers knew their best men and would assign leadership responsibilities for each campaign. When Saul became king, he formed the nucleus of a standing army, and his successor David developed the organization even more. In fighting God's battles, faith and courage are important, but so are authority and order.

WAR OUTSIDE THE LAND (20:10–20; 21:10–14)

Moses has been instructing the people how to wage war in the land of Canaan, but now he deals with the battles they will fight outside the land. The Lord wanted to enlarge Israel's borders (19:8), and this would involve military engagements away from the Promised Land.

Taking a city (vv. 10–18). It's important to note that Israel's approach in attacking distant cities was different from their approach when they attacked the cities in the land of Canaan. God commanded Israel many times to destroy the people in the Canaanite cities and show them no mercy (vv. 1–18; 3:6; 7:1–11). During their invasion of Canaan, not only were the Jews to slay all the citizens, but they were also to destroy everything connected with the wicked Canaanite religious system, including temples, idols, and altars. This policy would help remove dangerous temptations from the Jewish people who were always prone to follow idols.

Upon arriving at a foreign city, the officers' first responsibility was to offer terms of peace. If the people accepted the terms, then the city and its inhabitants would be spared but the city would be put under tribute to Israel. This involved paying an annual levy to Israel and making their citizens bond servants to the Israelites (see Josh. 9:16–17; 16:10; 17:13). During King David's reign, there was a special officer in Israel who was in charge of the "forced labor" (2 Sam. 20:24). Because of his extensive building programs, King Solomon expanded this office and even included Israelites in the workforce (1 Kings 5:13–18; 2 Chron. 2:17–18). It was this burden that made Judah finally revolt against Solomon's son Rehoboam and secede from the kingdom (1 Kings 12).

If the people refused Israel's offer of peace, then the Jewish army was permitted to besiege the city, trusting God to give them the victory. The males in the city would be slain (Num. 31:7), the women and children would be taken as servants, and the spoils in the city would be divided among the soldiers.

Though some well-meaning people don't like the military metaphors in the Bible, the church today is in a battle against the world, the flesh, and the Devil (Eph. 2:1–3; 6:10–18; 2 Tim. 2:3–4). But we are also ambassadors of peace who wear the shoes of "the preparation of the gospel of peace" (Eph. 6:15) and plead with rebellious sinners to be "reconciled to God" (2 Cor. 5:18–21). Jesus brought His message of peace to His own people (Luke 2:14) and they rejected it (13:34–35; John 1:11), so He had to replace the offer of peace with an announcement of judgment (Luke 12:51–56). In AD 70 the Roman army destroyed Jerusalem and killed, captured, or scattered the people, and there was no political nation of Israel until May 14, 1948.

Taking care of natural resources (vv. 19–20). Just as Israel was to be mindful of the God-given resources in their own land (Deut. 21:6), so they were cautioned not to waste natural resources in other lands. Defeating the enemy was important, but conserving natural resources was also important. When the Lord really wanted to humble a nation, He commanded His people to destroy the good trees (20:19), but this approach was an exception. The other trees could be used for making siege works, but the fruit trees had to be preserved, for "the tree of the field is man's life" (Deut. 20:19), whether that man or woman is an ally or an enemy. It would take years to replace wantonly destroyed trees.[2] War is destructive enough without adding to the ruin and waste.

Taking a wife (21:10–14). While Jewish men were not allowed to take wives from the Canaanite nations (7:3), they were permitted to marry women from the conquered cities located at a distance from the Promised Land (20:14–15). Of course, it was expected that these women would accept the faith of Israel and enter into the religious life of the nation. However, on returning home with his bride, the man had to wait a month before consummating the marriage. Knowing this would keep him from acting rashly and just taking an attractive woman to satisfy his desires, as if she were part of the spoils of battle. During that waiting period, the man could give serious consideration to what he was doing, and the woman could be emotionally prepared for a new beginning; for she had to shave her head, cut her nails, and put on different clothes.

Shaving the head was part of the rituals for cleansed lepers (Lev. 14:8–9) and the dedication of Nazarites who had fulfilled their vows (Num. 6:18). While shaving the head would be a humbling experience for the woman (see Deut. 21:14), it could also be the sign of a new beginning, as it was for the leper and the Nazarite.[3] She was renouncing her former religion, the worship of idols, and accepting Jehovah as her God. From a practical point of view, perhaps her appearance would encourage her to stay home and get better acquainted with her Jewish husband-to-be. During this waiting period, she was expected to express her sorrow over leaving her family and her native city. In short, the experiences of this month of waiting, painful as they might be, were designed to help the woman make the transition from the old life into the new.

If after the consummation of the marriage, the man was displeased with the woman, he couldn't just throw her out or sell her as though she were a slave. He had to divorce her and let her go wherever she desired.[4] It's assumed that another man could marry her or that she could return to her home city. Modern society wouldn't countenance a woman being forcibly taken captive to become the wife of a stranger, but the ancient world was accustomed to such things (Judg. 21). However, this law did protect her from being raped and discarded after the battle or being so cheapened by her husband that another man wouldn't want to marry her. Better that she go free than that she be forced to live with a man who didn't want her.[5]

ATONING FOR THE LAND (21:1–9)

The land belonged to God and the people living on it were His tenants. Their sins not only grieved the Lord but also defiled the land, especially the sins of sexual immorality (Lev. 18:24–28) and murder (Num. 35:30–34).

The shedding of innocent blood was a terrible crime in Israel (Deut. 19:10, 13; Jer. 7:6; 22:3, 17). When Cain killed his brother Abel, the ground received Abel's blood and cried out to God for justice (Gen. 4:10–12; Heb. 12:24). God keeps a record of the innocent blood shed by both animals and people, and one day will call for an accounting (Gen. 9:5–6). "When He avenges blood, He remembers them; He does not forget the cry of the humble" (Ps. 9:12 NKJV). When the Lord comes to judge, the earth will bear witness of the innocent blood that was shed (Isa. 26:21).

The "elders and judges" mentioned in Deuteronomy 21:2 are probably the "sanctuary court" mentioned in 17:8–13, and this would include the priests (21:5). This was the highest tribunal in the land and murder was a heinous crime. Furthermore, nobody had yet measured to see which city was nearest, so the elders and judges couldn't have come from that city. Once the nearest city had been determined, the elders of that city participated in the assigned ritual. We assume that the elders and judges investigated the case thoroughly before they took the steps outlined in these verses.[6]

The offering of the red heifer was not like the offering of a sacrifice at the sanctuary. For one thing, the priests didn't slay the animal and catch its blood; laymen beheaded the beast in the valley, and the priests only witnessed the deed. The officers washed their hands over the dead animal (Matt. 27:24), confessed their innocence, and prayed for the Lord to forgive His people, and He did. Of course, this didn't mean that the unknown guilty murderer was automatically forgiven, but rather that the Lord would cleanse the land and forgive Israel the sin that had been committed. God's justice was upheld and God's law was obeyed even though the culprit wasn't known.

That this ritual relates to Jesus Christ and His atoning work on the cross is clear from the elders' words, "Do not lay innocent blood to the charge of Your people Israel" (Deut. 21:8 NKJV). On that tragic day when Israel asked to have her Messiah crucified, Pilate washed his hands and said, "I am innocent of this man's blood," and the people replied, "Let his blood be on us and on our children" (Matt. 27:24–25 NIV). Like that innocent heifer, Jesus died for the nation and even prayed from the cross, "Father, forgive them; for they know not what they do" (Luke 23:34). Jesus fulfilled God's will and upheld His holy law, and God withheld His judgment from Israel for approximately forty years. Jesus died for the sins of the world (John 1:29; 1 John 4:14), He died for the church (Eph. 5:25–26), and for the people of Israel: "for the transgression of my people was he stricken" (Isa. 53:8).

The entire ritual speaks of the grace of God, for man's works could never earn God's forgiveness. The red heifer had never been worked, the ground in the valley had never been tilled, and the elders, judges, and priests had done nothing special to merit God's forgiveness for His people. The sacrifice wasn't even made at the sanctuary or offered by a priest. "For by grace you have been saved through faith, and that not of yourselves; it is the gift of God, not of works, lest anyone should boast" (Eph. 2:8–9 NKJV). The offering of the innocent red heifer pointed to the offering of the Son of God, whose death brought cleansing, forgiveness, and the annulment of God's judgment.

Reviewing this section of the law, we're impressed with the fact that God wanted His people to enjoy living in their land, and the secret of this enjoyment was obedience to His will. Crime and injustice defiled the land, and God didn't want His land defiled. The godless nations in Canaan so polluted the land that it "vomited them out" (Lev. 18:24–30). Apart from Israel, no nation of the world is in a covenant relationship with God, but the Lord still holds all nations accountable for their sins (Amos 1:3—2:3). One day God will judge the nations in righteousness (Joel 3:9–16) and nobody will escape.

QUESTIONS FOR PERSONAL REFLECTION
OR GROUP DISCUSSION

1. Of what comfort is it to you that God is completely and always just?

2. What was the function of the cities of refuge? What does this provision teach us about God?

3. What does the practice of capital punishment do and what does it not do? In what circumstances, if any, do you believe capital punishment is appropriate?

4. Why is truth so important in our system of justice? In what ways does our system try to protect the truth? How well do you think this works?

5. What is the law of retaliation? In contrast, how did Jesus instruct us in His Sermon on the Mount to deal with personal insults and offenses?

6. On what basis should we accept the encouragement to "fear not"?

7. What does it mean for a Christian to be "entangled with the affairs of this life"? How can we avoid this?

8. What lesson do we learn from the three exemptions given in the Israelites' military service? What do we learn about God from this?

9. What did it mean for a foreign wife to shave her head? What could a newly converted person do today to signal a new beginning?

10. In what different ways did the offering of the red heifer (Deut. 21:1–9) speak of the work of Jesus Christ and the grace of God?

Chapter Nine

DISPUTES AND DECISIONS

(Deuteronomy 21:15—25:19)

T he major emphasis in these chapters is on how the law of the Lord governed relationships in the nation of Israel. The material is so varied that perhaps the best way to study what Moses said is to arrange it in general categories.

PROTECTING THE FAMILY (21:15–21; 24:1–5; 25:5–10)

The foundation for human society is the family, a gift from God for which no successful substitute has been found. Sociologist Margaret Mead said, "No matter how many communes anybody invents, the family keeps creeping back." It was God who established the home and in so doing remedied the only thing that was "not good" in His creation, that the man was alone (Gen. 1:26–31; 2:18–25). The people of Israel were commanded to honor father and mother (Ex. 20:12), and since four generations might live together as an extended family, that honor covered a lot of territory.

The firstborn son (21:15–17). The original divine pattern for marriage was one man and one woman devoted to each other for one lifetime, and the two exceptions—polygamy and divorce—were permitted in

Israel because of the "hardness of men's hearts" (Matt. 19:3–9). The first polygamist was Lamech, a rebel against God (Gen. 4:19), and the men in Scripture who followed his example brought heartache and trouble into their homes. Jacob discovered that having multiple wives meant competition and friction in the home and brought a great deal of grief into the family (Gen. 29:30; 31:1ff.). God overruled the selfishness in the home and accomplished His purposes in building the nation, but some of the family members paid a price.

At Passover, God spared the firstborn Jewish males who were sheltered by the blood of the lamb. In honor of this gracious miracle, He commanded that all the firstborn of Israel, man and beast, should be dedicated to Him (Ex. 13:1–16). Israel was God's firstborn son (4:22–23), and Israel's firstborn also belonged to Him. It was also ordained that the firstborn son in the family would inherit a double portion of the estate. If there were two sons, the elder son received two-thirds and the younger son one-third. Nothing could change this law, not even the husband's love for his favorite wife.

In salvation history, it should be noted that God occasionally bypassed the firstborn son and chose the second born. Abraham's firstborn son was Ishmael, but God chose Isaac, and Esau was Isaac's firstborn, but God chose Jacob (Rom. 9:6–13). Jacob gave the special blessing to Ephraim, Joseph's second son, and not to Manasseh, the firstborn (Gen. 48). God doesn't accept our first birth, which is of the flesh, but offers us a second birth, a spiritual birth, that makes us His firstborn children (John 3:1–18; Heb. 12:23).

The rebellious son (vv. 18–21). This boy was the original "prodigal son" (Luke 15:11–32), except that he didn't leave home to disobey the fifth commandment, dishonor his parents, and disgrace his community. Day after day, he resisted the pleas, warnings, and chastenings of his parents as he refused to work, reveled with the drunkards, and contributed nothing to the home or the community. This kind of sin was so heinous that it was included in the curses read in the land of Canaan (Deut. 27:16; see Ex. 21:17).[1]

This was more than a family concern, for it involved the peace and reputation of the community. The solidarity of the people of Israel was an important element in their civil, social, and religious life, for the sin of a single person, family, city, or tribe could affect the whole nation (see Deut. 13; Josh. 7:1–15). This is also true of the church, for as members of one spiritual body (1 Cor. 12), we belong to one another and we affect one another (1 Cor. 5). The parents of the rebellious son were to take him to the local council at the gate, bear witness of his rebellion and obstinacy, and let the council decide. If the boy refused to change his ways, then the only verdict was death by stoning, with all the men of the community participating. Why? In order to "put away evil" and to warn other profligates of what might happen to them. The phrase "put away evil" is found nine times in Deuteronomy (13:5; 17:7, 12; 19:19; 21:21; 22:21–22, 24; 24:7), and the phrase "hear and fear" four times (13:11; 17:13; 19:20; 21:21). The Lord and Moses believed that the public punishment of offenders could be a detriment to others sinning. Furthermore, the future of that family was at stake if this son were allowed to continue in his sins.

This "law of the prodigal" helps us understand one aspect of our Lord's parable, the fact that the father ran to meet his son (Luke 15:20). In the East, it isn't customary for older men to run. Of course, the father's love for his son compelled him to hasten to meet him, but there was something else involved. The news of this boy's wicked life in the far country had certainly drifted back to his hometown, and the law-abiding citizens knew that he had disgraced their city. Seeing the boy approach, the elders at the gate might have been tempted to refuse to let him in, or in their anger, they might have picked up stones to stone him! But with the father holding the boy in his arms, kissing him, and welcoming him, the elders could do nothing. Had anybody thrown stones, they would have hit the father. This speaks to us of Calvary, where God took our punishment for us that He might be able to welcome us home.

Divorce (24:1–4).[2] It's bad enough when a family has a rebellious son to disturb the home, but it's even worse when the husband and wife don't get along and the marriage breaks up. The original Edenic law of marriage said nothing about divorce (Gen. 2:18–25). Marriage is fundamentally a physical union ("one flesh"), so only a physical reason can dissolve it, and there are two such reasons: the death of one spouse (Rom. 7:1–3; 1 Cor. 7:39) and adultery (Deut. 22:22; Lev. 20:10). The adulterous man and woman were killed, leaving the innocent spouses free to remarry. The law of Moses did not allow divorce for adultery because the guilty spouse was stoned to death for his or her sin.

Since the "uncleanness" ("something indecent," NIV) couldn't be adultery, what was it that it permitted a man to divorce his wife? In our Lord's day, the rabbinical school of Hillel took a very broad view and interpreted "uncleanness" to mean "anything that displeased the husband." But the school of Rabbi Shammai took the narrow view that "uncleanness" meant some kind of sexual sin. (See Matt. 5:31–32; 19:1–9; Mark 10:1–12.) Jesus didn't define "uncleanness" but made it clear that the Mosaic law of divorce was a concession and not a command. God permitted it because of the hardness of the human heart. However, it appears that Jesus did permit divorce if one of the spouses committed adultery. The assumption is that the innocent spouse was free to remarry; otherwise, why get a divorce?[3]

When our Lord permitted divorce because of adultery, He was equating divorce with death. The church doesn't have the right to kill people for committing adultery or any other sin, but they can accept divorce as the equivalent of death, thus leaving the innocent partner free to remarry. Jesus affirmed the priority of the original Edenic law of marriage, but He also granted this concession. Of course, it's better that the guilty party confess the sin, repent, and be restored and forgiven, but this doesn't always happen. Sin is the great destroyer, and where the privileges are the highest, as in marriage, the pain of that sin is the greatest.

The "bill of divorcement" was an official document that protected the women from slander and abuse and also gave her the privilege of a second marriage. The time that was required to secure this document would give the husband opportunity to think the matter through and possibly reconsider. He would lose what was left of the marriage price or dowry, and that might be costly. Too many separations and divorces are the result of built-up emotions, festering wounds, and thoughtless words that could have been avoided if the spouses had been honest with each other, talked things over, and sought the Lord's help earlier in the problem.

Should her second marriage end in divorce, the woman was forbidden to return to her former husband because she had been "defiled" (Deut. 24:4). Perhaps this means that the consummation of the second marriage was considered adultery, because only death or adultery could dissolve the marriage. (Adultery is called "defilement" in Lev. 18:20 and Num. 5:13–14.) For her to return to the first husband would cheapen her and make her nothing but a piece of property that could be bought and sold at will.

Deferment (v. 5). This law has been considered in Deuteronomy 20:7. Any able-bodied man could take the new husband's place in the army but nobody could take his place at home. His wife would suffer from the pain of separation from her beloved and, if he died in battle, the sorrow of bereavement. This law shows the high value God puts on human love and the responsibilities of marriage.

Levirate marriage (25:5–10). The word "levirate" comes from the Latin and means "a husband's brother," (i.e., a brother-in-law). It was this law that the Sadducees used when they tried to trip up Jesus (Matt. 22:23–33). Basically, this law required a deceased man's brother to marry the widow and have children by her so that the name of the deceased wouldn't perish from Israel. However, there were some special conditions to observe. First, the married brother and single brother had to live together; second, the married couple had to be childless; and, third, the single brother had to be willing to marry the widow and have children by her.

The first requirement—"living together"—didn't demand a common house but only that the brothers lived near each other (Gen. 13:6). The wife, therefore, wasn't a stranger to her brother-in-law. As to the second requirement, if the couple were not childless, there would be no need for the second marriage. In fact, it was against the law for a brother-in-law to marry his sister-in-law if they had children (Lev. 18:16). The third requirement was the critical one: Would the brother-in-law be willing to marry his brother's widow? The unnamed relative in the book of Ruth refused to marry Ruth because it would have jeopardized his own inheritance (Ruth 4:1–6).

If the man refused to marry her, the woman took her case to the elders at the gate, and they would try to reason with the man. No doubt they would point out that childless widows needed protection and that his late brother needed an heir to maintain the family name and property. If he still refused, then the widow could publicly humiliate him by spitting in (or before) his face (Num. 12:14) and removing his sandal. To put your foot down on land or cast your shoe on it meant to claim it for yourself (Gen. 13:17; Josh. 10:24; Ps. 60:8; 108:9), while to take off your shoe meant to relinquish any claim to the property. If the brother married later and had a family, that family would be known as "the house of the barefooted one." Only the poor, mourners, and prisoners of war went barefoot (Isa. 20:2–4; Mic. 1:8; Luke 15:22), but to get your shoes back was to be reinstated in society (2 Chron. 28:15; Luke 15:22). By refusing to honor his dead brother, the man brought dishonor on himself and his family.

HUMILIATING CRIMINALS (21:22–23)

The Lord used both positive and negative imagery to teach His people to respect and obey His law. On the positive side, the men wore blue tassels on the corners of their clothing to remind them that they belonged to the Lord and were privileged to have His law to obey (Num. 15:37–41). The weekly Sabbath and the annual feasts were reminders of all that the Lord had done for Israel, and the presence of God's sanctuary kept the Lord's presence before their eyes. The Levites scattered throughout Israel were living reminders of the law of the Lord and the importance of knowing it.

On the negative side, the offering of blood sacrifices was a vivid reminder that the basis of forgiveness and fellowship was the surrendering up of life (Lev. 17:11). Whenever the community stoned a lawbreaker to death, it would cause the people to "hear and fear." Isolating the lepers outside the camp, burning leprous garments, and tearing down leprosy-infested houses reminded the people that sin is like leprosy and must be dealt with. But the public exposure of a criminal's corpse would be an object lesson few would forget. A criminal found guilty of committing a capital crime was stoned to death, and if the officials wanted to make the judgment even more solemn, they could order the body hanged from a tree or impaled on a pole until sundown. What an object lesson that would be! (In seventeenth- and eighteenth-century London, the heads of executed criminals were sometimes displayed in public.) Since a dead body was unclean, it was taken down at sundown so as not to decay further and defile the land. Also, the Lord didn't want executed criminals to get too much attention lest they become heroes.

This rather gruesome symbolic act reminded the people that God cursed people who committed capital crimes. In Galatians 3:13, Paul applied this truth to our Lord's death on the cross: "Christ has redeemed us from the curse of the law, having become a curse for us (for it is written, 'Cursed is everyone who hangs on a tree')" (NKJV). Those who trust Christ cannot be condemned by the law (Gal. 3:10) because Christ bore that curse for them.

LOVING ONE'S NEIGHBORS (22:1–4, 6–8; 23:24–25)

These regulations are specific applications of Leviticus 19:18, "You shall not take vengeance, nor bear any grudge against the children of your people, but you shall love your neighbor as yourself: I am the LORD" (NKJV). The neighbor is a brother, which is even a greater motive for helping him, and God is the Lord of both, which is the highest motive of all. In fact, the Jews were to extend this same concern even to their enemies' animals (Ex. 23:4). Both Jesus and Paul admonish us to love our enemies and to manifest this love in practical ways (Matt. 5:43–48; Rom. 12:17–21).

Lost property (vv. 1–3). There were few fences and walls on Jewish farmland, so it would be easy for livestock to wander away. If you found such an animal, you were to return it to the rightful owner; if the owner lived too far away, you were to "board" the animal until the owner came to get it. Farm animals were both expensive and essential; neither the farm family nor the nation could survive without them. But Moses didn't limit the law to restoring strayed animals; he said that anything a Jewish person found was to be guarded and returned to the owner. A neighbor wasn't only someone who lived adjacent to you; he was anybody in need whom you could help. In His parable of the good Samaritan (Luke 10:25–37), Jesus followed this definition of "neighbor." However, God is concerned for the animal as well as for the owner, and we should be too.

The Lord is concerned that people find and restore lost animals, but He is also greatly concerned that we find the lost sinners who have strayed away (Luke 15:1–7; James 5:19–20). Certainly a human being made in the image of God is of more value than a beast (Matt. 12:12)!

Emergencies (v. 4). A heavily laden donkey wouldn't be easy to lift, but that's what neighbors and brothers are for. For the animal's sake and the owner's sake, the men would get together and turn this emergency into an opportunity to practice brotherly love. Emergencies don't make people; they show what people are made of. When a terrible storm destroyed thousands of trees in our town, some people took advantage of the situation and used their chain saws to collect exorbitant fees from helpless people. Love of money won over love for their neighbors. But others, including many teenagers, went from place to place donating their services to help those who couldn't help themselves.

Tenderness (vv. 6–7). Concern for fallen animals leads to concern for defenseless birds. It would be easy for the man to wipe out the nest and have wild birds and eggs for dinner, but God prohibited such wanton activity. If the man took the mother bird, the young would die from lack of food and care, so he was allowed to take the young and the eggs. The female bird could have another brood, and this would help to preserve the species. As you read the Mosaic law, you can't help but be touched by the Lord's concern for the natural resources He put on the earth, not only birds but also trees (20:19–20), donkeys (22:4), and hungry oxen (25:4). God preserves both man and beast (Ps. 36:6; 104:10–30), and He expects His people to assist Him in that important work. God provides food for mankind, but the greed of a few can destroy the supply for the many. The Lord promised that it would go well with the nation if they showed concern for helpless creatures (Deut. 22:7; see 4:40; 5:16; 6:3, 18; 12:25, 28; 19:13).

Safety (v. 8). The flat roof of a house in Israel was living space for the family, especially during the hot season when they slept on the roof where it was cooler. The owner of the house had to build a low wall (parapet) or a railing around the roof to protect people from falling. It wasn't enough to post a sign and warn people of danger; he had to put up a barrier to help protect the people. We commonly think of home as a haven from the assaults of the world, but safety specialists tell us that the home can be the scene of many accidents, injuries, and even deaths.

Generosity (23:24–25). The land belonged to the Lord and the harvests were His reward for His people's faithful work and their obedience to His law; therefore, He had every right to share His harvest with those who needed it. If hungry oxen could eat of the grain they were threshing (25:4), surely hungry people could eat from the Lord's fields (Matt. 12:1–8). This law didn't give people the right to take food from their neighbors' fields, vineyards, and orchards any time they wanted a snack. The privilege was reserved for the truly hungry and especially farm laborers, strangers, and the poor. This law especially helped travelers passing through the land. However, Moses made it clear that the food was to be carried away in the persons' stomachs and not in bowls or baskets. The law gave people the privilege of meeting their need but not satisfying their greed.

God encouraged the people of Israel to be generous to those who were less fortunate. The farmers weren't to harvest their fields and vineyards so conscientiously that nothing would be left for the poor and needy to glean (Deut. 24:19–22; Lev. 19:9–10; 23:22; see also Ruth 2). If Israel obeyed God's laws and loved their neighbors, God would abundantly bless them and provide abundantly for everybody. Even under the old covenant, people who gave to others would receive abundantly from the Lord (Prov. 11:25; 22:9; Isa. 58:6–7; Mal. 3:10; see also Matt. 5:42; Luke 8:38–39; Acts 20:35; 2 Cor. 9:6). How much more generous we should be who share the unsearchable riches of God's grace through faith in Jesus Christ!

MAINTAINING DISTINCTIONS (22:5, 9–10)

Because the Israelites were God's chosen people, separated from other nations, practices that were acceptable in pagan cultures were prohibited to the Jews. God set apart the priests and Levites to teach the people how to know right from wrong and the clean from the unclean, and this helped the people develop discernment. As they obeyed God and sought His blessing, they learned more and more of what was fitting and proper in Jewish society. The nation decayed spiritually because the priests and Levites failed to do their job, and the Jews began to imitate their heathen neighbors (Ezek. 22:23–29; 44:23).

Clothing (v. 5). The familiar and now accepted word "unisex" first appeared in print in *Life* magazine (June 21, 1968) in an article describing unisex clothing as "good fashion as well as good fun." In this verse, God calls it "an abomination." However, people who agree with Moses don't always agree with one another on how this law should be applied in the church. Since Christians aren't under the old covenant, some believers disregard the law completely, while others use it to tell the women in their churches how they should dress, both at home and in public. We can't ignore God's revelation in the Old Testament, because Jesus and the apostles used the Old Testament in their discussions of spiritual concerns.[4] Even if this law about clothing doesn't apply to the church in the same way it applied to Israel, there are spiritual principles behind it that are important to us (2 Tim. 3:16–17).

To begin with, this law doesn't focus only on clothing. Literally it says, "There shall not be man's things upon a woman, and a man shall not put on a woman's clothes."[5] The phrase "man's things" could refer to anything that was commonly associated with men in that culture, including clothing, tools, and weapons. If we apply this law strictly to believers today, then we have to determine in every culture and in every circumstance what things are feminine and what things are masculine, and that might not be easy to do. Semitic men wore earrings and other gold jewelry, a practice frowned upon by some churches today. That this verse is a prohibition of transvestitism is clear, but could a man in Western culture use a woman's umbrella or wear her raincoat?

Moses was reminding the people that there is a distinction between the sexes, established by God from the very beginning, and that God wants us to maintain this distinction. "So God created man in his own image, in the image of God created he him; male and female created he them" (Gen. 1:27). By divine wisdom, man and woman were made for each other but were made to be different from each other. Many nations in the ancient world approved and practiced homosexuality, even in their religion, but God prohibited it in Israel and made it a capital crime (Lev. 18:22; 20:13). The maintaining and honoring of sexual distinctions neither demeans the woman nor exalts the man. Both were created by God in His image and both shared in the creation blessing and mandate (Gen. 1:28–31). To blur their distinctives, so that men are no longer distinguishable from women is to bring confusion to God's order for His world (1 Cor. 11:1–16; 1 Tim. 2:9–15).

If men and women in Israel had been allowed to "cross dress," it would have made it easier for them to sin. All the adulterer had to do was put on women's clothing and nobody would know who was visiting the neighbor's house. In today's society, disguises are no longer needed. In fact, sexual sins are standard fare in media entertainment, and people don't seem to be ashamed of what they see or do. Furthermore, "cross dressing" would mean imitating the pagan nations that used such practices in their religious rituals. "Be not conformed to this world" (Rom. 12:2) doesn't mean that Christians should look like they came from another world or out of a time warp. Dedicated Christians will not only look and act like Christians, but they'll also look and act like men and women. This also applies to children and young people. Fashions change and cultures differ, but Christian girls and women should always dress modestly (1 Tim. 2:9) in garments suited to the occasion, and so should men and boys.

The principle behind the law is that of separation from the world and recognition of God's order for men and women. It's a principle that helps us honor God and avoid confusion and sin. To say that we have to obey the letter of this law today is to miss the point. Does this also mean we can't wear garments with mixed fibers (Deut. 22:11) or that we must sew tassels on our clothing (v. 12; see Num. 15:37–40; Matt. 23:5)? Perhaps the prohibition about mixed fabrics is a further reminder of Israel's responsibility to be separated from the other nations that practiced these things, perhaps as part of their religious system.

Farming (vv. 9–10; Lev. 19:19). By not yoking different kinds of animals together, the Jews were again recognizing God's order in nature. There was also the matter of separation, for the ox was a clean animal and the ass an unclean animal. From a practical point of view, the animals have different temperaments, and their being yoked together could only create problems. Keeping the various seeds separated when sowing the fields was also recognition of the principle of separation. It's possible that the pagan nations mingled their seed as a part of their fertility rites in connection with their gods.

Whether they were weaving garments, plowing with their farm animals, or sowing their seed, the Jewish people were to remember that they were God's people and therefore a separated people. This was the old covenant version of 1 Corinthians 10:31, "Therefore, whether you eat or drink, or whatever you do, do all to the glory of God" (NKJV).

HONORING PERSONAL PURITY (22:13–30)

"Sex has become one of the most discussed subjects of modern times," said Fulton J. Sheen. "The Victorians pretended it did not exist; the moderns pretend that nothing else exists." God created sex and has every right to control the way we use it, and if we obey Him, it will bring enrichment and enjoyment. One of the basic rules is that sex must not be experienced outside of the bonds of marriage. The law of Moses and the New Testament magnify personal purity and the importance of honesty and loyalty in marriage.

The slandered wife (vv. 13–21). The sexual purity of women was important in Israel in order to maintain the integrity of the family line and therefore the integrity of the tribes. The legitimacy of a man's sons guaranteed the protection and perpetuation of the family name and the family property. To us, this seems like a double standard, for there was no law by which the woman could test her husband's fidelity. But the issue here isn't just personal morality so much as family legitimacy, the preventing of an illegitimate son from entering the family. If on consummating the marriage the husband discovered that his wife was not a virgin, then it was possible that she was already pregnant. If the husband didn't act immediately to protect himself, he would have to accept a child fathered by another man, but how could he prove it?

On the marriage night, the wise bride provided herself with a marriage cloth that would be stained with her blood at the consummation of the marriage. This would be proof that she was indeed a virgin when she married. If later on her husband said otherwise,[6] she and her parents could present the marriage cloth as evidence. No faithful woman would want her reputation blemished or her future destroyed just because of a hateful man's lie. The elders would beat the husband, fine him twice the bride price (vv. 19 and 29), the equivalent of ten years' wages, and order that he could never divorce her. The law punished the man and protected the woman.

But if the accusation was proven true, the woman would be stoned to death in front of her father's house, because it was while she was living there that she had sinned. It's also possible that the parents already knew that their daughter was not a virgin and had lied to the husband. These parents could never walk out their front door without seeing the place where their daughter had been stoned to death. "The wages of sin is death."

Adultery (vv. 22–24). Fornication is intercourse between single people while adultery involves at least one married person. Those who were found committing adultery were stoned to death. (In the episode described in

John 8:1–11, we wonder what happened to the man.) A Jewish girl engaged to be married was considered to be a man's wife (Deut. 22:24), and if she had intercourse in a city, it was considered adultery and she was stoned. This was true even if the intercourse was more like rape, for she could have cried out for help. Even if nobody came in time to rescue her, her cries were evidence that she wasn't cooperating in the deed. Her silence would have implied consent.

Rape (vv. 25–29). An engaged woman attacked in the country could cry out and not be helped because nobody was there to hear and come to her aid. Therefore the man was stoned to death but the woman was allowed to live. Nothing is said about her future wedding, for perhaps her fiancé wouldn't want her if she had lost her virginity. About this, Moses is silent.

The man who raped a girl who was not engaged had to marry the girl and pay her father the bride price of fifty shekels, and he was forbidden to divorce her. We wonder how successful marriages will be that begin with lust and are held together only by law. But once again, the law protected the woman and punished the man.

Incest (v. 30). The woman here is stepmother to the man committing the sin and not his mother (see Lev. 18:7–8). Leviticus 20:11 condemns them both to death. This sin was among those condemned on Mount Ebal (Deut. 27:20). Apparently this was the sin of the man in the Corinthian church who needed to be disciplined (1 Cor. 5).

Various Laws (23:1—25:19)

Here we categorize several miscellaneous laws that were important to the life of the nation and that illustrate spiritual truths that are important to us today.

Entering the assembly (23:1–8; 25:17–19). It was a privilege to be a member of the Jewish nation and share in the blessings of God's covenant. The word "congregation" ("assembly," NIV) may refer to the worshipping assembly and not the nation as a whole. Gentiles could live within the confines of Israel's territory but that didn't give them the right to share in the feasts and other religious events. Gentiles who submitted to circumcision and confessed Jehovah as the true and living God could become proselytes (Ex. 12:43–51), but some of them were excluded for various reasons. The Lord has the right to determine who shall enter His holy nation.

For one thing, any emasculated male (eunuch) was rejected (Deut. 23:1). Priests who had similar defects were prohibited from serving at the altar, although they could eat of the holy food (Lev. 21:16–23), and Israel was a kingdom of priests (Ex. 19:5–6). Therefore, the men entering the nation had to be free from these defects. It's possible that some of the Gentile men had received this surgery as part of their devotion to a heathen God, while Jewish circumcision spoke of belonging to the true God of Israel. The prophet Isaiah looked forward to the day when eunuchs would be welcomed into the kingdom and be blessed of God (Isa. 56:3–5). We can rejoice today that physical blemishes and limitations are not a barrier to faith in Jesus Christ and participation in the blessing of the new covenant (Acts 8:26–39).

Illegitimate children (Deut. 23:2) were also excluded, although we're not sure what this term meant in ancient Israel. The rabbis interpreted it to mean a child "born of a forbidden marriage," as the NIV translates it, but what is "a forbidden marriage"? It could include incestuous marriages or marriages involving rejected nations (Ammonites, Moabites). Why the innocent child should be punished for the sins of the parents (24:16) is difficult to understand. The phrase "unto the tenth generation" means "forever" (23:3).

The Ammonites and Moabites (23:3–6) were descended from Lot, the nephew of Abraham, but they didn't show kindness to their Jewish relatives. The Ammonites wouldn't sell them food and water, and Balak, a king of Moab, hired Baalam to curse Israel (2:9–23; Num. 22—24). Because both nations were related to Israel, the Lord wouldn't permit the Jews to attack them. Their punishment was exclusion from Israel's national blessings forever. However, Ruth the Moabitess married Boaz and entered the nation of Israel and became the great-grandmother of King David (Ruth 4:17–22) and therefore an ancestress of Jesus Christ (Matt. 1:3–6). She had put her faith in Jehovah (Ruth 1:16–17), and the Lord accepted her.

The Edomites and the Egyptians (Deut. 23:7–8) could enter the nation in the third generation because the Edomites descended from Jacob's brother, Esau (Gen. 25:24–26), and the Egyptians received Jacob and his family into their land and cared for them (Gen. 46—47). In spite of later Egyptian hostility, God transformed the family of Jacob into a great nation while they sojourned in Egypt.

The Amalekites (Deut. 25:17–19) were rejected by the Lord and Israel was not to forget their evil deeds. They attacked Israel after the nation had come out of Egypt (Ex. 17:8–13), starting with the weary and feeble Jews bringing up the rear of the march. Joshua defeated them and God declared perpetual war on them. King Saul lost his crown because he failed to exterminate them (1 Sam. 15), and he was slain on the battlefield by an Amalekite (2 Sam. 1:1–16). It wasn't until the time of Hezekiah that the Amalekites finally disappeared from the scene (1 Chron. 4:41–43).

Sanctifying the army camp (vv. 9–14). This section applied to Israel's soldiers when they were encamped away from home. The basic principle was that they treat the camp as they would their land at home, for the Lord was with them even on the battlefield, walking in their midst. The idol-worshipping nations believed that they left their gods behind when they went to another country, but Israel's God was always with them, for He is the God of all the earth. If a soldier had become unclean at home, he would have to leave the community, wash, and return the next day, and that same rule applied in the camp.[7] The men were also to have a place outside the camp for disposing of their excrement. This would not only keep them from being defiled, but it would also promote hygiene.

No matter where we go, God goes with us, and we must not think that we can disobey Him and get away with it. God's admonition is, "Keep away from everything impure" (v. 9 NIV). Whether we're on vacation or away from home on business, the Lord watches us and desires us to be as careful where we're unknown as we are where we're known. Moses was on holy ground in Midian (Ex. 3:5) as was Joshua standing near Jericho (Josh. 5:13–15).

Sharing with the poor and needy (vv. 15–16, 19–20; 24:6, 10–15, 19–22; 25:4). This collection of laws relates to opportunities that the Jews would have to show kindness and generosity to both humans and animals. Contrary to the laws of other nations, the law of Israel allowed the Jews to harbor fugitive slaves and protect them. These slaves would not be Jewish, because the Jews were not allowed to enslave their brothers. Jewish servants were either released in the Sabbath Year or would agree to serve willingly for life (15:12–18). Also, Jewish masters were not allowed to abuse their servants so that they would want to flee. These fugitives would be from the surrounding nations, and assisting them would give the Jews opportunity to tell them about the God of Israel.

Jews were not permitted to charge interest when they loaned money or produce to their brothers, but they could charge foreigners (23:19–20; see Ex. 22:25–27; Lev. 25:35–37). The blessing God would send the lender would far surpass the interest he would make on the loan. This is another example of the principle expressed in Matthew 6:33.

If a lender needed collateral for a loan, he wasn't permitted to take the borrower's millstones (Deut. 24:6), because the man needed them in order to feed himself and his family. The lender was not to demean the borrower by going into his house to secure a pledge (vv. 10–15), and if that pledge was the man's cloak, the borrower had to return it by sunset (Ex. 22:25–27). Business transactions between Jewish brethren were to be humane and compassionate, to help the needy brother and not to enrich the lender.

The farmer was to leave some "gleanings" for the poor during the time of harvest (Deut. 24:19–22; see Lev. 19:9–10). This would give the aliens, orphans, and widows opportunity to gather food in a dignified way and not be forced to beg. As with the lender, so with the generous farmer: God would bless him in his work and reward him for his kindness to the poor (Ps. 41:1; Prov. 14:21, 31; 29:7). "It is more blessed to give than to receive" (Acts 20:35).

This generosity should also extend to one's animals (Deut. 25:4). To muzzle the ox that is threshing the grain is to frustrate him and make his work unnecessarily painful. Once again, the Lord shows compassion for animals and urges us to show pity to those under our care. "A righteous man regards the life of his animal, but the tender mercies of the wicked are cruel" (Prov. 12:10 NKJV). Paul used this verse to teach that those who labor in the gospel should be supported by God's people (2 Cor. 9:1–14; 1 Tim. 5:17–18).

Fulfilling religious vows (23:17–18, 21–23). The subject of vows is discussed also in Leviticus 27 and Numbers 30. A Jew could make a vow to give the Lord something, or do something for Him, in return for a special blessing. The vow could also involve abstaining from something in order to please the Lord. Vows were purely voluntary (Deut. 23:22), and they had to be declared openly and fulfilled obediently (v. 23). Whatever was promised had to be brought to the sanctuary and given to the Lord (Eccl. 5:4–6). To make the promise and not keep it would be taking the Lord's name in vain (Ex. 20:7; Prov. 20:25).

However, no vow could be paid to the Lord with money earned by committing sin (Deut. 23:17–18). "Playing the harlot" is a euphemism for idolatry (Ex. 34:15–16) because the pagan shrines did offer worshippers female and male prostitutes ("dogs"). No Jewish man or woman was ever to become a shrine prostitute, and no vow could be paid to the Lord with the hire of a prostitute. We don't do evil that good may come from it (Rom. 3:8). All money is defiled in a sense—Paul and Peter both called it "filthy lucre" (1 Tim. 3:3, 8; Titus 1:7, 11; 1 Peter 5:2)—but some money is especially filthy because of its origin.

Seeing that justice is done (24:7, 16–18; 25:1–3, 11–16). Kidnapping was prohibited (24:7) and was a capital crime (Ex. 21:16). To kidnap people and sell them is to treat them like merchandise and not like persons created in the image of God. The Jews were not to enslave one another or sell one another to be enslaved by the Gentiles. The Lord had delivered His people from Egypt so they could be free, and kidnapping was the reverse of God's purpose.

When an offender was found guilty and sentenced to be beaten, he was not to be humiliated but punished justly (Deut. 25:1–3). To beat him too little would be to minimize the offense, but to beat him too much would be to treat him in an inhuman manner and "degrade him" (NIV). The limit was forty stripes, but the Jews later made it thirty-nine (2 Cor. 11:24) so as not to accidentally go over the legal number. Whether it's a judge sentencing a criminal or a father chastening his child, the punishment must fit the offense and not demean the offender. As the United States "Bill of Rights" says, "Excessive bail shall not be required, nor excessive fines imposed, nor cruel and unusual punishments inflicted" (Amendment VIII).

Two men fighting (Deut. 25:11–12) is an invitation for more trouble; better they should seek help and settle their dispute in a more constructive way. It's understandable that the wife would want her husband to win, but her method of assistance was shameful, unfair, and grossly offensive. In describing this scenario, Moses prohibited all indecent methods of combat by either men or women. The penalty would certainly restrain anybody from doing such a thing.

Honest weights and measures (Deut. 25:13–16) were essential to the public good (Lev. 19:35–37). The prophets denounced dishonest weights and measures because their use made the poor poorer and the rich richer (Amos 8:5; Mic. 6:10–11; see also Prov. 11:1; 16:11; 20:10, 23). Once again, Moses reminded the people that their future security and blessing in the land depended on their obedience to God's law. When they cheated others, they only cheated themselves.

"Righteousness exalts a nation, but sin is a reproach to any people" (Prov. 14:34 NKJV).

QUESTIONS FOR PERSONAL REFLECTION
OR GROUP DISCUSSION

1. What do you think are the pros and cons of publicly punishing offenders today?

2. Why didn't the law of Moses allow for divorce in the case of adultery? How do you respond to this? What did Jesus teach about divorce, and why?

3. What positive and negative imagery did God use to teach His people to respect and obey His law? What reminders or imagery help you to obey the law?

4. In the command "Love your neighbor as yourself," who is meant by the term *neighbor*? What are some practical ways we can love our neighbors?

5. "Emergencies don't make people; they show what people are made of." When have you seen this to be true?

6. What distinctions between the sexes should be maintained today? What is the principle behind this distinction?

7. The Israelites were reminded that they were separated unto God in various ways. What could be a reminder to us that we are a separated or set-apart people?

8. The basic rule in the Bible concerning sexual relations is "No sex outside marriage." What are some reasons why this rule is good for people? Why are these reasons considered unconvincing in our society?

9. When you meditate on the truth that God is with you wherever you go, what feelings arise? Why?

10. Why do you think God made a point of insisting that business transactions were supposed to be humane and compassionate? Is there anything in this principle that applies today?

Chapter Ten

OBEDIENCE AND DISOBEDIENCE, BLESSINGS AND CURSES

(Deuteronomy 26:16—31:13)

Moses completed his exposition of the law in 26:15 and then began to bring his long farewell message to a close with a personal challenge to obedience. As we've seen before, the book of Deuteronomy is patterned after the ancient treaties given by kings to conquered nations. The Lord is the King and Israel is His chosen nation and special people. He took the Jews to Himself by defeating Egypt and setting Israel free to love Him and to serve Him. Moses has reviewed what the Lord did for Israel and said to Israel, and he has spelled out the terms of the covenant. Now he will explain the benefits of obeying the Lord and the disciplines that will come if Israel disobeys.

THE CHOICE PRESENTED (26:16—28:14)

In his brief introduction to this final section (26:16–19), Moses reminded the people that he had given them the Word of the Lord, the commandments of the true and living God. He also reminded them that at Sinai the nation had vowed to obey all that God said to them (Ex. 19:7–8; 24:3–8), and that the Lord had promised to bless them if they obeyed Him from the heart (Deut. 7:6–16). There on the plains of Moab, the Israelites would accept this solemn commitment a second time, and then they would affirm it a third time when they entered the Promised Land (Josh. 8:30–35). It isn't enough for God's people to enjoy the blessings and privileges of the covenant; they must also accept the responsibilities that are involved. Moses explained these responsibilities and called for the people to commit themselves wholly to the Lord.

The two mountains (27:1–13). Note that Moses joined with the elders (v. 1) and the priests (v. 9) in announcing the covenant to the people. Moses would soon leave the scene, but the nation would continue and the Lord's authority would operate through their civil and religious leaders. The people weren't committing themselves to Moses; they were committing themselves to the Lord to "keep all his commandments" (26:18).

Once Joshua had led the nation into the Promised Land, they were to interrupt their conquest and engage in a ceremony of reaffirming the covenant. It would take place near Shechem, with Mount Ebal to the north and Mount Gerizim to the south. The valley between the two mountains formed a natural amphitheater where the priests and Levites could assemble and declare God's Word. The six tribes that assembled at Mount Gerizim, the mount of blessing, were Simeon, Levi, Judah, Issachar, Joseph (Ephraim and Manasseh), and Benjamin, all Jacob's sons by his two wives Rachel and Leah. Assembled at Mount Ebal, the mount of curses, were Reuben and Zebulun (both sons of Leah) and the sons of the maidservants, Gad, Asher, Dan, and Naphtali.

Joshua was commanded to plaster some large stones on Mount Ebal and write on them the laws that God gave His people. This wasn't a symbolic gesture, for the words were to be written clearly for the people to read (27:8).[1] He was also to build an altar at the base of Mount Ebal where the priests would offer burnt offerings (total dedication to God) and peace offerings (joyful celebration of God's blessing). To have God's law without having a sacrifice for sins would be to bring condemnation and not consecration, for "by the law is the knowledge of sin" (Rom. 3:20). The location held sacred memories for the Jewish people, for Abraham had built an altar near Shechem (Gen. 12:6–7) and so had Jacob (33:17–20).

The curses (vv. 14–26). As the spiritual leaders read these curses, they weren't predicting what would happen if the people disobeyed God. They were calling upon the Lord to send these curses on His people if they turned away from Him.[2] And when the people said "Amen" after each statement ("so be it"), they were telling God that they were willing to be chastened if they disobeyed Him. Their "Amen" wasn't just their agreement with the words spoken; it was their acceptance of the terms of the covenant. These curses were closely related to the law Moses had delivered and explained, especially the Ten Commandments.

The first curse (v. 15) condemned idolatry and the violation of the first and second commandments (Ex. 20:1–6). To carve or cast an idol and worship it was to deny that Jehovah was the one true and living God, and it was this sin that finally brought the wrath of God on Israel. Even if a Jew worshipped an idol in secret and didn't try to persuade anybody to join him, it was still a great sin and had to be punished (Deut. 13). The second curse related to the family and the home (27:16; Ex. 20:12), and the third to property (Deut. 27:17; 19:14; Ex. 20:15). The fourth curse (Deut. 27:18) revealed God's special concern for people with disabilities. Leviticus 19:14 mentions both the deaf and the blind.

In the fifth curse (Deut. 27:19), the focus is on treating with kindness and justice the helpless and unfortunate in the land. Widows, orphans, and aliens were often abused and exploited in Israel and God called on His people to champion their cause and see that they received justice (24:17–18; Ex. 22:21–24; Luke 18:1–8). The Jews had been aliens in Egypt for many years and the Lord cared for them and judged the people who abused them. If Israel didn't care for the needy, God would also judge them. Among other things, this meant bringing their special tithes to the Lord every third year so the needy would have food to eat (Deut. 14:28–29).

Curses six through nine (27:20–23) have to do with sexual purity and relate to the seventh commandment (Ex. 20:14). These sins were prevalent among the nations in Canaan, and Israel wasn't to imitate their neighbors. Incest (Deut. 27:20, 22–23) was especially condemned in Israel (22:30; Lev. 18:8–9, 17; 20:11). Reuben lost his rights as the firstborn because he violated this law (Gen. 35:22; 49:3–4). Bestiality (Deut. 27:21; Lev. 18:23) was practiced in some pagan religions and "sacred animals" were used in the worship of their false gods. The perversion of sex is not only the abuse of a gift from God, but it threatens marriage and the family, which are foundational to the success of the nation.

The tenth and eleventh curses (Deut. 27:24–25) are an echo of the sixth commandment, "Thou shalt not kill" (Ex. 20:13). This command speaks of a deliberate deed (murder) and not accidental death (manslaughter; 21:12–14). Murder is the ultimate crime because its consequences can't be reversed, but to murder one's neighbor makes that crime even worse. The only thing more heinous would be to be paid to murder somebody! The law of Moses condemned those who accepted bribes to break the law, for making money is not more important than maintaining justice (Deut. 16:19; Ex. 23:8). The law taught the people of Israel to love their neighbors and do them good (Lev. 19:18; Deut. 22:1–4). But whether a neighbor or a total stranger is the victim, murder is wrong and murderers must be punished.

The twelfth curse (27:26) obligated the Jews to obey every law that God gave them, whether it was named in this list or not. Paul quoted this verse in Galatians 3:10 to prove that there could be no salvation by obeying the law, since nobody could obey everything God commanded. But the purpose of the law was not salvation but condemnation, the indictment of all people as sinners, and therefore the need of all people to trust Christ, "for the just shall live by faith" (Gal. 3:11).[3] There can be no true conversion without conviction, and conviction comes when we see the holiness of God in His law and the sinfulness of our own hearts. To say that we've kept some of God's laws doesn't excuse us, for to break one is to break them all (James 2:10–11). If you were hanging over a chasm holding to a chain of ten links, how many links would have to break for you to fall?[4]

When the Israelites in the Promised Land said their "Amen" to these twelve curses, they would be assenting to the law of God, promising to obey it, and agreeing that they deserved judgment if they disobeyed it. This would be a solemn hour in the history of Israel. At Sinai, Israel had agreed to obey God's law (Ex. 19:7–8; 24:3–8), and not long after, they made a golden calf and worshipped it! It takes more than pious words and good intentions to be a devoted and obedient child of God (Matt. 7:21–23).

The blessings (28:1–14). We don't read that the people were to say "Amen" to these blessings as they said "Amen" to the curses. The curses were not prophetic while this list of blessings is God's prophetic promise of what He would do for His people if they kept their commitment to Him. God's blessings are wholly of grace, whether or not His people assent to them or even appreciate them.[5] These blessings would lift Israel far above all the other nations (26:19) and make Israel "a light to the Gentiles" (Isa. 49:6). This would give the Jews opportunities to tell the other nations about the true and living God (Deut. 28:10).

God promised to bless His people in all places—the city, the field, and the home—with all that they needed.[6] As they went in and out in their daily work (v. 6; 8:17–18), He would care for them and prosper their efforts. He would give them victory over their enemies so that they could maintain possession of the land. He would supply rain for the fields, for water is a precious commodity in the East. God would send the "former rain" in October and

November, the "winter rain" from December to February, and the "latter rain" in April, and Israel's crops would grow abundantly. They would sell their surplus harvests to other nations but wouldn't have to buy from anybody.

We must keep in mind why the Lord promised these marvelous blessings. For one thing, the nation of Israel was still in its spiritual infancy (Gal. 4:1–7), and one way to teach children is by means of rewards and punishments. These material blessings were God's way of reminding His children that obedience brings blessing but disobedience brings chastening. However, it wasn't long before thinking Israelites discovered that wicked people were also receiving blessings, so there was something more to faith than just being rewarded. (See Ps. 73; Jer. 12:1–4; Job 21:7–15.)[7] Gradually God taught His people that their obedience was a witness to the other nations (Deut. 28:12) and brought glory to His name. Obedience also built godly character in the people so that they were indeed a holy nation and a kingdom of priests.

THE CURSES DESCRIBED (28:15–68)

This section is predictive; it describes the judgments God promised to send on the nation if the people refused to obey His law. The judgments are given in greater detail than are the blessings and are just the opposite of the blessings. (Compare vv. 1–14 with vv. 15–64.) God wanted His people to know that when these calamities struck, they would recognize the hand of the Lord and not think it was a series of coincidences.

Just as God promised to bless them in every area of life if they obeyed His covenant, so He warned that He would curse them in every area of life—their bodies, families, fields, flocks, and herds—if they disobeyed. They would be sick in body and mind, deprived of the necessities of life, defeated in battle, and scattered throughout the world. The word "destroyed" is repeated ominously (vv. 20, 24, 45, 48, 51, 61, 63) as are the words "smite" and "smitten" (vv. 22, 25, 27–28, 35). The Jews would be consumed by disease and famine and defeated in war, with their dead bodies left unburied to become food for birds and animals. (For a body to be left unburied was a terrible disgrace for a Jew.) They would experience the diseases and plagues they saw in Egypt; they would see their wives ravished and their children slain before their eyes. Finally, they would go into captivity and serve their enemies. Then they would learn that serving God wasn't so difficult after all, but then it would be too late.

Here is a summary of the judgments listed in these verses:

children cursed (v. 18); low birth rate (vv. 62–63)

crops ruined and animals killed (vv. 18, 22, 31–32, 38–40, 42, 51)

confusion of mind, madness, and fear (vv. 20, 28–29, 34, 65–69)

sickness (vv. 21–22, 27–28, 35, 59–61)

drought, hunger, and thirst (vv. 22–24, 48)

defeat in war (vv. 25, 49–50, 52)

wives ravished (v. 30)

oppression and slavery (vv. 29, 33, 48, 68)

cannibalism (vv. 53–57)

captivity (vv. 36, 63–64)

corpses not buried (v. 26)

plans shattered (v. 30)

poverty, debt, and nakedness (vv. 44, 48)

robbery (vv. 29, 31, 33)

children kidnapped (vv. 32, 41)

aliens take over the land (v. 43)

shame and scorn (v. 37)

It's quite depressing to read this long list of calamities, especially when you realize that Israel experienced all of them at one time or another and that innocent people suffered because of the sins of the guilty. Not only

Deuteronomy 28, but also Jeremiah's book of Lamentations is a solemn reminder that it doesn't pay to rebel against God and try to have your own way. And what was the reason for all this trouble? "Because you did not serve the LORD your God with joy and gladness of heart, for the abundance of everything" (Deut. 28:47 NKJV). They welcomed the blessings and enjoyed them, but they wouldn't honor the Lord who gave them the blessings (8:11–20). "Because, although they knew God, they did not glorify Him as God, nor were thankful" (Rom. 1:21 NKJV). Idolatry begins with a proud and selfish heart that loves the gifts more than it loves the Giver, and it ends by losing both the Giver and the gifts.

Who is the "nation … from far, from the end of the earth" that will swoop down like the eagle (Deut. 28:49)? In Scripture, the image of the eagle is often used to describe military invasion by different nations, including Babylon (Jer. 48:40; 49:22; Ezek. 17:3), Egypt (v. 7), and Assyria (Hos. 8:1). The Assyrians captured the northern kingdom of Israel in 722 BC and the Babylonians invaded the southern kingdom of Judah in 606 and destroyed Jerusalem and the temple in 586. Thousands of Jews were taken captive to Babylon and forced to live in that land of idols, and this cured them once and for all of idol worship. Perhaps the image in Deuteronomy 28:49 was meant to cover all the invasions that brought chastening to the Jewish people, including the Roman invasion in AD 70. The things described in vv. 49–57 certainly happened during both the Babylonian and the Roman sieges of Jerusalem. Being sold as slaves and not being purchased would be one of the Jews' humiliating experiences during these chastenings (v. 68). Nobody wanted them!

The Jews were not only a disciplined people, they were also a dispersed people (vv. 63–68; 2 Kings 17:6; 25:21). After the Babylonian captivity, in 538 BC they were permitted to return to their land, rebuild Jerusalem, and restore the temple (Ezra 1—6; the book of Haggai), and about 50,000 Jews took advantage of this opportunity. Israel had a temple, a priesthood, and a nation until the Roman invasion in AD 70; and after that, they were again a scattered people, found in almost every nation on earth. They had no homeland, no temple, and no priesthood, yet no matter in what nations they settled, they never lost their national identity. It would not be until May 14, 1948, that Israel would once again become a political entity on the world stage.

During these times of severe suffering, more than one Jew asked the Lord, "Why do Your people suffer when the wicked Gentile nations escape suffering? How can a holy God use godless Gentile nations to chasten His chosen people?" This is one of the themes of the book of Habakkuk, and it is discussed in several psalms (Ps. 74; 77; 79—80). But the fact that Israel is God's chosen people and a special nation explains why He chastens them, for the greater the privilege, the greater the responsibility. "You only have I chosen of all the families of the earth; therefore I will punish you for all your sins" (Amos 3:2 NIV). Divine election isn't an excuse for human rebellion. "For everyone to whom much is given, from him much will be required" (Luke 12:48 NKJV).

There's a sobering message here for the church in today's world. Like Israel of old, we are God's chosen people and a holy nation (1 Peter 2:9–10) and have been greatly blessed in Jesus Christ. We are here to "advertise" the virtues of the Lord and declare the good news of the gospel. If we fail to glorify God and obey His Word, He will chasten us just as He chastened Israel (Heb. 12:1–14). "For the time has come for judgment to begin at the house of God; and if it begins with us first, what will be the end of those who do not obey the gospel of God?" (1 Peter 4:17 NKJV). If God chastens His own people for their sins, what will He do to those who don't belong to the family and have resisted His will? But judgment will begin in God's family, and the only way we can avoid it is to turn from our sins and obey His will.

The church that thought it was rich, Jesus said was poor, and the church that thought it was poor, Jesus said was rich (Rev. 2:9; 3:17). What will Jesus reveal about our churches when the fire of chastening falls?

THE COVENANT RENEWED (29:1–29)

The word *covenant* is used seven times in this chapter; in fact, this chapter is the book of Deuteronomy in miniature. Moses reviewed the past (vv. 1–8), called the people to obey God's law (vv. 9–15), and warned them what would happen if they disobeyed (vv. 16–29). As we read and study Moses' farewell address, we may get weary of these repeated themes, but they are the essence of God's covenant with His people. While the priests and Levites had a copy of the law of Moses and could refer to it (17:18; 28:58; 29:20, 27; 31:26), the common people had to depend on their memories, and therefore repetition was important. "For me to write the same things to you is not tedious, but for you it is safe" (Phil. 3:1 NKJV). Too often God's people forget what they ought to remember and remember what they ought to forget!

The covenant declared in Deuteronomy wasn't different from the covenant given at Mount Sinai. Rather, it was an explanation and application of that covenant to the new generation and their new situation in the Promised Land. If what Moses taught in Deuteronomy had been a separate covenant, he would have offered blood sacrifices to seal the covenant as he did at Sinai (Ex. 24:3–8; Heb. 9:18–22). Many of the people who accepted the covenant at Sinai had perished in the wilderness, but there was still a "nation of Israel" that was accountable to the Lord to obey that covenant (Deut. 4—5). Future generations in Great Britain were both benefited and obligated when King John signed the Magna Carta in 1215, and so were future generations of Americans when the Constitution of the United States went into effect in 1789. Future generations of Jews were bound by the covenant made by their ancestors at Sinai, and that covenant wasn't annulled until Christ died on the cross (Col. 2:11–14).

Reviewing the past (vv. 1–8). Moses never seemed to tire of reminding the people of the grace and mercy of God bestowed on the descendants of Abraham, Isaac, and Jacob. God judged the land of Egypt and delivered Israel from bondage (vv. 2–3), cared for the people in their wilderness journey (vv. 5–6), and gave them victory over the nations east of the Jordan (vv. 7–8). Because of all God did for them, Israel was now on the verge of entering the Promised Land and claiming their inheritance. During their long journey, God kept their shoes and clothing from wearing out,[8] and gave them manna to eat and water to drink. A nomadic people wouldn't be able to harvest grapes for wine or grain for bread.

Calling for obedience (vv. 9–15). The secret of prosperity was the blessing of God, and the secret of receiving that blessing was obedience to God's law. Moses began with the leaders of the nation (v. 10), for if leaders don't set the example as spiritual people, there's not much hope for the followers. However, nobody in the camp was excluded, and this included the women and children, the resident aliens and the lowest servants. God could not truly be God to them if they refused to accept and obey His law. What He does for us depends a great deal on how we relate to Him (2 Cor. 6:14–18). The covenant He made with their fathers would stand forever, but their enjoyment of its promises depended on their obedience to the obligations.

It's important to note that what the Jews did that day affected their descendants in the years to come (Deut. 29:14–15). Just as Israel's decision at Sinai was binding to the new generation on the plains of Moab, so the new generation's decision would be binding to their descendants.

Warning of judgment (vv. 16–29). Moses reminded the people of the gross idolatry they witnessed while enslaved in Egypt and then while traveling through the wilderness. If they witnessed it with hearts devoted to the Lord, they couldn't help but be repulsed by what they saw, and they surely wouldn't want to participate in it. Nobody in Israel—no individual, family, or tribe—was to get involved in idolatry, for any idolater could become a "bitter root" that could defile the whole nation. Hebrews 12:15 applies this same warning to local assemblies of believers, for "one sinner destroys much good" (Eccl. 9:18 NKJV). Even if the offenders kept their sins hidden and were confident that they could escape judgment, the Lord would know and would judge. There could be no forgiveness; they would be plagued and killed, and their names would be blotted out from under heaven (Deut. 9:14; Ex. 32:32–33). They would suffer from all the plagues named in Deuteronomy 28.

If the nation followed the idolaters and disobeyed the Lord, the Lord would judge the whole land, and it would become an example to others of what happens when God's law is violated. Visitors would behold a country without people, farms without produce, land like the devastated land around Sodom and Gomorrah, and cities destroyed and left in ruin. The utter desolation of Israel would be a reminder that it's a costly thing to disobey the will of God.

Will Israel be an obedient people? Would God send these curses? What does the future hold for the nation? Some of the Jews might have been asking themselves those questions, but this was not a time for speculation; it was a time for dedication. "The secret things belong to the LORD our God: but those things which are revealed belong unto us and to our children forever, that we may do all the words of this law" (29:29). Our responsibility as God's people isn't to try to pry open the doors of the future but to obey God's will here and now. When a man asked Jesus, "Lord, are there few that are saved?" His reply was personal and not philosophical. "Strive to enter through the narrow gate, for many, I say to you, will seek to enter and will not be able" (Luke 13:24 NKJV). It's not necessary to know God's secrets, but it is essential that we obey what the Lord has clearly revealed to us.

THE BLESSINGS RESTORED (30:1–20)

So often in Scripture, the thundering voice of judgment is followed by the loving voice of hope. Alas, Israel did forsake the Lord and follow after idols, and the Lord did bring on His people the judgments stated in His covenant. No nation in history has suffered as much as the nation of Israel, and yet no nation has given so much spiritual wealth to the world. In this chapter, Moses looked down through the centuries and saw the future restoration of Israel in their land and under the blessings of God.

Promise (vv. 1–10). "Heart" is one of the key words in this chapter (vv. 2, 6, 10); the others are "command" or "commandment" (vv. 2, 8, 10, 11, 16), "turn" or "return" (vv. 2, 3, 8, 10), and "life" (vv. 15, 19, 20). The connection is obvious: If God's people turn from their sins and return with all their hearts to God and God's commandments and obey them, they will enjoy life as only the Lord can give. Moses is here looking forward to the time when a chastened Israel will repent, turn from their wicked ways, and come back to the Lord.

To some extent, a regathering occurred after the Babylonian captivity, when a believing remnant returned to the land and rebuilt the temple, but the fulfillment of this promise (vv. 3–6) will not take place until the end times. The people of Israel today are scattered throughout the world, while in the nation of Israel there are about six million people. But the Lord promises to regather His people, bring them back to their land, and bless them. But first, a spiritual "operation" must take place, the circumcision of their hearts so that they will receive their Messiah, love their Lord, and experience the spiritual life that He promised.

Bible scholars disagree about the future of Israel. Some say that the church is now "spiritual Israel" and that all of these Old Testament promises are now being fulfilled in a spiritual sense in the church. Others say that the Old Testament promises must be taken at face value and that we should expect a fulfillment of them when Jesus Christ returns to establish His kingdom on earth. Moses seems to be speaking here to and about Israel and not some other "people of God" in the future, such as the church. The church has no covenant relationship to the land of Israel, for God gave that land to Abraham and his descendants (Gen. 15), and the blessings and curses were declared to Israel, not the church. It would appear that there will be a literal fulfillment of these promises to Israel. When they repent, turn back to Jehovah, and open their hearts to the operation of His Spirit (Ezek. 37:1–14; Isa. 11:2; Joel 2:28–29), God will save them from their sins and establish them in Messiah's glorious kingdom (Zech. 12:10—13:1; 14:8–9).

Choice (vv. 11–20). Because we're created in the image of God, we have minds to think with, hearts to feel with, and wills to decide with, and God calls us to make right decisions. We're not robots; we can hear God's Word, learn God's will, and decide either to obey or disobey. Moses made it clear that making this decision isn't a difficult task. After all, we have the revealed truth of God in His Word, and that Word is available to us. We don't have to go up to heaven to get the Word, or even across the sea to another country, because God has brought His Word to us. Paul quoted this passage in Romans 10:6–10 to prove that righteousness isn't obtained by doing great feats but by exercising simple faith in Jesus Christ the Lord.

Furthermore, the choice is between life and death, and who would deliberately choose death? In Israel's case, the choice was between trusting God and enjoying the bounties of the land ("life and good"), or turning to idols and experiencing the curses given in the covenant ("death and evil"). It's either "life and blessing" or "death and cursing." Is this a difficult decision to make? Of course, today the choice is between eternal life and eternal death, salvation by the grace of God or condemnation by the righteousness of God. The only sensible decision is to choose life. "He who believes in the Son has everlasting life; and he who does not believe the Son shall not see life, but the wrath of God abides on him" (John 3:36 NKJV).

Moses called all creation to witness Israel's great opportunity to accept the covenant and enjoy its blessings (Deut. 30:19; 31:28; 32:1; Ps. 50:1; Isa. 1:2). God offered His people life, for God is our life (Deut. 30:20). "For in him we live, and move, and have our being" (Acts 17:28). We receive from Him not only physical life in our first births but also spiritual life through our second births (John 3:1–18).

This marks the end of Moses' farewell address, the review of the law, and the renewal of the covenant. He still has much more to say, and what he says is very important. Then Moses will die, and the Lord will bury him where nobody can find the body. Joshua will then take over and lead Israel to triumph in their Promised Land.

QUESTIONS FOR PERSONAL REFLECTION
OR GROUP DISCUSSION

1. What motivates you to obey God?

2. What was the choice Moses presented to Israel in his farewell message?

3. As the curses for disobedience were read, what did the people's "Amen" signify? What do you think it would have been like to participate in that ceremony? *p 195*

4. What do you make of the fact that God gave an explicit curse for treating the vulnerable with unkindness or injustice? Why was it so important? How important is this matter in your life?

5. Why did the Lord promise incredible blessings for Israel if they would obey? Do any of these promises apply today? Explain.

6. Jesus teaches in Luke 12:48 (NIV) that "from everyone who has been given much, much will be demanded." In what specific areas of life does this hold true?

7. What are some ways Christians today might be chastened?

8. What truths do you think Christians need to be reminded of often?

9. What does it mean to return to God with all your heart?

10. Why would anyone choose death and cursing over life and blessing?

Chapter Eleven

THE SONG OF MOSES

(Deuteronomy 31:14—32:47)

These people will soon prostitute themselves to the foreign gods of the land they are entering" (31:16 NIV).[1]

That's the message the Lord gave Moses after he finished his farewell address to the people he had served so faithfully for forty years.[2] Certainly these words grieved his heart, but Moses knew that Israel had a long history of turning away from the Lord and worshipping idols. At Sinai they had made a golden calf and indulged in a pagan orgy (Ex. 32), and at Kadesh-barnea they wanted to appoint a new leader and return to Egypt (Num. 14). In both rebellions, it was the intercession of Moses that saved the nation from being destroyed by God's judgment. During their wilderness journey, the Jews had frequently complained to Moses about the way he was leading them. When the new generation arrived at the border of Canaan, the men indulged in immorality and idolatry with the women of Moab, and God sent a plague that killed 24,000 Israelites (Num. 25). Israel's history was a tragic story indeed.

How could Moses encourage his beloved people to stay true to their Lord, who had done so much for them? Moses did what God commanded him: He appointed Joshua to be his successor; he gave the people the book of the law and told them how to use it; and he sang them a song of warning. What Moses did to help prevent apostasy in Israel needs to be done to prevent apostasy in the church today, for the church's record isn't much better than that of Israel.[3] We have three responsibilities before the Lord: to honor godly leaders, to hear the Word of God, and to heed the warnings God gives us.

1. HONORING GOD'S SERVANTS (31:1–8, 23)

Moses was 80 years old when God called him to lead His people (Ex. 7:7), and he was now 120, so he had been serving the Lord and His people for forty years. The time had come for him to step aside and let Joshua take over. Moses was still physically fit (Deut. 34:7), but the Lord had told him that, because of his sin at Kadesh, he wouldn't be allowed to enter Canaan (1:37–38; 3:23–27; 4:21–22; Num. 20:1–13). Moses had been a faithful servant in leading the people, delivering God's law to them, and building a nation, but Joshua was the man God chose to lead the army of Israel in conquering the land of Canaan. The phrase "go out and come in" (Deut. 31:2) describes the activities of a leader serving the people (Num. 27:15–17; Josh. 14:11), and Joshua would now be that leader.

Joshua wasn't a stranger to the people of Israel, for he'd been serving them well ever since they left Egypt. He was Moses' servant long before he became Moses' successor (Ex. 33:11; see Matt. 25:21). It was Joshua who led the Jewish army in defeating the Amalekites when they attacked the nation after the exodus (Ex. 17:8–16), and he had been with Moses on Mount Sinai (24:13; 32:17). Joshua was one of the twelve spies who scouted out Canaan, and he and Caleb stood with Moses and Aaron in encouraging the people to trust God and claim the land (Num. 13—14). In answer to Moses' prayer for a leader to succeed him, God appointed Joshua and Moses commissioned him before the whole congregation (27:12–23).

Moses encouraged Joshua by assuring him that God would go before His people and help them conquer the land and destroy the godless nations in Canaan (Deut. 31:3–6, 23). The "charge" in verse 23 is similar to the one the Lord gave Joshua after Moses died (Josh. 1:1–9). Joshua was to duplicate the victories the Lord had given Israel on the east side of the Jordan, when Israel defeated Sihon and Og, which meant destroying the Canaanite nations and everything connected with their religion. It's good to know that the same God who marched ahead of the armies of Israel still helps His people today (Heb. 13:5).

In the work of the Lord, there's no substitute for godly leadership. As Moses did with Joshua, Christ with His apostles, and Paul with Timothy and Titus, the older generation must equip the younger generation to take their place (2 Tim. 2:2). The Lord has given us the qualifications for leaders in the church (1 Tim. 3; Titus 1), and we must give ourselves to mentoring and training qualified people to become those leaders. "The final test of a leader," wrote political columnist Walter Lippmann, "is that he leaves behind him in other men the conviction and the will to carry on." Leaders must not only be qualified, but they must also be prepared and proved (1 Tim. 3:10) so that they aren't novices in serving the Lord (v. 6). The absence of gifted and qualified leaders is sometimes evidence of God's judgment on His people (Isa. 3:1–4, 12; 57:1). The situation is different today, but ancient Israelites would have been humiliated if young people and women were serving in places of leadership. It was the elderly men who had the wisdom and experience to lead the people.

2. HEARING GOD'S WORD (31:9–13, 24–29)

At Mount Sinai, the Lord made it clear to Israel that, unlike the nations around them, they were to be a people of the word who would hear God's voice and obey it. The pagans could see their man-made idols but couldn't hear them speak, because their idols were dead (Ps. 115:1–8). If Israel forsook the living words of the living God and bowed down to dumb idols, they would be living by sight and not by faith and forsaking divine truth for human superstition. It was by the Word that the Lord created the universe, and it is through that same Word that He accomplishes His purposes in history (Ps. 33:6–13).

During his long ministry, Moses had kept a record of what God had done and said (Ex. 17:14; 24:4–8; 34:27; Num. 33:2; Deut. 28:58; 29:20, 27), and he deposited that record with the priests who carried the ark of the covenant. He commanded them to put the book beside the ark in the Holy of Holies, where He was enthroned on the mercy seat between the cherubim (Ps. 80:1 NIV). God rules His world through His Word and God's people must respect His Word and obey it. In future years, Israel's king was required to write a copy of the law, study it, and keep it with him (Deut. 17:18–20). Each Sabbath Year, at the Feast of Tabernacles, the law was to be read and expounded publicly to every man, woman, and child, whether Israelites or strangers, so that they would hear, fear, and obey (Neh. 8). It was especially important that the children hear the word (Deut. 31:13) so they could learn it early and enjoy a long life in the Promised Land.[4]

Moses bluntly told the people what the Lord had told him: They were rebellious and stiff-necked and, after his death, would turn away from the Lord to worship idols (v. 27). When people are stiff-necked, they refuse to bow in reverent submission to the Lord, but harden themselves against the Lord and persist in doing what they want to do. (See Ex. 32:9; 33:3, 5; 34:9; Deut. 9:6, 13; 10:16.) Hearing God's Word, meditating on it, and obeying it was the best remedy against apostasy. Unfortunately, after the death of Moses and Joshua, the people of Israel listened to the false prophets and turned aside from God's truth and practiced idolatry (Judg. 2:6–12). Centuries later, Stephen accused his own nation of being "stiff-necked and uncircumcised in heart and ears" and always resisting the Holy Spirit as He spoke through the Word (Acts 7:51).

There's an important lesson here for the church today, for God has given His people the truth of His Word, and we must guard it, obey it, and pass it along to the next generation. (See 1 Tim. 1:11, 18–19; 6:20; 2 Tim.

1:13–14; 2:2.) The church of Jesus Christ is always one generation short of extinction, so it's important that each believer studies the Scriptures, receives the truth, practices it, and passes it on to others. We need faithful professionals like Ezra the scribe, who "prepared his heart to seek the law of the Lord, and to do it, and to teach in Israel statutes and ordinances" (Ezra 7:10). We also need dedicated and willing lay people like Priscilla and Aquila who can expound the way of the Lord more perfectly to believers who are confused (Acts 18:24–26).

The doctrines of the Christian faith, recorded in Scripture, weren't invented by the early believers but were given by God to His chosen servants. Jude 3 calls this body of sacred truth "the faith which was once for all delivered to the saints" (NKJV). In the local church, we are to teach no other doctrine (1 Tim. 1:3), nor are we to preach anything other than the inspired Word of God (2 Tim. 4:1–5). Paul called this treasure of truth "sound [healthy] doctrine" (1 Tim. 1:10; 2 Tim. 4:3; Titus 1:9; 2:1) and "sound [healthy] words" (2 Tim. 1:13). If we want to have spiritually healthy churches, the saints must feed on "healthy" doctrine; anything else is "vain jangling" (1 Tim. 1:6; 2 Tim. 2:16) and a spreading infection like gangrene (v. 17). While it's a good thing for believers to encourage one another, we must be careful that our "sharing times" promote the truth of the Word and not just what individuals think about the Word.

Local churches must imitate Israel and have special times when they meet together to read the Scriptures and hear them explained. In my own ministry, I've been privileged to address large Bible conferences attended by believers who had only one thing in mind: to hear from God's Word what the Lord wanted them to do. Today, many churches can't hold Bible conferences because the people won't attend. Everybody is too busy, and an hour or two on Sunday morning once a week is all the time they can spare for the Lord. The Word isn't read and taught in homes as once it was, and unless they attend a Christian day school, the children receive Christian education during thirty minutes of Sunday school and perhaps an hour in a midweek club. Is it any wonder that families and churches are drifting farther from the faith?

3. HEEDING GOD'S WARNINGS (31:14–22, 30; 32:1–43)

God instructed Moses to meet Him at the tabernacle and to bring Joshua, his successor, with him. Speaking from the glory cloud, the Lord told the two men that Israel would turn from the true and living God and worship idols ("play the harlot"), and that He would turn away from them and send the judgments named in the covenant (Deut. 28). The cause of their apostasy would be not only the pagan influence around them, but also their own prosperity in the land (31:20). They would forget God the generous Giver and cease to thank Him for His goodness. If the nation obeyed God and served Him joyfully, His face would shine upon them (Num. 6:22–27), but if they turned to idols, God would hide His face from His people and chasten them.

The Lord instructed Moses and Joshua[5] to write down a song that He would give them, a song that the people could easily learn and remember. This song would warn the new generation and generations to come against the perils of idolatry and the tragic consequences of apostasy. It would also remind them of the goodness and mercy of the Lord. After Moses and Joshua wrote down the song (Deut. 31:19), they taught it to the leaders (v. 28) and to all the congregation (v. 30).[6] Moses prefaced the song with the solemn reminder that, after his death, they would abandon the Lord and thereby invite the chastening of the Lord. This sounds something like Joshua's farewell speech to the officers and the people (Josh. 23—24), and Paul's last words to the Ephesian elders (Acts 20:17–37).

The song has four major divisions: the character of God (Deut. 32:1–4); the kindness of God to His people (vv. 5–14); the faithfulness of God to chasten His people (vv. 15–25); and the vengeance of God against

His adversaries (vv. 26–43). The song traces God's dealings with Israel and is a concise review of the nation's history, from their wilderness sojourn to the judgments in the end times. It has both historic and prophetic aspects.

(1) The character of God (32:1–4). Moses did the speaking, although Joshua was with him (vv. 44–45 NIV), and he opened the song with two interesting images: a courtroom (v. 1) and a rain shower (v. 2). He called heaven and earth to bear witness to his words (30:19; 31:28), for the song would indict Israel for turning away from their God and breaking the covenant. This was the most serious offense the people could commit. Everything in creation obeys the Lord except His own people! (See Ps. 119:89–91; 148:5–9; Isa. 1:1–3.) But Moses didn't call for a storm; he gave his message as a quiet shower, trusting that the Word would soften the hard soil and produce fruit in the hearts of the people (Isa. 55:10–11). "Speaking the truth in love" (Eph. 4:15) is the best way to proclaim God's Word.

Learning the character of God should be our major concern in the school of life, and Moses was a star pupil (Ex. 33:12—34:9; Ps. 90). To the Jew, the name of the Lord was "Jehovah," the name God revealed to Moses at the burning bush (Ex. 3:13–15). Moses didn't proclaim his own name, for he was a humble man (Num. 12:3); his desire was to honor the name of the Lord. The other "Song of Moses" (Ex. 15) also magnifies the attributes of God. In two brief verses, Moses ascribes to the Lord perfection, greatness, justice, truth, faithfulness, and righteousness, and he describes Him as "the Rock" (Deut. 32:4, 15, 30–31). This is a familiar biblical image for God that speaks of Him as stable, strong, unchanging, faithful, and enduring. Jacob called Him "the stone" (Gen. 49:24), and Jesus is frequently spoken of as "the Stone" or "the Rock" (Matt. 21:42–44; Acts 4:11; Rom. 9:32–33; 1 Peter 2:4, 7–8; see Dan. 2).

At the very beginning of the song, Moses focused their attention on the greatness of God, for if they understood His greatness, the people wouldn't want to worship man-made idols. A. W. Tozer used to remind us that "no religion has ever been greater than its idea of God."[7] He also said, "The first step down for any church is taken when it surrenders its high opinion of God."[8]

(2) The kindness of God to His people (vv. 5–14). You would think that Israel would have exalted such a great God and counted it a privilege to know Him and serve Him, but they didn't. Instead, they turned to idols and corrupted themselves and blemished their own name and standing. "When they act so perversely, are they really his children? They are a deceitful and twisted generation" (v. 5 NLT). What a way to repay their Father for all He had done for them![9] We expect unconverted people to be twisted and corrupt (Phil. 2:15), but not the people of God (Matt. 17:17; Luke 9:41).

One more time, Moses invited the people to remember what God had done for them in "the days of old." The younger ones could ask the older people what they remembered, because it's the responsibility of older believers to teach the younger (Ps. 78:5–8). The Lord is the God of history and geography; He divided the nations (Gen. 10) and put them on the earth where He wanted them (Acts 17:26). But He had a special plan for Israel, for they were His own people; and He made sure that they had a land adequate for them.[10] The drama of salvation would be enacted in the land of Israel, so that land was very special to the Lord.

The Lord delivered Israel from Egypt and then came to them in the wilderness at Sinai. They were a helpless people and He claimed them for Himself. They were "the apple of his eye," referring to the pupil of the eye (Ps. 17:8; Prov. 7:2; Zech. 2:8).[11] Moses used the image of the eagle to illustrate God's care for His people (Deut. 32:11–13a). At a certain stage in the lives of the young, the parents destroy the nest and force the young to fly. To make sure the young don't fall, the adult birds stay close to the young as they "try their wings," flying beneath them and even carrying them in their strong claws. It's a beautiful picture of the difficult process of maturity that God puts all of us through just as He did the nation of

Israel. Israel was made to "ride on the high places" (v. 13) and not grovel in the mire like the pagans. Every experience they had during their wilderness journey was another opportunity for them to grow up, but too often they regressed and acted like babies.

Israel's enjoying the land of Canaan is the theme of verses 13b–14. God gave them a rich land, one that produced honey out of the rocks and in which olive trees could thrive in stony soil and produce much oil. Flocks and herds multiplied in the pastures and the fruit and grain prospered in the fields, orchards, and vineyards.[12] Indeed, the Lord gave them a good land and nothing was lacking.

(3) The faithfulness of God to chasten His people (vv. 15–25). Moses warned the people that their undeserved prosperity in the land would tempt them to become proud and forget the Lord (Deut. 8), and then He would have to chasten them, and that's exactly what happened. "Jeshurun" is a nickname for Israel (33:5, 26; Isa. 44:2) and means "the upright one." As far as their standing before God was concerned, "He has not observed iniquity in Jacob, nor has He seen wickedness in Israel" (Num. 23:21 NKJV), but when it came to their conduct, God stood ready to chasten His beloved people for not living up to their standing. He has a similar problem with the church today, for we don't always walk worthy of our high calling (Eph. 4:1ff.).

God's "jealousy" is that of a loving, faithful husband whose wife has betrayed him. (This is the story in the book of Hosea, and see Jer. 2:25.) To worship idols is to worship demons (1 Cor. 10:20), so Israel was not only grieving the Lord but also playing right into the hands of the wicked one. They forgot their Rock, who was both their Father ("who begot you") and their Mother ("who formed you," i.e., "gave you birth"). The Jewish people are His "sons and daughters" (Deut. 32:19). Their attitudes and actions prevented Him from loving them as He longed to do, so He had to show His love by chastening them.

Since they moved Him to jealousy by following other gods, He decided to move them to jealousy by blessing and using other nations (v. 21; Hos. 1). Historically, this refers to God using various Gentile nations to chasten Israel in their land (the book of Judges), and then Babylon to take them into captivity. But prophetically it refers to God calling the Gentiles to salvation after Israel had turned against the message of the gospel (Rom. 10; 11:11ff.). Today, God wants to use the church to make Israel jealous of the spiritual blessing that we have that the Jews once had (9:1–5; 11:13–14). We're to "advertise His virtues" (1 Peter 2:9) so that the lost will long to share in the blessings we have in Christ. It's sad to see words like fire, arrows, hunger, fever, beasts, serpents, swords, and calamities ("mischiefs," KJV) applied to God's special people, but those were the judgments He sent them (Lev. 26:14ff.). After the Roman conquest in AD 70, the nation was scattered, and today we find Jewish people all over the world.

(4) The vengeance of God against His adversaries (vv. 26–43). On two previous occasions, the Lord had threatened to destroy His people, and Moses reminded Him of His covenant promises and of the fact that the Gentile nations were watching (Ex. 32:11–14; Num. 14:11–25). If God destroyed Israel, the Gentiles would say, "Their God isn't strong enough to take them into their land and care for them!" Moses was concerned about the glory of the Lord as well as the good of the nation. God knew that the Gentiles would boast about defeating and humiliating Israel, so He intervened and saved His people (Ezek. 20:8–29). He also severely punished the Gentile nations because they went too far and were cruel in their treatment of the Jews (Jer. 50:10–13, 17). It was the Lord who permitted Assyria and Babylon to capture His people, and the nations acted as though they were the great conquerors.

The reason for Israel's plight was not the strength of their enemies but their own lack of wisdom (Deut. 32:28–29; Isa. 1:3). They possessed the Scriptures that recorded the covenants, and all they had to do was obey God's laws and He would have blessed them. Those same Scriptures predicted the coming of their Messiah, yet when He arrived, Israel didn't know Him (John 1:26). Today there is a veil over their hearts when they read the Old Testament, and they cannot see Christ in their Scriptures (2 Cor. 3:12–18; Rom. 11:25–36; John 5:39).

If Israel had been faithful to the Lord, He would have given them victory over their enemies, and one Jewish soldier would have been worth twenty or even a hundred enemy soldiers (Lev. 26:6–8). Alas, their rebellion caused their Rock to "sell them" to the enemy, even though the enemy had nothing compared to what Israel had in Jehovah (Deut. 32:31–33). Their gods (rock) were certainly not like the living God of Israel, and their vine (nation) wasn't planted, as was Israel in the land (Isa. 5). To eat the enemy's grapes and drink their wine was to be poisoned, yet Israel worshipped their gods! "They are a nation void of counsel" (Deut. 32:28).

God doesn't overlook the evil deeds of Israel's enemies but has His weapons ready so that He can vindicate His people (vv. 34–35). "This" in verse 34 refers to God's vengeance on the enemies of Israel and of God, something He had planned long ago. Here we have God presented as the righteous Warrior who will defeat Israel's enemies and at the same time judge ("vindicate") His own people and have compassion on them ("repent himself," v. 36). This is a message of hope for Israel, for His chastening is the first step toward restoring His people and returning to them the blessings that they forfeited when they turned to idols.[13] The false gods that they trusted won't be able to help Israel, but the Lord will show His great power on behalf of His helpless people and deliver them from the Enemy. We may have in verses 39–43 a description of the battle of Armageddon (see Rev. 14:17–20; 16:12–16). We have no record in Scripture or in history of any special time of vengeance when God vindicated the Jews by defeating the Gentile nations, so this prophecy has yet to be fulfilled.

The thrust of the closing section of the song (Deut. 32:34–43) is the ultimate vindication of Israel before the Gentile nations that have attacked her, humiliated her, and abused her. To some extent Israel was vindicated when Babylon was taken by Darius the Mede and the Jews were allowed to return to their land, but surely these verses describe something far more extensive and dramatic than that event. The vivid language makes us think of the Old Testament descriptions of the day of the Lord and the slaughter that will take place (Isa. 2:10–21; Amos 5:18–20; Zeph. 1:7–18). While it will be a day of judgment on the Gentiles for the way they have treated Israel (Joel 3:1–3), it will also be a time of refining for Israel; and in the end, they will see their Messiah, repent, and be converted (Zech. 9—14).

Moses closed the song, Joshua standing with him, by appealing to the people to take the message to heart and teach the song to their children, so that future generations would obey the law and avoid idolatry. (See Deut. 4:9–10; 6:7; 11:19; Ex. 10:2; 12:26.) The Word of God is the life of God's people, just as God is our life (Deut. 30:20), for the Word communicates to us the truth about God and His gracious blessings. To receive and obey the Word is to share in the life of God. "They are not just idle words for you—they are your life" (32:47 NIV). "For the word of God is living and powerful" (Heb. 4:12 NKJV).

QUESTIONS FOR PERSONAL REFLECTION
OR GROUP DISCUSSION

1. How did Moses try to encourage the Israelites to remain faithful to the Lord?

2. Why is godly leadership so important in preventing a church from drifting away from commitment to the Lord?

3. Why is idolatry a symptom of living by sight instead of faith?

4. What does it mean to be stiff-necked?

5. Besides church on Sunday morning, what do you do to grow in your understanding of the Word and sound doctrine? How have you tried to encourage others to grow in this?

6. What songs remind you of God's goodness and mercy? What song warns you of the consequence of disobedience? Why does music often work so powerfully in people?

7. What would you say is your "major concern in the school of life"?

8. Why is learning God's character vital to a well-lived life?

9. How can God's faithfulness be seen in His chastening of Israel?

10. What does it mean to say that the Word of God is the life of God's people? If a person doesn't find it life-giving, what would you recommend?

Chapter Twelve

THE END
OF AN ERA

(Deuteronomy 32:48—34:12)

S o teach us to number our days, that we may apply our hearts unto wisdom" (Ps. 90:12). Moses wrote those words probably after the great crisis at Kadesh-barnea, when Israel rebelled against God and He numbered the days of the older generation (Num. 13—14). But Moses was now numbering his hours, for it would soon be time to leave the camp of Israel, climb Mount Nebo, and surrender into the loving arms of God to be put to sleep. Moses left the camp and left this life, but he also left behind some wonderful gifts for his people and for us today.

A BLESSING FOR ISRAEL (33:1–29)

The "Song of Moses" had been a lesson in theology, history, and personal obedience, with several strong warnings included, but the final blessing Moses bestowed on his people is saturated with grace and mercy. It's quite a contrast to the "blessing" Jacob gave his sons before he died (Gen. 49), revealing their hidden character and exposing sin.[1] Moses opened and closed his speech by extolling the greatness of the Lord he was about to meet on top of the mount (Deut. 33:1–5, 26–29), and then he named each tribe except Simeon[2] and gave them a blessing from the Lord. Moses wrote and spoke of himself in the third person (vv. 1, 4), the same way David spoke to the Lord in 2 Samuel 7:20 when he was so overwhelmed by the promises of God. Both Moses and David were like little children, who often use their own names when speaking to adults.

The glory of God (vv. 1–5). As Moses looked back over his long life, the one scene that gripped his mind was the revelation of God's glory at Mount Sinai (Ex. 19:16–25; 24:15–18; Heb. 12:18–21) and the giving of the law. But he had seen God's glory up close when he had been on the mount interceding with the Lord (Ex. 33—34). This same description is used in Deborah's song in Judges 5:4–5, and also by the prophet Habakkuk as he praised the Lord (Hab. 3:3). The better we know the Word of God, the more able we are to express proper worship to Him. There is no substitute for "psalms and hymns and spiritual songs" (Eph. 5:19; Col. 3:16) that are founded on Scripture.

God came from[3] the myriad of angels in heaven to meet with sinful Israel! Why? Because "he loved the people" (Deut. 33:3). Throughout the book of Deuteronomy, Moses has emphasized God's special love for Israel and His grace in choosing them to be His special people (4:31–40; 7:6, 13; 14:2; 26:19; 28:9). God's sovereign grace and love are never reasons for pride on the part of sinful people. Rather, they are truths that should humble us and make us want to serve Him with all our hearts. The "saints" (holy ones) in 33:2 are the angels, but the "saints" in verse 3 are the people of Israel, God's set-apart ones, Jeshurun "the upright one." In spite of their frequent disobedience, Israel is seen by God as His special people. "He has not observed iniquity in Jacob, nor has He seen wickedness in Israel" (Num. 23:21 NKJV). There was much sin in the Corinthian church, yet Paul addressed the people as "saints" (1 Cor. 1:1–2). Our standing before God is that of being righteous in Jesus Christ (2 Cor. 5:21), but our present state in this world is that of being tempted and frequently failing. The victorious Christian life means living up to our standing through faith in the power of God.

Moses describes our exalted position because of God's grace: loved by God, secure in His hand, and submissive at His feet (Deut. 33:3). We also dwell between His shoulders (v. 12) and have His everlasting arms beneath us (v. 27). No wonder Moses exclaimed, "Who is like unto thee, O people saved by the LORD" (v. 29). Moses didn't see the law as a burden from God but as a rich inheritance (v. 4). Israel would inherit a good land, but their greatest inheritance was the Word of God that nourished them, protected them, and guided them. "Your testimonies I have taken as a heritage forever, for they are the rejoicing of my heart" (Ps. 119:111 NKJV). Unlike the nations around them, Israel didn't have a human king ruling the people, for God was their King, and His throne was the mercy seat on the ark of the covenant (Deut. 33:5; Ps. 80:1 NIV). How tragic that later Israel asked for a king and put their faith in the arm of flesh (Deut. 17:14–20; 1 Sam. 8—9).

God's blessings for the tribes (vv. 6–25). God saw not only the entire nation, the people of Israel, but He also saw the individual tribes and assigned blessings to them. Like the high priest, the Lord carried the names of the tribes individually over His heart (Ex. 28:15–30). We've already noted that Simeon is not mentioned, but all the other tribes are, including Joseph along with his two sons Ephraim and Manasseh. The order is:

Reuben, Judah, Levi—sons of Leah (Deut. 33:6–11)

Benjamin, Joseph—sons of Rachel (vv. 12–17)

Ephraim, Manasseh—sons of Joseph (v. 17)

Zebulun, Issachar—sons of Leah (vv. 18–19)

Gad—son of Zilpah (vv. 20–21)

Dan, Naphtali—sons of Bilhah (vv. 22–23)

Asher—son of Zilpah (vv. 24–25)

Since Reuben (v. 6) was Jacob's firstborn, he's mentioned first, although Reuben's sin (Gen. 35:22) cost him the rights of the firstborn (49:3–4), which were then given to Joseph (1 Chron. 5:1–2). But Moses says nothing about this! Jacob said that the tribe wouldn't excel, but Moses prayed that the tribe would live, i.e., grow and prosper. Hebrew students don't agree on the translation of the last clause. Is it "nor let his men be few" or "and let his men be few"? Is he asking blessing or judgment? In spite of his sin against his father, Reuben interceded for Joseph (Gen. 37:19–22; 42:22) and was willing to provide his sons as surety for Benjamin (42:37). The Reubenites settled with Gad and Manasseh in the territory east of the Jordan, but they marched at the head of the army in conquering Canaan (Josh. 4:12) and didn't return to their own land until after the conquest was completed (22:1–9). Between the first and second censuses in Numbers (Num. 1 and 26), Reuben lost 2,770 men, but the tribe had a reputation for being courageous soldiers (1 Chron. 5:10). It's interesting that no great civil or military leader or prophet ever came from the tribe of Reuben.

Judah (Deut. 33:7) was the royal tribe (Gen. 49:10), but it was also a military tribe, for the men of Judah marched at the front of the army during the nation's journeys (Num. 2:9). Moses prayed that God would hear Judah's prayers, give them victory on the battlefield, and bring their armies back home safely.

The tribe of Levi (Deut. 33:8–11) was set apart to be the priestly tribe (priests and Levites), and the Levites assisted the priests at the sanctuary. Jacob linked Simeon and Levi (Gen. 49:5–7) and announced that, because of their sins, these two tribes would be scattered in Israel. Simeon became a part of Judah, and the Levites lived in forty-eight special cities assigned to them (Josh. 21). Scattering the Levites turned out to be a blessing for the Jews because the Levites knew and taught the law and could instruct the people. Oddly enough, dying Jacob said nothing about the spiritual ministry of Levi's descendants.

The priests had the Urim and Thummim (Ex. 25:7; 28:30), which were probably two precious stones kept in the high priest's breastplate and used to determine the will of God (1 Sam. 23:6–9). The "holy one" in Deuteronomy 33:8 ("the man you favored," NIV) is probably Moses, who with Aaron came from the tribe of Levi. Moses was sorely tested at Massah (Ex. 17:1–7) and at Meribah (Num. 20:1–13), and the priests and Levites stood with him. It was the Levites who slew the idolaters after the golden calf episode (Ex. 32:25–29), showing their zeal for the Lord. They put obeying God's will ahead of their love for their own families and their own nation (see Matt. 10:37; Luke 14:26). It would be the privilege and responsibility of the priests to guard and use the Urim and Thummim, teach the people the law, and be in charge of worship at the sanctuary. Moses prayed that the tribe of Levi—his own tribe—would be given strength for their many ministries and be protected from their enemies.

Jacob's youngest son, Benjamin (Deut. 33:12), was greatly beloved by his father (Gen. 35:18; 44:20) and also beloved of the Lord and protected by the Lord. The little tribe of Benjamin was situated adjacent to Judah's northern boundary, and the city of Jerusalem was on the northern border of Judah and the southern border of Benjamin. Since the sanctuary would be at Jerusalem, Benjamin would be close to the Lord, who dwelt there with His people. Like a father caring for a son, God would carry Benjamin on His back, between his shoulders,[4] and shelter him from danger. The men of Benjamin had quite a reputation as warriors (Judg. 5:14).

More space is devoted to Joseph, Ephraim, and Manasseh (Deut. 33:13–17) than to any other tribe, but Jacob followed the same pattern (Gen. 49:22–26). Jacob had given the rights of the firstborn to Joseph and had also made his younger son Ephraim firstborn over Manasseh (Gen. 48). Moses blessed Joseph with "precious [choice] things" in terms of plenty of water, good land, fruitful harvests, and valuable timber and minerals from the hills and mountains. He spoke of the "sun and moon" because these were the lights God put in charge of the seasons (1:14). The one who "dwelt in the bush" (Deut. 33:16) was the Lord Himself when He appeared to Moses (Ex. 3). The phrase "separated from his brethren" can also be translated "a prince among his brethren." This was true not only literally in Egypt but also spiritually and morally in the family. He was a godly man.

Moses compared Joseph and his sons ("his glory") to a beautiful first-born bull with sharp horns that defeat every enemy. The word "firstborn" ("firstling") is significant, because Joseph inherited the blessing of the first-born when Jacob rejected Reuben, and Ephraim was made firstborn over his brother Manasseh. The tribes of Ephraim and Manasseh were known for their fruitful lands, their large flocks and herds, and their military power. Unfortunately, they were proud of their ancestry and occasionally refused to cooperate with the other tribes and thereby created problems for the nation.

Zebulun and Issachar (Deut. 33:18–19) are described as two tribes who will receive rich blessing from land and sea. Jacob identified Zebulun with the sea (Gen. 49:13) and Issachar with the land (vv. 14–15), although Issachar was near the Sea of Galilee and Zebulun just a few miles from the Mediterranean Sea. The two phrases "going out" and "in your tents" cover all of daily life: going out to work, coming home to rest. Moses was blessing every aspect of their lives, what we might call the "routine tasks of life." The picture in Deuteronomy 33:19 is that of worship followed by a communal feast, but the Jews had to bring their sacrifices to the central sanctuary where they could enjoy family feasts. Some think it's a picture of the two tribes sharing their bounties with their brothers and sisters and giving thanks to God for His generosity, a Jewish version of a family picnic.

The tribe of Gad (vv. 20–21) was located east of the Jordan (3:12–16) with Reuben and Manasseh. Moses knew that Gad had chosen the best land for their flocks and herds. But Gad was also a brave tribe that sent warriors into Canaan to help conquer the land (Josh. 1:12–18; 4:12–18;

22:1–4). When Israel defeated the nations east of the Jordan, Gad took a "lion's share" for themselves.

Comparing Dan (Deut. 33:22) to "a lion's whelp" suggests that the tribe wasn't quite mature yet, but it showed great promise and had great strength. A lion's cub grows up to be a lion! The second clause has been translated "he shies away from the viper." Jacob compared Dan to a serpent (Gen. 49:16–17), and the serpent and the lion are both associated with Satan (Gen. 3; Rev. 12:9, 14–15; 20:2; 1 Peter 5:8). The tribe of Dan became idolatrous and apostate (Judg. 17—18).

Naphtali (Deut. 33:23) is promised the fullness of the Lord's blessing and expansion to the south, where the Sea of Galilee is located, and the west, toward the Mediterranean Sea. Barak came from this tribe, and soldiers from Naphtali assisted him and Deborah (Judg. 5:18) and Gideon (7:23). Naphtali is mentioned in messianic prophecy (Isa. 9:1; Matt. 4:13–16).

The name Asher (Deut. 33:24–25) means "blessed," and Moses asked that the Lord bless the tribe with many children, the favor of his brothers, and great prosperity. To use precious olive oil on your feet would be a mark of wealth, and Asher's territory was blessed with many olive groves. The word translated "shoes" is also translated "bolts," referring to strong security at the city gates. So, the tribe would enjoy fertility, brotherly love, prosperity, and security, and the Lord would give them daily strength to accomplish their work. What more could they want?

The happiness of God's people (vv. 26–29). These are the last written words of Moses, and they focus on the happiness of the people of God because of His blessings. As Moses finished blessing the tribes, he visualized the whole nation and the joy Israel ought to have because they know the true and living God. Their God isn't a dead idol sitting in a temple; He rides the heavens to come to the aid of His people! (Ps. 18:10; 68:33.) But even more, God is Israel's "home" and dwelling place (see 90:1), and they abide in Him no matter where they go. As we go forward by faith, He defeats the Enemy and holds us up in the battle.

Israel would face many enemies and fight many battles as they conquered the Promised Land, but God would give them victory. They would dwell in a safe and productive land, separated from the pagan nations but bearing witness to them about the God of Israel. God would be their helper, their shield, and their sword, so they had nothing to fear. Israel's greatest danger wasn't the armies around them so much as the appetites within them. Their hearts needed to be weaned away from their love for idols and the sins associated with idol worship. In the end, the Jews accepted and worshipped the gods of the nations they defeated, and this led to the spiritual and moral decay of the nation. Instead of "treading on their high places" (Deut. 33:29), Israel sank lower and lower into the pits of sin, until God had to send them into captivity.

A WARNING FOR GOD'S SERVANTS (34:1–8)

The imminent death of Moses is a repeated theme in these closing chapters (31:1–2, 14, 16, 26–29; 32:48–52; 33:1; 34:1–8, 10, 12). Moses knew what was coming, for death is an appointment (Heb. 9:27), not an accident. Moses had begun his ministry as a lonely shepherd, caring for his sheep near Horeb (Sinai), the mountain of God (Ex. 3), and now he would end his ministry, leaving his sheep with Joshua and going up Mount Nebo alone to meet God.

But the emphasis in these verses isn't so much his death as the fact that the Lord couldn't allow him to enter the Promised Land because of his rash sin at Kadesh (Num. 20). Instead of speaking to the rock, Moses struck the rock in anger and said, "Listen, you rebels, must we bring you water out of this rock?" (v. 10 NIV). His attitude, his actions (hitting the rock), and his words were all generated by the flesh and not the Spirit and were intended to glorify him and Aaron and not the Lord. Moses did not sanctify God in what he said and did, and for this he was kept out of the Promised Land (Deut. 1:37–40; Num. 20:12–13). He prayed earnestly that the Lord would change His mind, but the Lord refused to do so (Deut. 3:23–26; the verb indicates that Moses had often prayed this prayer). On Mount Nebo, Moses was perhaps six miles from the border of the Promised Land, but the Lord wouldn't allow him to go in.

Was the punishment greater than the offense? Not at all. "Any offense of Moses cannot be a small offense," said Alexander Maclaren. Moses was the leader of God's own people; he was the lawgiver and the architect of the Jewish nation and the Jewish religion. He knew that the greater the privileges, the greater the responsibilities. In what he did, Moses failed to glorify God, and for that sin he had to suffer chastening. God in His grace forgives our sins, but God in His government allows our sins to work out their sad consequences in our lives.

God gave Moses the ability to view the whole land, with Naphtali on the north, Ephraim and Manasseh in the central area, and Judah, the Negev, and Zoar in the south. The Lord assured Moses that he would keep His covenant with the patriarchs and give Israel this wonderful land. However, all was not lost, for Moses did arrive in the Holy Land centuries later when he and Elijah joined Jesus in glory on the Mount of Transfiguration (Matt. 17:1–3; Luke 9:28–31). Moses even talked with the Lord Jesus about "His decease [exodus]" that He would accomplish on the cross at Jerusalem. (Moses knew something about an exodus!)

After viewing the land, Moses died and the Lord and the archangel Michael (Jude 9) buried him on Mount Nebo, in a grave that nobody could ever locate or identify. What the dispute was between Michael and the Devil isn't explained anywhere in Scripture. The main reason Jude mentioned this strange event was to refute those who speak evil of dignitaries (vv. 8, 10), something that even a holy archangel wouldn't do, though the "dignitary" was Satan himself! This event is not recorded in Scripture;

it comes from an apocryphal book called *The Assumption of Moses*. Michael has a special ministry to the Jewish nation (Dan. 10:13, 21; 12:1) and is also an enemy of Satan, because Satan wants to destroy the Jewish people (Rev. 12:7–9). The name Michael means "Who is like God?" and Satan had said, "I will be like the Most High" (Isa. 14:14). Did Satan want to use Moses' dead body to create problems in the Jewish nation that was about to invade his strongholds in Canaan? Could he tempt the Jews to worship their dead leader? We don't know, and it's useless to speculate.

Moses died "according to the word of the LORD" (Deut. 34:5), and that should be the goal of every believer. The death of God's saints is very precious to Him (Ps. 116:15), and therefore He'll not permit it to happen by accident, unless the believer is rebelling against His will. The days that God has "ordained for [us]" are written down (139:16 NIV), and though we can't live beyond them, we can by our foolishness and sin hasten our own deaths.

AN EXAMPLE FOR GOD'S SERVANTS (34:9–12)

There were times when Moses complained to God because his work was difficult, and more than once he was ready to quit, but in spite of these very human weaknesses, Moses was a faithful servant. In fact, in the matter of faithfulness, Moses is even compared with Christ (Heb. 3:1–6).

Moses was faithful to walk with God, and he spoke to God as a man speaks to his friend (Ex. 33:11; Num. 12:7–8). The secret of his life wasn't his own abilities—he claimed he had none—or even his education in Egypt (Acts 7:22), but his humble walk with the Lord. He spent time with God, he listened to God's Word, and he followed God's orders.

Another exemplary thing about Moses was his devotion to his people. On two occasions, God offered to wipe out the Jewish people and begin a new nation with Moses, and Moses rejected the offer (Ex. 32:9–14; Num. 14:10–25). Moses was a true shepherd who was willing to lay down his life for his sheep (Ex. 32:30–35). Too many so-called "Christian leaders" are really only hirelings who do their work for what they can get out of it (John 10:12–14). When there's trouble or danger, the hireling flees to a safe place, but the true shepherd flees to the Lord for the strength needed to get the job done.

Moses was a faithful intercessor. Many times he fell on his face and pleaded with God not to judge the people, and on the mountain, he prayed until he was certain the Lord would go with them on their journey. Like the apostles, Moses was a man who focused on "prayer and the ministry of the word" (Acts 6:4). As Jesus with His apostles, he taught the people the Word and then he prayed for them to receive it and grow.

The Lord prepared Moses for his ministry and took eighty years to do it. He was raised as a prince in Egypt and taught all that the wise men in Egypt knew. Some scholars believe that Moses was in line to be the next Pharaoh. Yet Moses gave all this up to identify with the people of God in their suffering (Heb. 11:24–27). God gave Moses a forty-year "post-graduate course" as a shepherd in the land of Midian, a strange place for a man with all the learning of Egypt in his mind. But there were lessons to be learned in solitude and silence, and in taking care of ignorant sheep, that Moses could never have learned in the university in Egypt. God has different ways of training His servants, and each person's training is tailor-made by the Lord.

In many respects, Moses comes across as a very Christlike person. Like Jesus, he was born into a godly home at a difficult time in Jewish history, and like Jesus, his life was threatened. When Moses gave up the treasures of Egypt, it was like Jesus, who became poor that He might share spiritual riches with many (2 Cor. 8:9). Like Jesus, Moses was rejected by his people when he tried to help them the first time (Ex. 2:11–15), but he was accepted by them when he came to them the second time (4:29–31; Acts 7:23–36). Israel rejected Christ at His first coming, but they will receive Him when He comes again (Zech. 12:10—13:1).

Moses was a meek man, and Jesus said, "I am meek and lowly in heart" (Matt. 11:28–30). Moses finished the work God gave him to do (Ex. 39:42–43; 40:33) and so did the Son of God (John 17:4). Before He returned to heaven, Jesus left trained disciples behind to continue the work of world evangelism, and Moses left Joshua and the elders behind to guide the people in the ways of the Lord. Our Lord's face shone on the Mount of Transfiguration, and Moses' face shone when he came down from meeting God on the mount (Matt. 17:2; Ex. 34:29–30). Moses was "mighty in words and deeds" (Acts 7:22), and so was Jesus when He was ministering on earth (Luke 24:19).

The only perfect example is Jesus Christ, but when we read about Moses, he reminds us of our Lord and encourages us to become more like our Savior in all things.

QUESTIONS FOR PERSONAL REFLECTION
OR GROUP DISCUSSION

1. What, if anything, enables you to focus on God's glory as something real?

2. Moses described our exalted position (through God's grace) as loved by God, secure in His hand, and submissive at His feet. How real are these truths in your mind and life?

3. Moses communicated God's blessings to the tribes of Israel. If you were to bless a child who is special to your heart, what would you say?

4. What were the Urim and Thummim, and what were they used for? How can we determine the will of God?

5. How should knowing the living and true God affect the way we live?

6. Idolatry was Israel's greatest danger. What do you feel is your greatest danger?

7. What does Wiersbe mean when he says "death is an appointment (Heb. 9:27), not an accident"? What do you believe about the timing of death?

8. Why is it that people often fail in the area of their strengths? What is your area of strength? Where might you be vulnerable because of that strength?

9. What was the secret to Moses' faithfulness?

10. What preparation did the Lord use to get Moses ready for ministry? How has the Lord been preparing you for ministry?

Chapter Thirteen

LEARNING TO REMEMBER— REMEMBERING TO LEARN

(Review of Deuteronomy)

M y memory is nearly gone," wrote John Newton at age eighty-two, "but I remember two things: that I am a great sinner, and that Christ is a great Savior."

That's the purpose Moses had in mind when he delivered the addresses we call the book of Deuteronomy: He wanted the people to remember the things that were really important. If they would remember who they were—sinners saved by God's grace and power—and what God had done for them, they would be able to enter the new land triumphantly, defeat their enemies, avoid the dangerous temptations all around them, and enjoy the inheritance God prepared for them.

We can review the major lessons of Deuteronomy by noting what Moses tells us to remember.

"REMEMBER THE LORD" (8:18)

The Word of God was given so that we might better know the God of the Word.[1] Everything that Moses declared to the people was a revelation of the mind and heart of God. Each law, each ceremony, each prohibition, and each memory of past events pointed to Jehovah, the God of the Israelites. In mighty deeds of power and gracious words of truth, the Lord had revealed Himself to Israel as He did to no other nation, and Moses recorded these words and deeds for us to read today. The knowledge of God is life's most important knowledge.

Israel was to remember that the Lord was one Lord (6:4). They lived in a world of superstitious idolatry in which each nation had its own gods and goddesses, and when you moved from nation to nation, you changed your gods! But the people of Israel believed that there was one supreme God, the true and living God, whose name was Jehovah—"I am that I am." The first commandment said, "Thou shalt have no other gods before me" (Ex. 20:3), and the second commandment prohibited the Jews from making an image of their God or of any other thing in the universe that they might worship as a god.

This one Lord is the Creator of all things and possesses unlimited power. He demonstrated that power in sending the plagues to Egypt and then opening the Red Sea so that Israel could depart. He revealed His glory at Mount Sinai, but He also revealed His grace and mercy as He entered into a covenant with Israel (Deut. 4:32, 37). The Lord is the faithful God who keeps His word and will not be false to His people. The God of Israel loves His people and wants them to love Him. He is jealous over His people (v. 24; 5:9), the way a husband is jealous over his wife.

The God of Israel is the God who chastens His people if they disobey Him. His covenant makes it clear that He will bless when His people obey Him and send chastening when they disobey Him, and both activities are evidences of His love and faithfulness. In His mercy, He will forgive if the people repent and return to Him, but He will not tolerate rebellion.

God declares His Word through chosen servants like Moses, and He expects His people to listen to the Word, remember it, and obey it. Just as Israel is a people of the Word, so the church today is a people of the Word. Our faith isn't something that we manufactured ourselves, because it was graciously given to us in the Word of the Lord. God's Word is our life, and apart from that Word, we cannot know God, know the will of God, or worship and serve God acceptably. God's commandments are God's enablements. We're privileged to have the written Word in our own language and to enjoy the freedom to read it and share it with others. Like Israel, the church must be a "people of the Word," for everything we need for life and godliness is found in the inspired Word of God (2 Peter 1:3; 2 Tim. 3:16–17).

"REMEMBER THAT YOU WERE SLAVES" (5:15)

The admonition is also found in Deuteronomy 15:15; 16:3 and 12; and 24:18–22. Each time the Jews celebrated Passover, they were reminded of the trials the nation experienced in Egypt, and this should have led them to love the Lord all the more for what He did for them. When the journey became difficult, the Jews frequently wanted to return to the security and slavery of Egypt instead of trusting the Lord and enjoying the freedom He gave them. While we don't want to repeat the sins of the past, it does us good to remember what the Lord saved us from when we trusted Christ. The Jews were to remember the day that the Lord brought them out of their slavery (16:3). There's nothing wrong with setting aside special "remembrance days" when we review the goodness of the Lord toward us.

The fact that the Jews were once strangers in a foreign land should have motivated them to be especially kind to the strangers in their land (10:19). It should also have encouraged them to be kind to their own servants

(24:14). "Love one another" simply means that we treat others the way the Lord treats us.

"REMEMBER HOW GOD LED YOU" (8:2)

"And you shall remember that the LORD your God led you all the way" (NKJV). God didn't desert Israel when they came out of Egypt, but led them by a pillar of cloud by day and a pillar of fire by night. The Jews didn't always understand the route that the Lord took, but He never led them astray. We can be sure that the will of God will never lead us where the grace of God cannot keep us or the power of God cannot enable us to glorify the Lord.

One of the hardest lessons God's people must learn is to accept God's will and obey Him without protest or complaint. If the Jews had taken time to look back and recall their journey from Egypt to Canaan, they would have seen that each stage in the journey taught them more about themselves and about the Lord. They would see themselves as living in the past and afraid of the future, doubting God's love and His ability to see them through. Their frequent complaining revealed their lack of love for the Lord, and their rebellion showed their lack of submission to His will.

Wherever he lived, missionary J. Hudson Taylor put up a plaque that read: "Ebenezer—Jehovah-Jireh." These Hebrew words mean, "Hitherto the LORD has helped us—the LORD will see to it" (1 Sam. 7:12; Gen. 22:14). As God's people look back, we see that the Lord has been faithful, and as we look ahead, we know He will provide; so, why worry and fret?

"REMEMBER MOUNT SINAI" (4:9–13)

The Lord didn't lead Israel directly from Egypt to Canaan because they weren't ready to enter the land and confront the Enemy. Liberty isn't the same as maturity; in fact, without maturity, liberty is a dangerous thing. God didn't give His law to Israel as a means of salvation because He had already redeemed them by the blood of the Passover lamb. He gave them His law to mature them, for they were like little children who needed a babysitter (Gal. 4:1–7).

What did the people of Israel learn at Mount Sinai? Of first importance, they learned that God is a holy God who must be feared and honored. God demonstrated His great power and glory at Sinai and the people shook with fear. But unless that fear becomes reverence in the heart, it can never transform the life. Israel also learned that God was a gracious and merciful God who provided forgiveness and a means to worship and serve Him.

However, it was also at Mount Sinai that the people discovered their impatience and unbelief when Moses stayed on the mount so long. In their hearts they had a craving for idols, and they worshipped the golden calf. They saw how swiftly God judged their terrible sin, but they also learned that Jehovah would forgive them and give them a new beginning.

Every believer must learn to submit to the will of God as it is expressed in the Word of God. One test of our submission is a willingness to wait on the Lord and not run after substitutes. Even though the golden calf was approved by the high priest, it was wicked and contrary to the will of God.

"REMEMBER HOW YOU PROVOKED GOD" (9:7)

"Remember! Do not forget how you provoked the Lord your God to wrath in the wilderness" (NKJV). On at least two occasions, the Lord threatened to destroy all the people and make a new nation from Moses. And yet, what did the Jews have to be provoked about? The Lord who graciously delivered them from Egypt also gave them everything they needed on their journey, defeated their enemies, and gave them a land flowing with milk and honey.

Their basic problem was unbelief (Heb. 3—4); they simply didn't trust God. They didn't believe His promises or obey His commands but tried to go their own way, and this led to rebellion and chastening. And they never seemed to learn their lesson! Like stubborn and rebellious children, the Jews took their spankings and went right back to their sins!

As God's children, we need to confess that apart from God's grace, nothing good dwells in us (Rom. 7:18), and that our fallen nature can't be changed. "That which is born of the flesh is flesh" (John 3:6)—and it always will be flesh! The ability to sin is still with us, but we should have less of an appetite to sin. Through the sanctifying work of the Spirit and the Word (John 17:17; 2 Cor. 3:18), our inner person should conform more and more to Christ, desiring and delighting in the things of God.

"REMEMBER YOUR ENEMIES" (25:17)

This isn't a command to carry grudges but to recognize the true enemies that oppose the Lord and us. The Amalekites attacked Israel after the exodus, and Joshua and the Jewish army defeated them (Ex. 17:8–16). It was then that God declared war on every generation of the Amalekites until the memory of the nation would be wiped off the face of the earth. The Israelites weren't attacked in Egypt but after the Lord had set them free from bondage. This reminds us that the world, the flesh, and the Devil don't assault dead sinners because they already have them under their control (Eph. 2:1–3). However, once the Lord has set us free, these enemies come after us, and the war will go on until we see Jesus Christ.

A young Scottish minister attended a "victorious Christian life" conference and came to believe that he had "gotten the victory" over the enemies of the spiritual life. He shared this good news with Alexander Whyte, noted minister in Edinburgh, who said, "Aye, it's a sore battle up to the very last!" It's a solemn thought that some of the men in Scripture who sinned greatly against the Lord didn't do so when they were young men: Abraham fleeing to Egypt and lying about his wife, Moses losing his temper, Aaron making a golden idol, David committing adultery and murder, and Peter denying his Lord. We never outgrow temptations and battles.

"REMEMBER WHAT THE LORD DID TO MIRIAM" (24:9)

The story of Miriam's rebellion is found in Numbers 12. While Aaron was implicated with her, it seems that she was the ringleader in the matter because she was the one who was punished. Miriam was envious of Moses' wife and critical of her brother because of his marriage.[2] God saw her heart and heard her words and punished her sin by giving her leprosy. Displaying his usual meekness and love, Moses interceded for her and God healed her. However, the leprosy had made her unclean, and she had to leave the camp for a week until the priest could verify that the leprosy was gone. Her sin held up the march of Israel, for sin always hinders the progress of God's people.

Sins of the spirit are as destructive as sins of the flesh, and sometimes they are worse. Miriam was guilty of pride, envy, evil speaking, and lack of love. But even more, sins within families are especially painful, as are sins among the leaders of God's people. If God gave leprosy to every leader who envied other leaders and criticized them, there wouldn't be many healthy people left!

These special reminders apply to us today. Bad memories can lead to bad attitudes and actions and often to unfaithfulness to the Lord. While the book of Deuteronomy is a long book, filled with a variety of material, the spiritual lesson that stands out is that we must be equipped by the Lord to face the challenges and opportunities of the future. That equipping comes from hearing His Word, cherishing it, and obeying it. While there are some things we must forget, there are also some things that we must remember if we're to please and glorify the Lord and accomplish the work He's given us to do.

QUESTIONS FOR PERSONAL REFLECTION
OR GROUP DISCUSSION

1. What seven important truths did Moses want the Israelites to remember? Explain each in your own words.

2. What truths about God do you feel are most crucial to remember?

3. If we didn't have God's Word, what else wouldn't we have?

4. Which, if any, special remembrance days help you to remember how the Lord saved you?

5. Wiersbe says one of the hardest lessons God's people must learn is to accept God's will and obey Him without complaint. Why is this hard to learn? Has this been true for you? If so, in what way?

6. What is the relationship between liberty and maturity? Where have you witnessed the danger of having the first without the second?

7. What truths and lessons did the Israelites learn on Mt. Sinai?

8. Unbelief was the underlying sin that led to the Israelites' provoking God time and again. What do you think they didn't believe?

9. Who or what are our enemies? Why should we remember our enemies?

10. What are the main things you will take away from your study of Deuteronomy?

NOTES

CHAPTER 1

1. George Santayana, *The Life of Reason*, vol. 1, chap. 12.
2. For an exposition of the book of Numbers, see my book *Be Counted* (David C. Cook).
3. This is the first time the title "the LORD your God" is used in Deuteronomy (v. 10), and you'll find it used almost 300 times in the book. Moses used it to remind the Jews that they belonged to the Lord and were His special people.
4. When Joshua was conquering Canaan, twice he relied on human information alone, and both times he failed: when he attacked Ai with a small force (Josh. 7) and when he made a covenant with the Gibeonites (Josh. 9). It isn't sinful to obtain human information, but it is sinful to lean on our own understanding and not seek God's direction (Prov. 3:5–6). When Israel asked for a king, God gave them one, but they suffered because of it (1 Sam. 8—9).
5. There was more to this judgment on Moses than just personal chastening. Moses represented the law, and God's people cannot claim their blessings by obeying the law. It's a matter of faith in God's promises, claiming the grace of God. Joshua represented Jesus, for both names

mean "Jehovah is salvation." It is by trusting Christ that we enter into our spiritual inheritance, represented by Canaan (Heb. 4:1–8).

6. Numbers 33 lists without comment the places where Israel camped during those sad years.

7. As with Pharaoh, the process of hardening involved Sihon's personal response to God's will. The Lord doesn't assault people and force them to act against their own wills. The news of Israel's march had reached Sihon long before the Jews arrived on the scene, and the king had already decided to declare war. As he resisted God's Word, he experienced a hardening of his heart.

CHAPTER 2

1. Abraham Joshua Heschel, *I Asked for Wonder: A Spiritual Anthology*, edited by Samuel H. Dresner (New York: Crossroad, 1996), 73.

2. Roy Zuck, *Biblical Theology of the Old Testament* (Chicago: Moody, 1991), 232. Job, Proverbs, and Ecclesiastes are the leading "wisdom books" in the Old Testament, and James in the New Testament.

3. We must not read into this an assurance that obedient saints today will automatically experience all the special blessings mentioned in God's covenant with Israel, such as freedom from sickness, guaranteed material wealth, and a long peaceful life (Lev. 26; Deut. 27—30). No such benefits are promised under the new covenant, for our wealth is primarily spiritual and not material (Matt. 5:1–12; Eph. 1:3ff.).

4. God doesn't judge the children for the sins committed by the parents (Ezek. 18:1–20), but the consequences of those sins can greatly affect the children. Furthermore, children tend to follow the example set at home and will imitate their parents' sins. But we must also remember that the godliness of grandparents and parents will bring blessing to their descendants (Ps. 90:16; 103:17–18; Gen. 18:17–19).

5. In the tabernacle and the temple, God did permit the Jews to have

copies of various things in nature, but these were there to bring beauty to God's house and not as objects of worship. God doesn't prohibit the making of artistic things as such, for He's the Author of beauty, but only prohibits the making of things that become gods to us. See *Art and the Bible* by Francis A. Schaeffer (InterVarsity Press).

6. A. W. Tozer, *The Knowledge of the Holy* (Harper, 1961), 9, 11.

CHAPTER 3

1. When Korah, Dathan, and Abiram rebelled against God and Moses, they called Egypt "a land flowing with milk and honey" (Num. 16:13 NIV), but God compared Egypt to an iron furnace (Deut. 4:20; 1 Kings 8:51; Jer. 11:4). Israel's bondage in Egypt helped to refine them ("an iron-smelting furnace," Deut. 4:20 NIV) and prepare them for their new life as a nation. However, all that the older generation seemed to remember about Egypt was the food they ate so freely (Ex. 16:1–3; Num. 11:4–6). The pain of their slavery in Egypt was overlooked or forgotten.

2. Moses often reminded the people of God's promises to the patriarchs: Deut. 1:8, 11, 21, 35; 6:3, 10, 19; 7:8, 12; 8:18; 9:5, 27; 11:9; 19:8; 26:3; 29:13; 30:20; 34:4.

3. The Scriptures written on four pieces of parchment and put into the phylacteries are Exodus 13:1–10; 11—16; Deuteronomy 6:4–9; and 11:13–21. The mezuzah contains 6:4–9; 11:13–21, plus the phrase, "The LORD our God is the LORD."

4. In verse 5, the "groves" (KJV) or "wooden images" (NKJV) were "Asherah poles" (NIV) dedicated to the goddess Asherah, the consort of Baal. The poles were designed to be phallic symbols, and her worship was associated with grossly immoral practices. The word translated "destroy" is a Hebrew word *(herem)* that means "to be devoted to God, to be under a ban." When Joshua conquered Jericho (Josh. 6—7), the city was

put under a ban and nothing could be taken as spoils of war. Because Achan took some of the spoils, he robbed God and led the nation into defeat at Ai.

5. We must remind ourselves that the promise of health and material blessing belonged only to Israel under law; it is not promised to the church under the new covenant. Nor should we conclude that the absence of health and material blessing is an evidence of God's displeasure. This was the error Job's friends committed when they tried to explain his suffering, and their suggestion was, "Get right with God and He will restore all your blessings." Of course, that was also Satan's philosophy (Job 1—2), a philosophy I call "commercial Christianity." "Commercial Christians" worship and obey God only because He rewards it. In the childhood of the Jewish nation, God used rewards and punishments to teach them obedience, and then He sought to lift them to a higher level.

6. Deuteronomy 20 is the key chapter on Israel's conduct of war. In verses 10–15, Moses deals with how Israel should attack cities outside the land of Canaan, and verses 16–18 apply to cities in the land of Canaan.

CHAPTER 4

1. Horace Walpole, *Anecdotes of Painting in England*, vol. 3, chap. 1.

2. In His sermon on the Bread of Life (John 6), Jesus pointed out that, like the manna, He came down from heaven, but that He came to give life while the manna only sustained life. God sent the manna to Israel alone, but He sent His Son to the whole world. Unless we receive Jesus within our hearts, just as the body receives bread, we are not saved. Our Lord's sermon in John 6 has nothing to do with the Lord's Supper (Eucharist) or any other religious ceremony. It focuses entirely on having a personal relationship with Jesus through faith. "Eating His flesh

and drinking His blood" is metaphorical language for receiving Him personally within.

3. However there are many recorded incidents of God's provisions for His people in ways that are just as miraculous as anything He did for Israel. For more than thirty years, George Mueller of Bristol, England, trusted God to feed thousands of orphans, and he was never disappointed. Without promoting for funds, J. Hudson Taylor trusted God to provide support for the missionaries of the China Inland Mission, and the Lord was faithful.

4. Hebrews 12:1–15 is the classic text on God's disciplining of the believer. For an exposition, see chapter 11 of my book *Be Confident* (David C. Cook).

5. "The outskirts of the camp" was where the "mixed multitude" lived, the non-Jewish people who had left Egypt with Israel (Ex. 12:38). According to Numbers 11:4, it was this crowd that caused the problem, just as unsaved people and carnal believers create problems in churches today. However, the Jews shouldn't have listened to them and joined them in their complaining.

6. "I Sing the Mighty Power of God" by Isaac Watts.

7. The persons in Jacob's family are listed in Genesis 46:8–25 according to his wives: Leah—33; Zilpah—16; Rachel—14; Bilhah—7, which totals seventy persons. But Er and Onan were dead (v. 12), so we have a total of sixty-eight, and Joseph was already in Egypt with his two sons, which gives us sixty-five. Adding the daughter, Dinah, gives us sixty-six persons who went to Egypt with Jacob, as stated in 46:26. When you add Jacob and Joseph and Joseph's two sons, you have a total of seventy persons (Deut. 10:22). Stephen used the number seventy-five (Acts 7:14), which was taken from the Septuagint, the Greek translation of the Old Testament, which was popular among the Hellenistic Jews.

The Septuagint number includes the five grandsons of Joseph (Num. 26:28–37; 1 Chron. 7:14–15, 20–25).

8. Dathan and Abiram lost their lives, their families, and their possessions; but Numbers 26:8–11 indicates that the family of Korah wasn't judged. The sons of Korah served as Levites and are credited with writing at least eleven psalms (42; 44—49; 84—85; 87—88).

9. The phrase in verse 10 ("watered it with thy foot") suggests that one of the tasks of the enslaved Jews in Egypt was to keep the irrigation ditches open so the water flowed into the fields. There's no evidence that the Egyptians had foot-powered irrigation equipment that lifted water from the Nile and distributed it in the fields.

10. Dr. and Mrs. Howard Taylor, *Hudson Taylor's Spiritual Secret* (China Inland Mission, 1949), 114. Every believer should read this classic book on faith and spiritual victory.

11. Since Mount Ebal was the mount of cursing, the altar was needed there for sacrifices that could bring forgiveness and restore fellowship with God. The Old Testament sacrifices speak of the work of Jesus Christ on the cross (Heb. 10:1–18), and He bore the curse of the law for us (Gal. 3:10–14).

CHAPTER 5

1. The phrase "in the land" is used five times in chapter 12 (vv. 1, 10, 19, 29). In verses 1 and 19, it's translated "upon the earth" in the KJV, but "in the land" is the better translation.

2. See Leviticus 1—7 for a description of the various sacrifices the Lord ordained for His people to bring. All of these sacrifices and the rituals connected with them point to Jesus Christ and various aspects of His person and atoning work (Heb. 10:1–18). For an explanation of these sacrifices, see chapter 2 of my book *Be Holy* (David C. Cook).

3. These laws explain the meaning of Jewish "kosher meats" (also spelled

"kasher"), from a Hebrew word that means "fit, right." The meat is soaked in water for at least half an hour, then covered with salt and allowed to drain on a grate for at least an hour. After the salt is washed away, the meat is ready to be eaten. Obeying the dietary laws in Leviticus 11 is also a part of maintaining a kosher home.

4. Andrew A. Bonar, *The Memoirs and Remains of Robert Murray M'Cheyne* (London: Banner of Truth, 1966), 29.

5. Bible students don't agree on whether this man was a true prophet who turned false or a false prophet from the beginning. If he were known to be a false prophet, he would have been killed, but the Jews didn't always obey the laws involving capital punishment. I take it from 13:1 that the man was a true prophet, which would make the temptation even more insidious.

6. Not everything published about demonism is biblical and dependable, but you may want to read some of these studies: *Demons in the World Today*, by Merrill F. Unger (Tyndale); *The Invisible War*, by Donald Grey Barnhouse (Zondervan); *The Adversary* and *Overcoming the Adversary*, by Mark I. Bubeck (Moody); *Spiritual Warfare*, by Timothy M. Warner (Crossway); *Powers of Evil*, by Sidney H. T. Page (Baker); and *The Bondage Breaker*, by Neil T. Anderson (Harvest House).

7. For a vivid description of false teachers and their methods, read 1 Timothy 4; 2 Timothy 3; 2 Peter 2; and the epistle of Jude. The closer we come to the return of Christ, the more false prophets and false teachers will appear on the scene (Matt. 24:3–5, 23–27).

Chapter 6

1. God had promised that if the people obeyed Him, He would keep from them the diseases they had seen in Egypt (7:15; Ex. 15:26), so perhaps the diet was related to this promise. Common sense tells us that if people have allergies and become ill from eating certain foods,

they ought to avoid them. But to find hidden mystical meanings in the cloven hooves, chewing the cud, fins and scales, and the other distinctives in this list is to get more out of the text than the Holy Spirit put into it.

2. The law prohibited Jews from charging interest when they loaned money to fellow Jews (Ex. 22:25; Lev. 25:37; Deut. 23:19), but the NIV margin translates Exodus 22:25 "excessive interest." Apparently this law wasn't always obeyed (Neh. 5:10–12; Ezek. 18:8, 13, 17).

3. On the day after the Sabbath following Passover, which would be the first day of the week, the Jews celebrated the Feast of Firstfruits (Lev. 23:9–14). The priest went into the harvest field and waved a sheaf of the grain before the Lord, indicating that the entire harvest belonged to Him. Passover pictures Christ in His death, but the Feast of Firstfruits pictures Christ in His resurrection (1 Cor. 15:20–24). He was the "grain of wheat" that was planted in the ground and produced much fruit (John 12:24). Because Christ is risen from the dead, His people will be raised from the dead and be like Him (1 Thess. 4:13–18; 1 John 3:1–3). The sheaf was waved on the first day of the week, and Jesus arose from the dead and appeared to His disciples on the first day of the week (Matt. 28:1–8; John 20:19ff.). This is one reason why Christians gather together for worship on the first day of the week (Acts 20:7; 1 Cor. 16:1–2).

Chapter 7

1. Israel's social structure was very masculine, as were the societies of most if not all the nations in the ancient world. However, God's law gave great protection and special care to women and children so that they couldn't easily be abused and treated like helpless slaves. Moses' sister, Miriam, was a leader in Israel (Ex. 15:20–21) and Deborah was a famous judge (Judg. 4—5).

2. Isaiah 59 gives a graphic picture of judicial corruption in Judah, and it looks very contemporary!

3. Doing away with idols is one aspect of devotion to the Lord, but giving Him our best is also important (Deut. 17:1). If we truly love the Lord, we will bring Him the very best that we have and not settle for whatever is left over. See Malachi 1:6–14.

4. Quoted in Gwynn McLendon Day, *The Wonder of the Word* (Fleming H. Revell, 1957), 165–66.

5. Ibid., 170.

6. The description of Solomon's kingdom in 1 Kings 10 makes it look like a paradise, but it was decaying from within. After Solomon's death, the people cried out for relief from the heavy burdens they had to carry in order to support Solomon's luxurious way of life (1 Kings 12). There are hints in the book of Ecclesiastes that, no matter how glorious the kingdom appeared to visitors, there was corruption among the officials, injustice in the courts, and a facade of success that was soon to crumble.

7. Deuteronomy 17:20 suggests that the king was to be "first among equals" and not elevated above his brothers. This was true of Saul in the early days of his reign. After he was anointed king, he returned to his home to help his father (1 Sam. 10:26). When news came to him of the invasion of the Ammonites, Saul was plowing with the oxen (11:4ff.). Unfortunately, Saul became proud and defensive, disobeyed God's command, and lost his crown. Deuteronomy 17:20 also states that the king would establish a dynasty (see NIV), and if he obeyed God, his descendants would reign after him. Saul's sons, including Jonathan, were slain on the battlefield (1 Sam. 31; 2 Sam. 1). God had chosen David as the new king (1 Sam. 16; Ps. 78:70–72) and with him established the dynasty through which Jesus Christ came into the world.

CHAPTER 8

1. The priests marched with the Jewish army around Jericho and blew trumpets (Josh. 6:4–21), and a Levite named Jahaziel gave a message of encouragement to King Jehoshaphat before the king went out to battle (2 Chron. 20:14–19). Benaiah, son of Jehoiada the priest (1 Chron. 27:5), one of David's mighty men, was leader of the king's body-guards (1 Kings 1:38) and succeeded Joab as captain of the army when Solomon became king (2:35; 4:4). Priests could become soldiers!

2. The NIV reads, "Are the trees of the field people, that you should besiege them?" God permitted the Jews to wage war against rebellious people but not against His creation.

3. For a man, the shaving of the head and beard would be a humiliating experience (Isa. 7:20; 2 Sam. 10:4–5), and it would certainly be for a woman (1 Cor. 11:15). While in mourning, Jewish men were not allowed to imitate the pagans by shaving their heads and cutting their beards (Lev. 19:27–28), and this especially applied to the priests (21:1–5).

4. The verb translated "let her go" is translated "put her away" (divorce) in 22:19 and 29. Since the marriage had been consummated, they were man and wife, and the marriage could be legally dissolved only by divorce (24:1–4).

5. Some commentators suggest that the husband divorced her because she wouldn't accept the religion of the Israelites and worship the true and living God. However, nothing in the text suggests this.

6. The fact that a certain city was the nearest to the corpse didn't mean that one of its citizens was guilty of the crime. It was necessary to involve the leaders of a neighboring city because the elders there knew the terrain and would represent the local citizens. The sanctuary court was in charge, but they respected the local authorities.

CHAPTER 9

1. What the rebellious son did to his parents, the nation of Israel did to the Lord. They disobeyed His law and turned to idols, they wasted the good gifts He gave them, and they hardened their hearts against His chastening. Instead of destroying them, the Lord exiled them in Babylon, allowed them to return to their land, and ultimately sent them His own Son.

2. The main thrust of these verses is that the woman couldn't return to her first husband. "If a man marries a woman ... if he finds some uncleanness in her ... if he gives her a certificate of divorce ... if she marries another man who subsequently divorces her, THEN she may not return to the first husband." Moses is assuming that a policy of divorce had been a part of Israel's life for a long time, and he did not rescind it. This law was given to protect the woman, not to make it easy for the man to divorce her.

3. Under the Jewish law, a woman could not divorce her husband, but in Mark 10:11, Jesus lifted that ban. Mark was writing especially to Gentiles in the Roman world.

4. For example, Jesus and the apostles used principles from the creation account (Gen. 1—3) to explain the relationship of male and female in marriage, in the home, and in the church (Matt. 19:1–12; Mark 10:1–12; 1 Cor. 11:1–16; 1 Tim. 2:9–15).

5. C. F. Keil and F. Delitzsch, *Commentary on the Old Testament*, vol. 3, 409.

6. Why would a man pay the bride price (v. 29) and then later try to get rid of his wife? Apparently he had quickly grown to dislike her and wanted to get his money back. Perhaps his wife had discovered something about him that he didn't want known, and he hoped to get her out of the way. But surely he knew that the marriage cloth would prove

him to be a liar. However, when love turns to hatred, people do strange things. See 2 Samuel 13:1–22.

7. Verse 10 describes something unforeseen that happened at night over which the man had no control, but it made the man unclean. It could have been a bodily emission (Lev. 15:16) or defilement from touching something unclean (22:4–9).

Chapter 10

1. How much of Exodus, Leviticus, and Deuteronomy Moses included in "all the words of this law" is not stated. Certainly the Ten Commandments would be written on the stones as well as the "book of the covenant" (Ex. 20:22—24:8).

2. The predictions of the curses God threatened to send on His disobedient people are given in 28:15–68. When God sent judgment to His people for their sins, He was only doing what they agreed for Him to do.

3. "The just shall live by faith" is one of the pivotal verses in Scripture (Hab. 2:4). It's quoted in the New Testament in Romans 1:17; Galatians 3:11; and Hebrews 10:38. Romans explains "the just," Galatians tells us how they "live," and Hebrews expounds "by faith."

4. The minimizing of God's holy law today has produced a shallow evangelism and brought into the churches "religious sinners" who have never repented of their sins because they've never felt conviction for their sins. "The person who will not repent still has his or her back turned on God" (A. W. Tozer, *Men Who Met God*, 45).

5. "Observe and to do" (KJV) is translated "carefully follow" in the NIV and is found also in 16:12; 17:19; 19:9; 24:8; 28:1, 13, 15, 58; 29:9; 31:12.

6. God hasn't promised to make His spiritual children wealthy, but He has blessed His church with "all the blessings of the Spirit" (Eph. 1:3),

and in Christ He has lifted us up "far above all" (vv. 20–23). We must not apply to the church today the covenant promises God gave only to Israel.

7. Job's friends criticized him because their theology said, "God always blesses the obedient and curses the disobedient." Since Job had lost his wealth, family, and health, he had to be a disobedient man, for God was punishing him. They didn't see that God might also be perfecting him. Even our Lord's disciples thought that if anybody would be saved, it would be the rich people (Matt. 19:16–30). Jesus became poor to make us rich (2 Cor. 8:9), and He promised to bless the poor in spirit (Matt. 5:3; see 2 Cor. 6:10; Rev. 2:9; 3:17).

8. We must not assume that the children's clothing "grew" with them. God kept the garments from wearing out so that the children coming along had something suitable to wear. The clothing of the adults wouldn't require that much alteration since the nation was on a simple diet.

Chapter 11

1. Idolatry was described as prostitution because Israel had been "married" to Jehovah when she accepted the covenant at Mount Sinai. When condemning idol worship, the prophets often compared the nation to an unfaithful wife. See Hos. 1—2; Isaiah 54:5; Jeremiah 2:1–3; 3:14; 31:32. The New Testament equivalent is loving the world (James 4:4).

2. It isn't easy to minister when you know that people will reject your messages, but we must be faithful to the end. Years before, Moses knew that Pharaoh would harden his heart (Ex. 7:1–7). Isaiah knew that the nation would become more blind and deaf (Isa. 6), and Jeremiah understood that calamity and captivity would come in spite of his ministry (Jer. 1:13–19).

3. At the end of the apostolic age, several of the churches addressed in Rev. 2—3 were already infected with false doctrine, idol worship, unspiritual leadership, and immorality. By the time you get to the church at Laodicea, Jesus is outside the church trying to get in (3:20)!

4. Modern educational philosophy advises us to use an age-graded approach, but there are times when the whole church needs to be together to hear the Word of God. If the Word is presented with clarity and simplicity, even the children can understand it and learn something from it, and it's good for families to worship together. The church today needs a John the Baptist who will "turn the hearts of the fathers to the children" and unite our homes and our churches (Luke 1:17).

5. The verb "write" in verse 19 is plural. Both men were involved.

6. In a society that didn't have printed books or convenient writing materials, a good memory was essential to success. Unlike people in our modern digital age, the Israelites knew how to listen carefully and remember accurately what they heard.

7. A. W. Tozer, *The Knowledge of the Holy* (Harper, 1961), 9.

8. Ibid., 12.

9. The Lord isn't called "Father" too often in the Old Testament: Deuteronomy 32:6, [18–19]; Isaiah 63:16; 64:8; Malachi 2:10. See also Exodus 4:22.

10. It's not likely that verse 8 refers to Genesis 10 and the seventy nations that came from Shem (v. 21ff.), Ham (v. 6ff.) and Japheth (vv. 2–5), and the seventy in Jacob's family who traveled to Egypt (Gen. 46). Throughout history, nations have come and gone and their number changed.

11. Literally it says, "The little man of the eye," that is, the reflection of someone who is looking into another person's eye. The Hebrew word implies "something precious and irreplaceable that must be guarded jealously." The English word "pupil" comes from the Latin *pupillam*,

which means "apple." When the word was coined, people thought that part of the eye was a sphere like an apple.

12. "Fat of kidneys of wheat" (v. 14 KJV) simply means "the very finest wheat." In the sacrifices, the fat of the kidney was a choice part (Ex. 29:13, 22; Lev. 3:3–4, 9–10, 14–15). "Blood of grapes" refers to the richness of the grape juice and the wine (Gen. 49:11).

13. Verse 36 is quoted in Hebrews 10:30 and applied to God's new covenant people. The phrase in verse 35, "Their foot shall slide in due time," is the text of Jonathan Edwards' famous sermon, "Sinners in the Hands of an Angry God."

CHAPTER 12

1. Genesis 49:28 calls Jacob's speech a "blessing," but the only son to whom the word was applied was Joseph (vv. 25–26). Jacob saw his words as a prophecy (v. 1), and he had some hard things to say to and about his sons.

2. The tribe of Simeon was later absorbed into Judah (Josh. 19:1–9). Jacob had exposed the anger of Simeon and Levi and announced that they would be scattered among the tribes (Gen. 49:7).

3. While angels were involved in the giving of the law (Gal. 3:19), the text indicates that the Lord came from the angelic hosts (Dan. 7:10) to Mount Sinai. See NIV margin.

4. Some translate the last clause "between his weapons," suggesting that God would protect Benjamin in their battles for the Lord.

CHAPTER 13

1. One of the paradoxes of Jewish history is that the Jewish scribes honored the Scriptures and studied them meticulously and yet failed to recognize their Messiah when He appeared. Jesus said, "You search the Scriptures, for in them you think you have eternal life; and these

are they which testify of Me" (John 5:39 NKJV). The old hymn said it best: "Beyond the sacred page / I seek thee, Lord / My spirit pants for Thee / O living Word." ("Break Thou the Bread of Life" by Mary A. Lathbury.)

2. Moses' first wife had died and he took another wife. "Ethiopian" means "Cushite" and need not be seen as a woman of the black race, although the Bible doesn't prohibit such marriages (Acts 17:26). Miriam saw the new wife as a competitor to fear instead of a sister-in-law to love.

The "BE" series . . .

For years pastors and lay leaders have embraced Warren W. Wiersbe's very accessible commentary of the Bible through the individual "BE" series. Through the work of David C. Cook Global Mission, the "BE" series is part of a library of books made available to indigenous Christian workers. These are men and women who are called by God to grow the kingdom through their work with the local church worldwide. Here are a few of their remarks as to how Dr. Wiersbe's writings have benefited their ministry.

"Most Christian books I see are priced too high for me . . .
I received a collection that included 12 Wiersbe
commentaries a few months ago and I have
read every one of them.
I use them for my personal devotions every day and they
are incredibly helpful for preparing sermons.
The contribution David C. Cook is making to the
church in India is amazing."
—Pastor E. M. Abraham, Hyderabad, India